MW01295226

Unless otherwise noted, the scripture quotations contained herein are from the New Revised Standard Version Bible, copyright circa 1989 (or when noted, the circa 1973 edition) by the Division of Christian Education of the National Council of the Churches of Christ in the U.S.A., and are used by permission. All rights reserved.

All information pertaining to Nazarenes/Essenes, unless otherwise noted, comes from, or is based on, various publications of The Essene Church of Christ, Box 516, Elmira OR 97437 and are used by permission; esseneinfo@aol.com

Cover illustration from Broderbund's Printmaster Gold 15 Suite

Copyright © 2003 Paula Gott
All rights reserved.

ISBN 1 59457 205-4

To order additional copies, please contact us.
BookSurge, LLC
www.booksurge.com
1-866-308-6235
orders@booksurge.com

Gabriel's Gift

The Messages And Mysteries
In Luke And Acts

Gott

Gabriel's Gift

Contents

"...leave the stump and roots of the tree...
the kingdom will be reestablished when you learn...
the Most High is All."
Daniel 4:26

"...The holy seed is its stump."
Isaiah 6:13

Jesus Said:
"To everyone who understands my words and acts accordingly,
I will give permission to eat from the tree of life..."
Revelation 2:7

The quotations above are from multiple versions of The Holy
Bible, combined to best express the author's understanding of
the meanings.

To the Angels in all dimensions, with gratitude, reverence, and awe.

INTRODUCTION

Almost from the time I first learned to read, I have loved mysteries. I quit my day job in 1999 so I could try my hand at writing mystery novels. I wrote just one; it was called *Enchanted Circle*. It was during that experience that I became aware of the presence of some unknown and unnamed energy force working through my mind. That changed everything.

I never liked mathematics or numbers. But there *is* something about numbers that makes them unique. Numbers are *the* universal language. It doesn't matter if the language is Greek, Hebrew, Spanish, Italian, English, or Martian, numbers are universal. If there are six apples sitting on a table, it doesn't matter what the word-symbols are that represent *six*. When *six* is translated into each language, the words used will be those that symbolize *six*.

When I discovered that many biblical numbers were related to scientific knowledge I was stunned. And I was instantly curious about what other information might be hidden within them. It also occurred to me that there might be mysteries within the words that filled the spaces between the numbers.

I decided to delve into the stories as if they were chapters in a mystery novel and to write about what I found. I spent over a year tracking down the clues that became easier to spot once I got the hang of it, and I still haven't unraveled all of it. In fact I feel as if I've just begun. But enough of the mystery has been solved that I can at least start telling it. I have no idea how many more books are waiting to be revealed. I'm certain I've just scratched the surface of Luke and Acts, and I haven't even looked at Matthew, Mark and John!

My first *Jesus* book, *Jesus: Master of Science, Lessons of Light*, focused on the numbers in the book of Revelation. At that time I hadn't even realized there were numbers elsewhere in the New Testament. But one day last year I noticed the numbers in Luke's gospel, and it occurred to me that they seemed totally irrelevant to the stories. I decided to underline each number in the first chapter of Luke; there were only five. And then I picked up my little calculator and multiplied them.

That was how this book came to be, and here's what I now know: *The Gospel According to Luke* is, in fact, *The Gospel of Lux*, or *The Gospel of Light*. (*Lux* rhymes with *Luke's*.)

With help from what I can only describe as an *Energy* that works through the electrical impulses in my brain, I will prove to you that the author of Luke and Acts cleverly created books designed to carry Jesus' true message and knowledge to the "*educated*" people who lived in the first century, and to all people who want to know *The Truth* for all times.

I use the word *educated* in reference to first century men and women because few were privileged enough to receive any form of education, other than learning the skills that would feed, house, and clothe a family. Reading classical literature was not an option for the average person at that time.

Modern men and women, at least those who live in developed countries, are virtually all educated, some more than others, but most are able to read and comprehend simple to complex information. And television, although not utilized to its maximum potential, provides facts, figures, and knowledge that educates even people who choose not to read.

Most people love a good mystery, and whoever wrote Luke was a master of mysteries and puzzles. Here's an example of what I mean: If a first century, Greek speaking teacher wanted to **covertly** address educated people who were interested in finding religious truths and knowledge, what term might he use in his address? Hint: The Greek word which refers to religion is *theo*, from which the word *theology* is derived. In Greek, *philo* means *lover* and *sophistes* means *wise one*. The highly educated were called *philosophers*, meaning, of course, "*lovers of knowledge*"; remember Plato, Aristotle, Socrates, and Pythagorus, who invented the word *philosopher.*

We're looking for a subliminal name not easily identified by the people in power who were determined to destroy all knowledge of Universal Truths in order to keep the masses ignorant and subservient to them.

What would it be?

How about, *Theological Philosopher*, or *Theophilosoph*? Too obvious? How about *Theo-philos*?

Luke 1:1-4: "*Since many have undertaken to set down an orderly account of the events that have occurred among us, just as they were handed on to us by those who from the beginning were eyewitnesses and servants of the word, I too decided, **after investigating everything carefully for a long time**, to write an orderly account for you, **most excellent Theophilus**, so that you may know **the truth** concerning the things about which you have been instructed.*"

Theophilus is pretty close to *Theo-philos*. In fact, I think I like it better.

Second question: If you knew that Jesus taught scientific knowledge, and you knew the primary information was about the importance of light in the creation process (remember Einstein's E=mc^2), how would you hide that information for the *Theological Philosophers* in a gospel referred to as *Luke's*?

Hint: What are two objects that would be symbols of light for a first century person? Perhaps the sun and the moon? The sun provides light during the day, the moon during the night. What about the unique use of numbers in Luke's Chapter 1? No other gospel writer inserted numbers throughout in the same way Luke did. Could there be a hidden message here?

Luke 1:24: "*...his wife Elizabeth conceived, and for **five** months she hid herself...*"

Luke 1:26: "*In the **sixth** month the angel Gabriel was sent from God...*"

Luke 1:36: "*...this is the **sixth** month with her who was called barren.*"

Luke 1:56: *"And Mary remained with her about **three** months..."*

Luke 1:59: *"And on the **eighth** day they came to circumcise the child..."*

Those are **all** the verses in the first chapter of the gospel of Luke that contain numbers. The numbers are 5, 6, 6, 3, and 8.

5 x 6 x 6 x 3 x 8 = 4320. Does this number have any relationship to the sun and/or the moon?

Fact: The diameter of the sun is 864,000 miles.

Fact: The diameter of the moon is 2,160 miles.

Halve 4320 = 2160, the diameter of the moon.

Double 432 000 = 864 000, the diameter of the sun.

The number 432 is the ONLY number that can be manipulated one time to reach the numbers contained in the diameter of both the sun and the moon.

Oh! One more thing. Square 432: 432 x 432 = 186,624. That just happens to be the speed of light in miles per second if there were no friction or resistance. Of course men and women in the first century couldn't have known about that. Or could they?

Can it be just a coincidence that the ONLY numbers in the first chapter of Luke, when all are multiplied, equal a number that, when halved is the diameter of the moon, when doubled (add two zeros) is the diameter of the sun, and when squared (drop the zeros) is the speed of light?

Oh, by the way, Lux was the **goddess** of Light in Greek mythology.

Among the items found at Nag Hammadi in 1945, in addition to ancient Jewish texts and texts with Gnostic undertones, was a short excerpt from *Plato's Republic*. This item is, in my opinion, far more important than has been previously acknowledged. This puts Greek philosophy into the hands of the people of Jesus' time and location and strengthens the argument for his knowledge of, and probable indoctrination into, the ancient Secret Schools that taught the Pythagorean philosophy that *"Number is All."*

But if you think these numbers in Chapter 1 are merely coincidence, have a look at Luke's Chapter 2.

Luke 2:21: *"And at the end of **eight** days..."*

Luke 2:24: *"...and to offer a sacrifice...'a pair of turtledoves, or two young pigeons.'"*

Luke 2:36 *"And there was...Anna...**seven** years from her virginity..."*

Luke 2:37: *"...and as a widow till she was **eighty-four**."*

Luke 2:42: *"And when he was **twelve** years old..."*

Luke 2:46: *"After **three** days they found him in the temple..."*

The *ONLY* numbers mentioned are: 8, 2, 84, 7, 12, and 3.

The functions required here become a little more complex than simple multiplication and addition. You will recall that "pi" is the number necessary to determine the circumference of a circle when you know its radius or diameter. Most of us used 3 1/7 or 3.14 in our manual calculations. That is the same as 22/7, and more precisely, it is 3.1428571. Mixing the ONLY numbers used in Chapter 2 with pi, we find the following:

84 x 2 x pi = 528. One statute mile is 5280 feet.

84 x 3 x pi = 792. The mean diameter of the earth is 7920 miles.

84 x 12 x pi = 3,168. A square drawn around the earth will measure 31,680 miles.

Now, using all the numbers in Chapter 2 EXCEPT 84:

8 x 7 x 12 x 3 divided by 2 = 1008 x pi = 3168.

In addition to being the total of the sides of a square drawn around the earth, students of *gematria* will immediately recognize 3168 as being the number of *Lord Jesus Christ*. (*Gematria* is the process of replacing Greek letters with corresponding numbers, then adding the numbers together. The Greek letters for *Lord Jesus Christ*, when converted to numbers, total 3168.)

Chapter 1 tells us that the Truth Jesus taught pertained to light; Chapter 2 tells us they had knowledge about the earth, as well, and that the units used to measure the earth, moon, sun, and the speed of light, were miles of 5,280 feet each.

Still think these numbers are simply coincidental? I'll make one more attempt to prove this hidden message via the numbers, then I have to move on with the rest of the story and the secret message encoded within the words.

Perhaps the best proof that the numbers aren't merely

coincidental can be found by looking at Luke's Chapter 9. There are fifteen numbers greater than one in Chapter 9. The specific verses that contain these numbers are listed and quoted in Chapter 6, along with the itemization of numbers and verses for all other chapters of Luke's gospel.

The numbers, in order, are: 12, 2, 12, 5, 2, 5000, 50, 5, 2, 12, 3, 8, 2, 2, 3.

12 x 2 = 24
24 x 12 = 288
288 x 5 = 1440
1440 x 2 = 2880
2880 x 5000 = 14 400 000
14 400 000 x 50 = 720 000 000
720 000 000 x 5 = 3 600 000 000
3 600 000 000 x 2 = 7 200 000 000
7 200 000 000 x 12 = 86 400 000 000
86 400 000 000 x 3 = 259 200 000 000
259 200 000 000 x 8 = 2 073 600 000 000
2 073 600 000 000 x 2 = 4 147 200 000 000
4 147 200 000 000 x 2 = 8 294 400 000 000
8 294 400 000 000 x 3 = **24 883** 200 000 000

Ridiculous!!! But wait. Take a closer look at that last number. For convenience, ancient mathematicians frequently used 22/7 (3.1428571) as pi. But a more accurate pi is 864/275. It takes a little more work to manually calculate the circumference of a sphere using this larger number, but sometimes, they did use it. Using the mean diameter of the earth, 7920 miles, and this slightly more accurate number for pi, the results are truly amazing, considering from where that last product above was derived:

7920 miles x 864/275
7920 times 864 = 6 842 880
6 842 880 divided by 275 = **24,883.2** miles.

That's the circumference of the earth to one decimal point! And that's the very number reached after multiplying all fifteen numbers in Luke's Chapter 9 after the zeros are dropped from the end.

Anybody still claiming coincidence? Do you have any idea how I felt and how long it took me to catch my breath when these numbers started doing what they do? I've been studying sacred numbers and sacred geometry for almost four years now, and no one to my knowledge has recognized the truth about Lux gospel (that is the correct spelling!) and what it contains.

$\mathcal{S}$

I hope I've piqued your curiosity enough to keep you reading. There are volumes of information in Luke and Acts (same writer), and someone was willing to risk his or her life to pass it on to us.

He, or she, or they, also left clues as to who they were and the truth about the other biblical narratives and about what was being done to Jesus' message and to those who attempted to save it. History tells us that many early Christians were killed for teaching what Jesus taught. History also tells us that the Gnostics (*gnosis* means *knowledge*) were declared heretics by the early church leaders and their doctrines and teachings destroyed. Even some modern fundamental Christians still use the word *Gnostic* synonymously with *heretic*.

Wouldn't it be something if the Gnostics had actually infiltrated the Church and left the message of their truth about Jesus encoded in two books selected to be a part of the official doctrine of the early Church, and at exactly the same time the Church was killing the Gnostics and destroying their books?

We provide overwhelming proof that they did just that! And we prove it using the "official church doctrine," the *Holy Bible*.

The "*we*" I refer to is that Energy force I previously mentioned. In the beginning I tried to deny Its existence. I kept using words like *coincidentally* and *accidentally*. Then the doorbell started ringing and the lights started blinking and I started thinking--and reading.

Einstein's equations actually point to what John Dobson calls "*an apparitional Universe*." (More information about Dobson can be found at several websites, including:

www.space.com/scienceastronomy/astronomy/dobson_
astronomer_000507.html)

Many scientists agree with Dobson's *apparitional
universe* theory, and if I understand it correctly, it means that
mass, matter--commmonly known as *stuff*--is nothing but
invisible energy spinning rapidly to create a standing wave of
vibrations. These vibrations enter our eyes and get labeled by
our programmed brain: *house, car, baby*. In other words, the
human body can be described as *"a standing wave of spinning and
vibrating energy in which consciousness resides."*

Look on the Internet for Brian Green's work on *String
Theory*, or buy his book, *The Elegant Universe*. Science appears to
be on the verge of confirming the existence of *"parallel universes."*
The implications are beyond our wildest imagination.

If the human body is nothing more than rapidly spinning
energy which obeys certain Laws of our physical Universe, it
stands to reason that the same energy could spin at different
speeds, faster or slower, and the *stuff* that's formed would be
invisible to me. I can't see It or hear It, and It doesn't control my
fingers on the keyboard; It affects the electrical impulses firing
in my brain. The communication is purely energetic or electric.
I still have to do the hard research, but It gives me the ideas and
directs me to the sources.

Ancient cultures, and even some modern cultures, call
these energies or forces *angels*. Christianity tells many stories
of angels and their intervention in the lives of the faithful. The
prolific biographer, philosopher, and Greek of high standing,
Mestrius Plutarchus (a.k.a., *Plutarch of Chaeronea*--circa. 45-125
ACE), believed that there was an infinite hierarchy of beings
that resided between the one unitary *God* and mortal men
and women. These spiritual beings experienced longer cycles
of birth and rebirth than mortals, but they had weaknesses of
the mortal kind and could be demoted into men or women in
a subsequent existence, just as men and women, he believed,
could be promoted into angels. This is a common feature of
the doctrines of various Mystery Schools, both ancient and
modern.

I now know that angels do exist and function in an invisible, but parallel, Universe. And by the time I completed this book, it was apparent to me that the *Energy Force* that directed me had been given a name by others before me. They called It *"Gabriel."* And now, so do I.

PART ONE

LUX GOSPEL

(ALSO KNOWN AS "LUKE'S GOSPEL")

CHAPTER ONE

"O Timothy, guard what has been entrusted to you,
avoiding worldly and empty chatter and the opposing arguments
*of what is falsely called "**gnosis**."*
1 Timothy 6:20.

PYTHAGORAS AND PLATO

After the excitement of discovering the meaning of the numbers in Chapters 1 and 2, I went to work on Chapter 3. It is sorely lacking in numbers and presented the first challenge in my search for the hidden knowledge in the numbers scattered throughout Luke's gospel.

Luke 3:1: *"In the **fifteenth** year of the reign of Tiberius Ceasar, Pontius Pilate being governor of Judea..."*

Luke 3:11: *"And he answered them, 'He who has **two** coats, let him share with him who has none; and he who has food, let him do likewise...'"*

Luke 3:23: *"Jesus, when he began his ministry, was about **thirty** years of age..."*

That's it. Only three numbers: 15, 2, and 30.

15 x 2 x 30 = 900. And, 15 + 2 + 30 = 47. Nothing there, either. All I could do was look around. It occurred to me that it might be time to combine some of the numbers in the first three chapters. So I looked back at Chapter 2. I wondered what would happen if I multiplied all the numbers in Chapter 2, except 84, by 900:

8 x 7 x 12 x 3 x 2 x 900 = 3 628 800. That didn't mean anything to me either. But I continued pondering the problem. I wondered what would happen if I multiplied all the numbers in chapter 1 by 84:

5 x 6 x 6 x 3 x 8 x 84 = 362 880. Add one zero and you have the same number. That was interesting, but I didn't have a clue what the number might represent.

Maybe this is a good time to describe how "*Gabriel*" has participated in this project. That's probably not exactly accurate. It's more like this is Gabriel's project, and I've been drafted to help. What happens is that I feel strong urges. A thought occurs to me to try something with the numbers, or to look someplace in the Bible or in some other book, and I feel as though I have to do it. It's stronger than just *Maybe I should*; it's more like *I have to*. And so I do it.

What I just did with the numbers in Chapters 1, 2, and 3 is a perfect example. There is no logical reason to "*multiply all the numbers in Chapter 2 except 84,*" by the 900 total in Chapter 3, and then to "*multiply all the numbers in Chapter 1*" by only the 84 found in Chapter 2. I just *felt an urge* to do it. Sometimes I recognize immediately what the numbers are about. But sometimes I don't have a clue. That's what happened with this number, 362 880. It meant nothing to me. But it turned up twice, so I suspected it meant something to someone.

When this happens, there's a "*Phase 2*" process of urges. In this case, I had an urge to review *The Dimensions of Paradise*, by John Michell. Why? I don't know why. I just did. Let's just say, "The Angel *made* me do it."

From *The Dimensions of Paradise*, Adventures Unlimited Press, 2001, page 97:

"*The earth's deviation from the form of a true sphere means that the length of each successive degree of latitude increases from the equator towards the poles. At about 10 degrees latitude north or south the length of a degree is 362 880 (=9!) ft., making the length of a minute of arc 6048 ft. This is equal to 10 stades of 604.8 ft., of which there are 5 in the perimeter of the (Great) Pyramid.*"

(Gott Note: 9! Means 1 x 2 x 3 x 4 x 5 x 6 x 7 x 8 x 9 = 362 880;

10! Means 1 x 2 x 3 x 4 x 5 x 6 x 7 x 8 x 9 x 10 = 3 628 800.)

Back to Michell, p. 97:

"*At about 50 degrees North or South the length of the nautical mile has increased to 6082.56 ft., approximately the value used by modern navies. It is equal to 6000 longer Greek feet of 1.01376 ft. or to 6250 longer Roman feet of 0.973 209 6 ft. or to 5280 longer Egyptian feet of 1.152 ft. The shorter nautical mile of 6048 ft. is made up of 6000 shorter Greek or 6250 shorter Roman or 5280 shorter Egyptian feet, and it is also divided by their respective cubits and stades. The difference between the longer and shorter nautical miles is 34.56 ft. or 30 Egyptian feet of 1.152 ft.*

"*Multiplying the length of the average nautical mile, as indicated by ancient metrology (6082.56 ft.) by 21 600, the number of minutes in a circle, produces the traditional value of the length of the meridian, the great circle passing through the poles. It proves to be 131 383 296 ft. or 24 883.2 miles...*"

What does this tell about the number, 362 880? Converting 131 383 296 feet per nautical mile to Egyptian feet (131 383 296 divided by 1.152) is 114 048 000 feet. And a sphere with a circumference of 114 048 000 feet would have a diameter of 36 288 000 feet (114 048 000 divided by 3.1428571).

It's right there, hidden for all *theological philosophers* to discover, in Luke's gospel! There's more.

Mitchell, page 154: "*In describing the process by which the Creator fabricated that quality called Soul which gives life to the world, Plato was at his most explicit on the nature of Pythagorean arithmetic and the traditional canon of number. The World-soul was compounded from three ingredients, the two Opposites, called the Same and the Other, together with Essence.*"

Philosophers from the time of Plato (circa 428-347 BCE) to the present have labored to solve the mystery of Plato's *World-soul* number. Michell provides a good argument (pp. 154-69) that the mystery number and answer to the puzzle is 1140480. That makes the number 362 880 highly significant in Plato's equation.

What I'm suggesting is that the writer of the gospel of *Luke* (or *Lux*) was a student of Plato and fully aware of his *World-soul* number puzzle. And/or, Luke knew the length of a degree at 10 degrees latitude north or south, and/or the diameter in feet of the great circle passing through the poles. Take your pick.

Any student of Plato would have also been familiar with Homer's *Iliad* and *Odyssey*, Plutarch's works, the scientists and mathematicians of ancient times, including Aristarchus, Pythagoras, Appolynius of Perga, Pliny the Elder (who would probably have been Luke's contemporary), and others. Most certainly Luke would have known the Torah through and through. And Plato's student would have known that only the educated of the time, and of subsequent times, would be familiar with all those sources.

So Luke did the only thing that had any chance of getting the knowledge and truth passed on through history. Luke buried the numbers for the sun, moon, earth, the speed of light, and other numbers of scientific significance, in the stories in the gospel. And within the same stories, Luke buried references to the Torah; Homer, Plutarch, and Euripides; the scientists and philosophers of ancient times, and of the same time in history as the text was being written.

By reading the stories covertly referenced by Luke, a good detective can unravel the coded message buried throughout both Luke and Acts. And for reasons that will be made clear in later chapters, from this point forward, except when quoting biblical chapters and verses, *Luke* will sometimes be referred to as *Lux*, and I may refer to the writer, or writers, using the plural pronoun, *they*.

CHAPTER TWO

*"All who believed were together and had all things in common;
they would sell their possessions...and distribute the proceeds to all,
as any had need."*
Acts 2:44

CONSPIRATORS' CODED CLUES

I thought it stood to reason that the person, or persons, who addressed the *Theological Philosophers*, and who hid significant numerical clues to their knowledge throughout the texts, would also reveal who they were and why they hid the message. With this goal in mind I began to read each word and line in Luke's gospel with the sole purpose of discovering who had written the message. I made notes of the information that seemed to be *"more than I need to know."* There was a lot! In fact, most of both Lux and Acts contained information that just seemed to be out of place and unnecessary for the transmission of the various stories. But that was what I had set out to find, and as the pages of notes piled up, I began to see how big the project would be.

I've tried to pare down quotations from various sources to only what's required to convey the information. Chapter 6 is dedicated to the numbers scattered throughout Luke's gospel and how they link to scientific data or philosophical exercises, primarily Plato's Academy and the Pythagorean schools.

When it was necessary to quote large portions of biblical texts or other sources, I highlighted the portions that are critical to solving the mystery. This is an exciting mystery and it moves quickly once you know what to look for.

I was certain that Lux would include a code early in the text to indicate that *Theophilos* had been given a mystery to unravel. I expected it would appear in the first chapter, and I was right:

Luke 1:5-7: *"In the days of King Herod of Judea, there was a priest named* **Zechariah**, *who belonged to the priestly order of* **Abijah**. *His wife was a descendant of Aaron, and her name was Elizabeth. Both of them were* **righteous before God**, *living blamelessly according to all the commandments and regulations of the Lord. But they had no children, because Elizabeth was barren, and both were getting on in years."*

Luke 1:8-11: *"Once when he was serving as priest before God and his section was on duty, he was chosen by lot, according to the custom of the priesthood, to enter the sanctuary of the Lord and offer incense. Now at the time of the incense offering, the whole assembly of the people was praying outside. Then there appeared to him* **an angel of the Lord**, *standing at the right side of the alter of incense."*

Luke 1:19: *"The angel replied, 'I am* **Gabriel**. *I stand in the presence of God, and I have been sent to speak to you and to bring you this good news.'"*

I was surprised to learn that the angel Gabriel is named only four times in the bible--twice in the book of Daniel, twice in Luke's gospel:

Daniel 8:16: *"And I heard a man's voice...and it called,* **"Gabriel..."**;

Daniel 9:21: *"...while I was speaking in prayer, the man* **Gabriel**, *whom I had seen in the vision at the first, came to me in swift flight at the time of the evening sacrifice."*

Luke 1:19: "...'I am Gabriel'...";

Luke 1:26: *"In the sixth month, the angel* **Gabriel** *was sent by God..."*

Working under the assumption that the writer of Lux was referring the *theophilosophers* to the book of Daniel to find more information about who they were, I began reading from Chapter 1. But something happened that interfered with this process. Quite by accident, (yeah, right!) I flipped open the 1994 edition of *The New Oxford Annotated Bible with the Apocrypha* to page 173 of the apocrypha section. The title? *The Additions to the Greek Book of Daniel.*

Although I'm curious about, and interested in, all things biblical, I didn't know there were additions to the Greek Book of Daniel. Considering there are over two thousand pages in this particular edition of the Bible (large print for weak eyes), opening it to this particular page was just another example of the *"incidents"* that have occurred during the writing of this book.

So what were *The Additions to the Greek Book of Daniel?* And when were they added? And when were they removed?

I needed some background on the meaning of *Apocrypha*, and the editors of The New Oxford provided a definition:

Introduction, page iii AP: *"Etymologically the word means 'things that are hidden,' but why it was chosen to describe certain books is not clear. Some have suggested that the books were 'hidden' or withdrawn from common use because they were* **deemed to contain mysterious or esoteric lore, too profound to be communicated to any except the initiated**...*Others have suggested that the term was employed by those who held that such books deserved to be 'hidden' because they were* **spurious or heretical**. *Thus it appears that in antiquity the term had an honorable significance as well as a derogatory one, depending upon the point of view of those who made use of the word.*

"According to traditional usage 'Apocrypha' has been the designation applied to the fifteen books, or portions of books..."

Page 173 AP: *"Although Theodotion 'corrected' in many particulars the Greek text of Daniel to the emerging proto-Masoretic text of the beginning of the second century BC, he nonetheless retained all the so-called additions of the Septuagint, albeit in a more suitable order for biographic purposes. Jerome's Latin Vulgate followed Theodotion basically, but made the story of Susanna ch 13, and the account of Bel and the Dragon ch 14, thus inverting the Greek order."*

Included in the list of "Apocryphal Books" are these three which are additions to Daniel:

The Prayer of Azariah and the Song of the Three Jews, Susanna, and *Bel and the Dragon.*

The editors note, Introduction, page v AP: *"Ostensibly historical but actually quite imaginative are the books of Tobit, Judith, Susanna, and Bel and the Dragon, which may be called moralistic novels.* **In fact, the last two are noteworthy as ancient examples of the _detective story_.***"*

There it is: the coded message to Theophilos that this is a mystery to be unraveled and solved. Unless the Greek copies of biblical texts in the first century didn't contain Susannah and Bel and the Dragon.

So when were these books in use, by whom, and when were they removed from common usage? And by whom were they removed? And the most important question: were these three books in use at the time Luke's gospel was written? If they were, there may be something in them that could help unravel the mystery of who, specifically, wrote gospel:

Introduction, page v-vi AP: *"Ecclesiastical opinions concerning the nature and worth of the books of the Apocrypha have varied with age and place.*

"None of the authors of the books of the New Testament makes a direct quotation from any of the fifteen books of the Apocrypha, though frequent quotations occur from most of the thirty-nine books of the Hebrew canon of the Old Testament. On the other hand, **several New Testament writers make occasional allusions to one or more apocryphal books...***"*

Introduction, page vi AP: **"During the early Christian centuries most Greek and Latin Church Fathers, such as Irenaeus, Tertullian, Clement of Alexandria, and Cyprian (none of whom knew any Hebrew), quoted passages from the Greek text of apocryphal/deuterocanonical books as 'Scripture,' 'divine Scripture,' 'inspired,' and the like.** *In this period only an occasional Father made an effort to learn the limits of the Palestinian Jewish canon (as Melito of Sardis)* **or to distinguish between the Hebrew text of Daniel and the addition of the story of Susanna in the Greek version** *(as Africanus).*

"In the **fourth century** *many Greek Fathers (including Eusebius,*

*Athanasius, Cyril of Jerusalem, Gregory of Nazianzus, Amphilochius, and Epiphanius) came to recognize a distinction between the books in the Hebrew canon and the rest, though the latter were still **customarily cited as Scripture**. During the following centuries usage fluctuated in the East, but at the important Synod of Jerusalem in 1672 the books of Tobit, Judith, Ecclesiasticus, and Wisdom were expressly designated as canonical..."*

"At the close of the fourth century, Jerome spoke out decidedly for the Hebrew canon, declaring unreservedly that books that were outside that canon should be classed as apocryphal. *When he prepared his celebrated revision of the Latin Bible, the Vulgate, he scrupulously separated the apocryphal, "Additions to Daniel" and "Esther," marking them with prefatory notes as absent from the original Hebrew."*

I think the primary question has been answered: the three *Additions to Daniel* were added during the second century BCE, and were included until some time in the fourth century ACE, probably toward the end of the century, and they were declared apocryphal by Jerome. They were part of the book of Daniel when Luke's gospel was written. That is the information necessary in order to know if there might be some of the hidden message in one of these apocyrphal, or hidden, chapters from Daniel.

But are any of these three stories likely to help us solve the mystery Lux has placed before us? Lux answers that question:

Luke 8:1-3: *"Soon afterwards he went on through cities and villages, proclaiming and bringing the good news of the kingdom of God. The twelve were with him, as well as some women who had been cured of evil spirits and infirmities: Mary, called Magdalene, from whom seven demons had gone out, and Joanna, the wife of Herod's steward Chuza, and **Susanna**, and many others, who provided for them out of their resources."*

Other than in the hidden chapter of Daniel, the name *Susanna* appears just this one time in the scriptures. And she's with Jesus, the twelve, Mary Magdalene, and Joanna. I think Lux might have been sending the message that Susanna's story is relevant to solving the mystery.

The editors of *The New Oxford Annotated Bible with the Apocrypha*, write on page 179 AP:

"It is difficult to determine if the account concerning Susanna was composed in Greek or rests upon a Semitic original. Puns based on the Greek in vv. 54-55 and 58-59 might indicate a Greek original, though good translators often try to match puns from original compositions in the receptor language. The Greek text, like other purely Greek portions of Daniel, is full of semitisms; most scholars have thought in terms of a Semitic original, a few thinking of two separate ones lying behind the Theodotionic and the Septuagint versions. The date of the composition would have been sometime in the second century BC."

(The verses 54-55 and 58-59, referenced above, will be quoted completely very shortly, and the puns referenced here, which contain critical clues to our mystery, will be fully explained at that time.)

Some highlights from *Susanna* begin to shed some light on the hidden messages in Luke's gospel.

The setting of the story is Babylon. Susanna is married to Joakim, who was very rich and *"had a fine garden adjoining his house; the Jews used to come to him because he was the most honored of them all."*

Two elders were appointed as judges to govern the people. They were frequently at Joakim's house, and *"all who had a case to be tried came to them there."*

"When the people left at noon, Susanna would go into her husband's garden to walk." These two elders watched her each day, and as time passed, their lust for her grew and grew. They confessed their lust to each other, then arranged for a time when they could get Susanna alone in the garden.

One day they were watching and saw her dismiss her maids, leaving her alone in the garden; they approached her:

"Look, the garden doors are shut, and no one can see us. We are burning with desire for you; so give your consent, and lie with us. If you refuse, we will testify against you that a young man was with you, and this was why you sent your maids away.'"

"*Susanna groaned and said, 'I am completely trapped. For if I do this, it will mean death for me; if I do not, I cannot escape your hands. I choose not to do it; I will fall into your hands, rather than sin in the sight of the Lord.'*"

As they promised they would do, the judges accused her of adultery; she was convicted and sentenced to death.

"*Then Susanna cried out with a loud voice, and said, 'O eternal God, you know what is secret and are aware of all things before they come to be; you know that these men have given false evidence against me. And now I am to die, though I have done none of the wicked things that they have charged against me.'*

"*The Lord heard her cry. Just as she was being led off to execution, God stirred up the holy spirit of a young lad named Daniel, and he shouted with a loud voice, 'I want no part in shedding this woman's blood!'*

"*All the people turned to him and asked, 'What is this you are saying?' Taking his stand among them he said, 'Are you such fools, O Israelites, as to condemn a daughter of Israel without examination and without learning the facts? Return to court, for these men have given false evidence against her.'*"

Back to court they all go. Daniel separates the two judges, then summons the first:

"*'You old relic of wicked days, your sins have now come home, which you have committed in the past, **pronouncing unjust judgments, condemning the innocent and acquitting the guilty, though the Lord said, 'You shall not put an innocent and righteous person to death.'** Now then, if you really saw this woman, tell me this: Under what tree did you see them being intimate with each other?' He answered, 'Under a **mastic tree**.' And Daniel said, 'Very well! This lie has cost you your head, for the angel of God has received the sentence from God and will immediately **cut** you in two.'*"

The other judge was then brought in:

"*'You offspring of Canaan and not of Judah, beauty has beguiled you and lust has perverted your heart. This is how you have been treating the daughters of Israel, and they were intimate with you through fear; but a daughter of Judah would not tolerate your wickedness. Now then, tell me: Under what tree did you catch them* *being intimate with each other?' He answered, 'Under an **evergreen oak**.' Daniel said to him, 'Very well! This lie has cost you also your head, for the angel of God is waiting with his sword to **split** you in two, so as to destroy you both.'"*

Footnotes explain that the Greek words for *mastic tree* and *cut* are similar; the Greek words for *evergreen oak* and *split* are similar, thus forming an ironic wordplay. The annotation puts it this way: *"The wordplay of the original may be also represented in English by the paraphrase, 'Under a **clove** tree...the angel will **cleave** you'; 'under a yew tree...the angel will **hew** you asunder."*

Luke has used a similar device with the title of the entire gospel: *Luke's Gospel* is *Lux Gospel*. And that works in both Greek and English.

Daniel saved Susanna, and she and Joakim lived happily ever after, I suppose.

Since *Bel and the Dragon* has also been classified as an ancient mystery novel, there's probably some additional evidence to be found there.

Bel and the Dragon, Chapter 14 of the Greek Version of Daniel, is also about corruption. It, too, is set in Babylon, and it is the story of seventy priests of Bel, their wives and children.

Bel ate a lot of food, and Daniel tried to tell the king it was not the god Bel who ate the food, since Bel was just an idol made of clay inside and bronze outside. He accused the priests of eating the food and set about to prove it. He and the king dusted the floor of the temple with ashes and then locked it and sealed it. The priests and their families had a secret tunnel that entered the temple under the table. They came in the night, ate all the food, and left before morning. The king and Daniel checked the seal and saw that it had not been broken, entered, and found the food all gone. The king proclaimed that Bel had eaten the food in the night, but Daniel showed him the footprints of the priests, their wives, and the children. The king arrested the priests and they showed him the secret door under the table. The king put them to death.

The third missing book of Daniel is *The Prayer of Azariah and the Song of the Three Jews*. It expands on the story in Daniel wherein Shadrach, Meshach, and Abednego are thrown into the fiery furnace. The Hebrew names of these three men were *Hananiah, Mishael,* and *Azariah,* and in Greek, they were **Ananias, Azarias,** and *Misael.* The name *Ananias* becomes very important later, and *Azariah* will be found in another apocryphal scripture also linked to by Lux very shortly.

The information that seems most pertinent from this *hidden* book, *The Prayer of Azariah,* is verse 26: *"But **the angel of the Lord** came down into the furnace to be with **Azariah** and his companions, and drove the fiery flame out of the furnace, and made the inside of the furnace as though a moist wind were whistling through it. The fire did not touch them at all and caused them no pain or distress."*

Since Gabriel is named at Daniel 8:16 and 9:21, I thought it was reasonable to assume that this *"angel of the Lord"* who saved the three friends was also Gabriel. But later discoveries changed my mind about this angel's identity. There is another possibility, and he's about to make an appearance.

ॐ

As I looked through the other books in the Apocrypha, one of them caught my attention because of its title: *Tobit.* I've had two dogs named *Toby,* and one of them is still with us.

I was sharing *"snuggles"* with Toby when I realized she is my second dog to carry that name. The first of the two, a male, I chose the name; this one, a bitch, was pre-named before she moved in and assumed control. Then the apocryphal *Tobit* popped into my head. *Interesting coincidence,* I thought. The next thought has become something of a *mantra* for me: *There are no coincidences.*

It didn't take long to prove out that mantra:

Tobit 1:1-2: *"This book tells the story of Tobit son of Tobiel son of **Hananiel** son of Aduel son of **Gabael** son of **Raphael** son of Raguel of the descendants of Asiel, of the tribe of Naphtali, who in the days of King Enemessaros of the Assyrians was taken into captivity from Thisbe, which is to the south of Kedesh Naphtali in Upper Galilee, above **Asher** toward the west, and north of Phogor."*

The first link to Lux which I recognized is the word *Asher.*

Luke 2:36: *"...there was a prophetess, **Anna**...of the tribe of **Asher**."*

The second link is the righteousness of the characters in both Lux and Tobit:

Tobit 1:3: *"I, Tobit, walked in the ways of truth and righteousness all the days of my life."*

Luke 1:6: *"...they (Zechariah and Elizabeth) were both righteous...walking in all the commandments and ordinances of the Lord blameless."*

And then this:

Tobit 1:9: *"When I became a man I married a woman, **Anna**, a member of our own family, and by her I became the father of a son whom I named Tobias."*

The discovery of Anna in *Tobit* is extremely significant since it is Anna whom Lux places with the newborn baby Jesus. There are no other Anna's in either the Old or New Testaments, so it's certain that *Tobit* is the story of Anna that Lux wanted Theophilus to read. (The Infancy Gospel of James found at Nag Hammadi describes *Anna* as the mother of the Virgin Mary, but James' gospel was written *decades after* Luke's and probably based his *Anna* on Luke's.)

Some of the highlights of Tobit and Anna's circumstances:

Tobit 1:10-12: *"After **I was carried away captive** to Assyria and came as a captive to Nineveh, everyone of my...people ate the food of the Gentiles, but I kept myself from eating the food of the Gentiles. Because I was mindful of God...the Most High gave me favor and good standing with Enemessaros."*

Tobit 1:17-18: *"I would give my food to the hungry and my clothing to the naked; and if I saw the dead body of any of my people thrown out behind the wall of Nineveh, I would bury it. I also buried any whom the King put to death when he came fleeing from Judea in those days of judgment that the king of heaven executed upon him because of his blasphemies. For in his anger he put to death many Israelites; but I would secretly remove the bodies and bury them."*

Tobit tells the story of some of the Judeans fleeing and others being killed by the king.

Tobit 1:19: *"...when I realized that the king knew about me and* *that **I** was being searched for to be put to death, I was afraid and ran away. Then all **my property was confiscated**; nothing was left to me that was not taken into the royal treasury except my wife Anna and my son Tobias."*

Tobit reports that all who resisted or disobeyed the king's orders were threatened with death. And if they fled they were stripped of everything they owned. Then Tobit's bad luck gets worse. After burying another dead body he showers and falls asleep by the wall of the courtyard:

Tobit 2:10: *"I did not know there were sparrows on the wall; their fresh droppings fell into my eyes and produced white films. I went to physicians to be healed, but the more they treated me with ointments the more my vision was obscured by the white films, until **I became completely blind**..."*

Tobit was left with no money, no land, and no home. He is blinded by bird droppings and is unable to provide for his own family:

Tobit 2:11: *"...my wife Anna earned money at women's work."*

Then Tobit remembers that he had left a sum of money with a relative in Media decades earlier. He tells his son Tobias that he is to retrieve the money. But the road to Media is dangerous and Tobias doesn't know the way:

Tobit 5:4: *"So Tobias went out to look for a man to go with him to Media, someone who was acquainted with **the way**. He went out and found the angel Raphael standing in front of him; but he did not perceive that **he was an angel of God**."*

Perhaps it's a stretch to consider that Lux might have wanted to lead *Theophilus* to *The Way* in this context, but it is associated with *"an angel of God."* It jumped out at me, and I believe it was intended to do just that. Lux wanted to emphasize the importance of angels in *The Nazarene Way*.

When Tobit interviews Raphael to determine if Tobias would be safe with him, he asks about his family and who his father was.

Tobias 5:13: *"He (Raphael) replied, 'I am **Azariah**, the son of the great **Hananiah**, one of your relatives.'"*

In Hebrew *Azariah* means *God helps*, and Azariah is

prominent in both Daniel and Tobit. The angel who protected Shadrach, Meshach, and Abidnego in the fiery furnace must have been Raphael, rather than Gabriel. Both have now become important figures in Luke's story.

Note the interconnectedness of the three biblical books, *Tobit, The Song of Azariah,* and *Daniel.* Hananiah was one of Daniel's three friends, and Daniel called him "*Shadrach.*" Also, the Greek for *Hananiah* is *Ananais,* and as already promised, that name will become quite relevant a little later.

During the trip to Media Raphael teaches Tobias the medicinal uses of fish organs to drive out evil spirits and to treat blindness. Tobias uses the formula to rid his new wife Sarah of an evil spirit that had killed her seven previous husbands on their wedding night. When he returns to his home with his new bride, he delivers an amazing gift to his father:

Tobit 11:10-14: "*Then Tobit got up and came stumbling out through the courtyard door. Tobias went up to him, with the gall of the fish in his hand, and **holding him firmly**, he blew into his eyes, saying, 'Take courage, father.' With this he **applied the medicine on his eyes**, and it made them smart. Next with both his hands he peeled off the white films from the corners of his eyes. Then Tobit saw his son and threw his arms around him, and he wept and said to him, 'I see you, my son, the light of my eyes!'*"

Lux uses this story in Tobit to draw another connection, this time at Acts 9:17-18: "*So **Ananias** went and entered the house. He **laid his hands** on Saul and said, 'Brother Saul, the Lord Jesus, who appeared to you on your way here, has sent me so that **you may regain your sight** and be filled with the Holy Spirit.' And immediately **something like scales** fell from his eyes, and his sight was restored. Then he got up and was baptized, and after taking some food, he regained his strength.*"

Fish gall was applied to Tobit's eyes, and "*something like scales*" fell from Saul's eyes, and Ananias appeared in both stories.

These books were declared apocryphal and removed from the gospels late in the fourth century. Why they were removed is said to be "*uncertain.*" But one thing *is* certain: their removal made it more difficult to discover Luke's primary purpose in writing to *Theophilus*. The primary purpose was to lead them to other texts that could tell the truth about what had happened to Jesus' message and what was happening to his disciples a generation or so later.

A good detective might suspect their removal was a cover up--an attempt to hide the truth that Lux promised to reveal to Theophilus. Did the fourth century church discover that two of their canonical books had managed to tell the truth about the evolution of Christianity and the truth about Jesus' message? Were they so fearful that someone would figure out the message, and learn the truth, that they removed the Old Testament stories to which Lux led Theophilus, hoping the trail would go cold? If that was the reason, it was successful--until now.

In addition to Anna in Tobit, we find another biblical woman named Sarah, and she becomes Tobias' wife. Lux wrote that Mary Magdalene was ridded of seven demons (Luke 8:2), and Tobit's Sarah was ridded of an evil spirit, Asmodeus, that had killed seven husbands.

A little Internet research uncovered Persian and Egyptian connections with *Asmodeus*. There seems to be virtually total agreement among scholars that *Asmodeus* is actually *Aeshma Daeva,* from Persian Zoroastrian mythology. He is one of seven evil spirits which balance seven angelic spirits that influence people's lives.

What might Lux have been trying to say about Mary Magdalene by adding this information about the seven demons? With this reference to the religion founded by Zoraster, which revolved around the struggle between good and evil, Lux reveals that Mary Magdalene became all good. Prior to this exodus of the seven demons, Mary Magdalene was like every other person, working to overcome negative tendencies and trying to be a good person. When the seven evil spirits departed from her she was left with no negative tendencies. According to Lux, once the connection is made to Tobit's *Sarah* and *Asmodeus*,

Mary Magdalene became the perfect feminine expression of goodness; a perfect expression of God in female form.

There are several more obvious connections between Luke/Acts and Tobit. Lux has the Virgin Mary say the following at Chapter 1 verses 46-53:

"My soul magnifies the Lord...his mercy is on those who fear him from generation to generation...He has scattered the proud in the imagination of their hearts, he has put down the powerful from their thrones, and exalted those of low degree; he has filled the hungry with good things, and the rich he has sent empty away."

Tobit's words are quite similar:

Tobit 13:7 : *"As for me, I exalt my God, and my soul rejoices in the King of heaven."*

Tobit 13:1-6: *"Blessed be God who lives forever, and his kingdom lasts throughout all ages. For he afflicts, and he shows mercy; he leads down to Hades in the lowest regions of the earth, and he brings up from the great destruction, and there is nothing that can escape his hand. Acknowledge him...O children of Israel; for he has scattered you among them...Exalt him in the presence of every living being...He will afflict you for your iniquities, but he will again show mercy on all of you. He will gather you from all the nations among whom you have been scattered. If you turn to him with all your heart and with all your soul, to do what is true before him, then he will turn to you and will no longer hide his face from you."*

The order of the words are a little different, but the word choices in many cases are identical and the meaning is clearly the same.

Tobit's story ends with Chapter 14:

Tobit 14:4-5: *"...All of our kindred, inhabitants of the land of Israel, will be scattered and taken as captives from the good land; and the whole land of Israel will be desolate, even Samaria and Jerusalem will be desolate. And the temple of God in it will be burned to the ground, and it will be desolate for a while. But God will again have mercy on them, and God will bring them back into the land of Israel; and they will rebuild the temple of God, but not like the first one until the period when the times of fulfillment shall come. After this they all will return from their exile and will rebuild Jerusalem in splendor; and in it the temple of God will be rebuilt, just as the prophets of Israel have said concerning it."*

By the time Lux prepared the two books for Theophilus, the temple at Jerusalem had been destroyed. It is possible that the last two chapters of Tobit were written *after* the fall of the temple. The editors of The New Oxford, page 16 AP: *"Some scholars believe that chs 13 and 14 were added to the book much later in order to give substance to the words of 12.22a and to round out the account of Tobit's life."*

Tobit 14:6: *"Then the nations in the whole world will all be converted and worship God in truth. They will all abandon their idols, which deceitfully have led them into their error; and in righteousness they will praise the eternal God. All the Israelites who are saved in those days and are truly mindful of God will be gathered together; they will go to Jerusalem and live in safety forever in the land of Abraham, and it will be given over to them. Those who sincerely love God will rejoice, but those who commit sin and injustice will vanish from all the earth."*

And then there are these two verses that simply left me shaking my head:

Tobias 5:16: "...and the young man's dog was with them." (From *The New Oxford Annotated with Apocrypha*, 1973 edition.)

Tobias 6:2: *"...and the dog came out with him and went along with them."*

Tobias 11:4: *"...And the dog went along behind them."*

I can assure you I did not choose the name for my first Toby because of this biblical dog. And since Tobit is apocryphal and unknown by even religious people, I doubt that the name for our current Toby was derived from this book either. Strictly coincidental!

❧

What could be Luke's purpose in referring us to these stories, most of which were removed by the Church leadership in the latter part of the fourth century?

First, as already noted two of them are mystery stories. That tells us we're working to solve a mystery. And the entire book of Daniel is dedicated to solving the mysteries and finding the meanings of a multitude of visions and dreams.

Second, Susanna is a woman forced by her integrity and faith into fighting ruthless, unethical men who have power over the lives of people. The two elders serving as judges had the power of life and death for Susanna and the other townspeople. They condemned innocent men and women and acquitted the guilty. That's a pretty powerful message, and history tells us it's accurate. The men and women who were faithful to Jesus and the Nazarene Way were fighting this same battle. Thousands were killed for heresies against the official church doctrine, when all they were doing was defending Jesus and his true message. By the time the killing had ceased, several million men, women, and children had died for various *"heresies"* as defined by the Church.

Bel and the Dragon tells us the temple priests were as corrupt as the government appointed judges in Susanna's story. History also tells us this was one of the reasons Jesus decided to take the Nazarene message to the people.

Luke 19:45: *"Then he entered the temple and began to drive out those who were selling things there; and he said, 'It is written, 'My house shall be a house of prayer; but you have made it a den of robbers.'"*

The *"things"* they were selling were the pigeons and doves for burnt offerings and sacrifices, one of the superstitions Jesus came to expose. Just as Daniel showed the lies and greed of the temple priests, so did Jesus. *Bel* was no more a false god than was the *god* described by the temple priests. Both required offerings and both were false. That's another message from Lux.

The Song of Azariah and *Tobit* introduce another angel: *Raphael*. And both tell more about what was happening to Jesus' disciples. But there are still more clues about what was happening:

Luke 1:13-15: *"But the angel said to him, 'Do not be afraid, Zechariah, for your prayer has been heard. Your wife Elizabeth will bear you a son, and you will name him John. You will have joy and gladness, and many will rejoice at his birth, for he will be great in the sight of the Lord, and **he shall drink no wine nor strong drink...**"*

The annotation for verse 15 references another book in the Old Testament:

Numbers 6:1-4: *"And the Lord said to Moses, 'Say to the people of Israel, 'When either a man or a woman makes a special vow, the vow of a **nazirite**, to separate himself to the LORD, he shall **separate himself from wine and strong drink; he shall drink no vinegar made from wine or strong drink**, and shall not drink any juice of grapes...'"*

This same phrase is found at Judges 13, and there are interesting parallels between this story and Lux, Chapter 1.

Judges 13:1-7: *"The Israelites again did what was evil in the sight of the Lord, and the Lord gave them into the hand of the Philistines for forty years. There was a certain man of Zorah, of the tribe of the Danites, whose name was Manoah. **His wife was barren**, having borne no children. And the **angel of the Lord** appeared to the woman and said to her, 'Although you are barren, having borne no children, **you shall conceive** and bear a son. Now be careful **not to drink wine or strong drink, or to eat anything unclean**, for you shall conceive and bear a son. **No razor** is to come on his head, for the boy shall be a **nazirite** to God from birth. It is he who shall begin to **deliver Israel** from the hand of the Philistines.' Then the woman came and told her husband, '**A man of God** came to me, and his appearance was like that of an angel of God, most awe inspiring; I did not ask him where he came from, and he did not tell me his name, but he said to me, 'You shall conceive and bear a son. So then **drink no wine or strong drink**, and eat nothing unclean, for the boy shall be a **nazarite** to God from birth to the day of his death.'"*

Would it be safe to assume this *"angel of the Lord,"* is also Gabriel? Or perhaps it's Raphael?

Numbers 13:24: *"The woman bore a son, and named him Samson. The boy grew and the Lord blessed him."*

A footnote adds: *"The name Samson is related to the Hebrew word for sun."*

Is the writer of Luke's gospel trying to tell us that they are descendants of the Nazarites described in the Old Testament, known as Nazoreans, or Nazarenes, during the time of Jesus?

Look at the similarities between Judges, Chapter 13, and Luke, Chapter 1:

Judges: *"There was a certain man of Zorah, of the **tribe** of the Danites, whose name was Manoah. His **wife was barren**..."*

Luke: *"...There was a priest named Zechariah, who belonged to the **priestly order** of Abijah. His **wife** was a descendant of Aaron, and her name was Elizabeth...But they had no children, because Elizabeth **was barren**. **Both of them were righteous before God, living blamelessly according to all the commandments and regulations of the Lord.**"*

Judges: *"**An angel of the Lord appeared** to the woman and said to her, '...You shall conceive and **bear a son**. Now be careful not to **drink wine or strong drink**, or to eat anything unclean, for you shall conceive and bear a son. No razor is to come on his head, for the boy shall be a nazirite to God from birth...'"*

Luke: *"Then there **appeared to him an angel of the Lord**...The angel said to him...'Your wife Elizabeth will **bear you a son**...He must **never drink wine or strong drink**; even before his birth he will be filled with the Holy Spirit...'"*

The only difference between the stories is that Judges states the child is a nazirite, and Luke does not. Is this what the writer wanted to convey by quoting a phrase that would send any student of theology to Numbers and Judges? Were they passing on the information that they were Nazarenes?

Why not just say it? Why not just say that Zachariah and Elizabeth were Nazarenes and that Baby John the Baptist was a Nazarene? Because the Nazarene Gnostics, teachers of the secret doctrine, were being persecuted, and the writer of Luke's gospel reveals this fact:

Luke 1:20-23: *"And behold, **you will be silent and unable to speak** until the day that these things come to pass, because **you did not believe my words**, which will be fulfilled in their time. And the people were waiting for Zechariah, and they wondered at his delay in the temple. And when he came out, **he could not speak to them**, and they perceived that he had seen a vision in the temple; and he **made signs to them and remained dumb.**"*

The names *Zechariah* and *Abijah*, appear in the same sentence in just one place in the Old Testament:

2 Chronicles 29:1-2: *"Hezekiah began to reign...in Jerusalem. His mother's name was **Abijah** daughter of **Zechariah**. He did what was **right in the sight of the Lord**, just as his ancestor David had done."*

In addition to the two names, the descriptions of the people are almost identical: This Zechariah *"did what was right in the sight of the Lord"*; Luke's Zechariah was *"righteous before God, living blamelessly according to all the commandments and regulations of the Lord."* What might Lux be leading the readers to find by duplicating names and descriptions first found in the Old Testament?

Here are some excerpts from 2 Chronicles 29:

"...our ancestors have been unfaithful and have done what was evil in the sight of the Lord our God; they have forsaken him, and have turned away their faces from the dwelling of the Lord, and turned their backs."

"They also shut the doors...and put out the lamps..."

"...Our fathers have fallen by the sword and our sons and our daughters and our wives are in captivity..."

Could this be more of the coded message from the Nazarenes that they were unable to speak openly because they did not accept the false teachings of the early church that denied their knowledge of God, and because of this their lives were being threatened at the time this gospel was written?

Luke provides more clues that point in this direction. After the child is named John, his father, Zechariah, begins to speak again, and here's what he says:

Luke 1:68-79: *"Blessed be the Lord God of Israel, for he has visited and redeemed his people, and has raised up a horn of salvation for us in the house of his servant David, as he spoke by the mouth of his holy prophets from of old, that we should be **saved from our enemies, and from the hand of all who hate us**; to perform the mercy promised to our fathers and to remember his holy covenant, the oath which he swore to our father Abraham, **to grant us that we, being delivered from the hand of our enemies, might serve**

**him without fear, in holiness and righteousness before him all
the days of our life.** *And you, child, will be called the prophet of the
Most High; for you will go before the Lord to prepare his ways,* **to give
knowledge** *of salvation to his people in the forgiveness of their sins,
through the tender mercy of our God, when the day shall dawn upon us
from on high* **to give _light_ to those who sit in darkness** *and in the
shadow of death,* **to guide our feet into the way of peace."**

Luke provided more information about why *"they could not
speak,"* and why they had to make *"signs...and remain dumb."* (Luke
1:22.) They had to write using code words and numbers because
they were hated by certain enemies of their faith. The reason
they were hated was because they attempted *"to give knowledge"*
and *"to give light"* and to teach *"the way of peace."*

Think about it. If Luke's gospel was written by the people
leading the early *"official"* church, writing the *"official"* church
doctrine, supporting the *"official"* church hierarchy, and
promoting the *"official"* church, why did they have to write in
coded words and hidden numbers? Remember, very early in
the formation of *"Christianity,"* the Gnostics became despised
because the *"official"* church taught that they were *"Pawns of
Satan"* and that their knowledge and teachings were heresies.
The earliest to do this was, of course, Saul, known as Paul:

I Timothy 1:19-20: *"By rejecting conscience, certain persons
have suffered shipwreck in the faith; among them are Hymenaeus and
Alexander, whom I have turned over to Satan, so that they may learn
not to blaspheme."*

I Timothy 5:15: *"For some have already turned away to follow
Satan."*

These people who *"turned away to follow Satan"* were the
Gnostics Paul warned his followers to avoid. And the *"Gnostics"*
were those who taught the numbers and the science of the
Universe--the same numbers and science hidden in Luke/Acts.

There is an interesting quotation in *The Case for Christ* by
Lee Strobel. On page 165 Strobel is quoting from his interview
with Gregory Boyd, Ph.D.

Boyd: *"Everyone concedes that this gospel (Thomas) has
been significantly influenced by Gnosticism, which was a religious*

*movement in the second, third, and fourth centuries that **supposedly** had secret insights, knowledge, or revelations that would allow people to know the **key to the universe**. Salvation was by what you knew--gnosis is Greek for 'know,' he said."* (Emphasis added. And, of course, both Strobel and Boyd argue that salvation has nothing to do with knowledge; salvation is by faith in the blood of Christ, Paul's doctrine upon which modern Christianity was founded.)

Boyd didn't say the reason this religious movement appeared in the second century was because it differed drastically from the *"official"* church doctrine that was beginning to become solidified at that time. Nor did he explain that it ceased to exist in the fourth century because the armies that fought under the direction of the church leaders, with help from the Roman government, managed to kill most of the Gnostics and drove the few who survived underground. It was also in the fourth century that Plato's Academy was closed permanently and its all books destroyed. Greek philosophy, for all intents and purposes, entered its 'dark winter' of fifteen hundred years.

It's time for a quick review of the clues gathered so far:

1. Lux first demanded our attention by inserting numbers in the first chapter that lead to the knowledge, or gnosis, they had about the sun, the moon, and the speed of light. This is knowledge the early church labeled, *"heresy,"* and denied until the 17th century.

2. Lux sent us to verses quoted from the Old Testament that were about nazirites. At the time Lux was writing, *nazirites* were known as *Nazarenes,* and they were being persecuted and killed for their *"heresies,"* which included knowledge about scientific and astronomical facts and figures.

3. Lux, using the angel of the Lord Gabriel, sent us to the Book of Daniel and, specifically, to the mystery novel *Susanna.*

4. Lux described Zecariah, apparently a Nazarene, as *"unable*

to speak" because he *"did not believe"* what he was being told.

6. Zechariah *"made signs"* in order to communicate with the people, just as Lux *"made signs"* using numbers and quotations to communicate a hidden message.

7. Lux indicated, through the use of the story about Susanna, that women played a prominent role in the drama unfolding at the time Luke's gospel was being written. There are very few biblical women who are portrayed as heroines, which may be one of the reasons Jerome decided *Susanna* should be hidden from the public.

8. *Susanna* reveals that the government officials, or judges, were corrupt, *"convicting the innocent and acquitting the guilty."*

9. Lux showed through the story of *Bel and the Dragon* that the temple priests were as corrupt as the government officials.

There's a lot of information in Lux Chapter 1. It tells us what was going on, who was trying to get *The Truth* out, and the challenges they were facing as they tried to accomplish this daunting task. In effect, we now know who the good guys and gals are, who the bad guys are, and what was happening between them.

CHAPTER THREE

"...your God is a God of gods...and a revealer of mysteries,
for you have been able to solve this mystery!"
Daniel 2:47

"MYTHSTERIES"
AND
MASTER MAGICIANS

The book of Daniel, which Gabriel's presence in Lux takes us back to, provides additional confirmation of the vegetarian lifestyle of the chosen people of God:

Daniel 1:8: *"But **Daniel resolved that he would not defile himself with the royal rations of food and wine**; so he asked the palace master to allow him not to defile himself."*

The palace master was fearful the king would be angry if Daniel and his three friends looked weaker and frailer than the other servants. (Daniel's three friends were Hananiah, a.k.a. Shadrach; Michael, a.k.a. Meshach; and Azariah, a.k.a. Abednego.)

But Daniel had a suggestion:

Daniel 1:12-13: *"Please test your servants for ten days. **Let us be given vegetables to eat and water to drink**. You can then compare our appearance with the appearance of the young men who eat the royal rations, and deal with your servants according to what you observe.'"*

The palace guard agreed to try it.

Daniel 1:15-17: *"At the end of ten days it was observed that they appeared better and fatter than all the young men who had been eating* *the royal rations. So the guard continued to withdraw their royal rations and the wine they were to drink, and **gave them vegetables.** To these four young men God gave **knowledge** and skill in every aspect of **literature and wisdom;** Daniel also had insight into all **visions and dreams.**"* (Emphasis added.)

This doesn't say they were wiser and more insightful because of their diet, but one could surmise the writer intended to show a connection. And notice one of the things they had knowledge of was literature. This becomes extremely important in later chapters.

(Note: The Nazarene/Essenes in Jesus' time were vegetarians, as are modern Essenes.)

Daniel 1:18: *"At the end of the time that the king had set for them to be brought in the palace master brought them into the presence of Nebuchadnezzar, and the king spoke with them. And among them all, no one was found to compare with Daniel, Hananian (Greek pronunciation, Ananiah), Mishael, and Azariah; therefore they were stationed in the king's court. **In every matter of wisdom and understanding concerning which the king inquired of them, he found them ten times better** than all the magicians and enchanters in his whole kingdom. And Daniel continued there until the first year of King Cyrus."*

Perhaps this refers, again, to the writer being Nazarene and having more *"wisdom and understanding"* than the others throughout the kingdom. This is the *gnosis* hated and ridiculed by early, and modern, church leaders.

Daniel 1:26-28: *"The king said to Daniel, whose name was Belteshazzar, 'Are you able to tell me the dream that I have seen and its interpretation?' Daniel answered the king, "No wise men, enchanters, magicians, or diviners can show to the king the **mystery** that the king is asking, **but there is a God in heaven who reveals mysteries,** and he has disclosed to King Nebuchadnezzar what will happen at the end of days. Your dream and the visions of your head as you lay in bed were these..."*

Note this reference to *"mysteries."* That word appears in the Old Testament only in the book of Daniel, and it is used there nine times. The word for *wise men* was *Magi,* the root word of *magician*. Daniel and his three friends are described as being *"ten times wiser"* than all the magicians and enchanters in the kingdom. Daniel is clearly the biblical Sherlock Holmes.

Daniel 2:37-38: *"'You, O king,...to whom the God of heaven has given the kingdom, the power, the might, and the glory, into whose hand he has given human beings, wherever they live, the wild animals of the field, and the birds of the air, and whom he has established as ruler over them all--you are the head of gold.'"*

The power wielded by this king is as great as the power of the Creator, and Daniel states that God gave the king this tremendous power.

Daniel 2:46: *"Then King Nebuchadnezzar fell on his face, worshiped Daniel, and commanded that a grain offering and incense be offered to him. The king said to Daniel, 'Truly, your God is God of gods and Lord of kings and a **revealer of mysteries**, for **you have been able to solve this mystery!**'"*

There's that word again: *mystery*. Two more times! Notice how many times the word *mystery* appears in these verses. I'm suggesting one of the messages Lux wanted to get across is, **"This book I've written is a mystery! Solve it!"**

Daniel's description of the king could very easily be a description of the religious and government leaders of Jesus' time. They had power over every aspect of life, and they had total control over the daily lives of all the people. And they claimed this power came from God.

Notice how the king responds to Daniel's knowledge and wisdom and his interpretation of the dream. At first, he praised and honored Daniel's God. But what happened next?

Daniel 3:1-7: *"King Nebuchadnezzar made a golden statue...The herald proclaimed aloud, 'You are commanded, O peoples, nations, and languages, that when you hear the sound of the...entire musical ensemble, **you are to fall down and worship the golden statue that King Nebuchadnezzar has set up**. Whoever does not fall down and worship shall immediately be thrown into a furnace of blazing fire.' Therefore, as soon as all the peoples heard the sound of the...entire musical ensemble, all the peoples, nations, and languages fell down and worshiped the golden statue..."*

The king's new knowledge about the "*True God*" that had just been demonstrated was immediately forgotten, and he created false idols and commanded his subjects to worship these idols to a false god with a horrific punishment if they failed to do so: burning in a furnace of blazing fire! Sound familiar?

And what was done to those, like Daniel, who refused to reject their God and worship the king's idols?

Daniel 1:8-30: "*...They said to King Nebuchadnezzar, '...you have made a decree, that everyone who hears the sound of the horn...shall fall down and worship the golden statue, and whoever does not fall down shall be thrown into a furnace of blazing fire. There are certain Jews whom you have appointed over the affairs of the province of Babylon: Shadrach, Meshack, and Abednego. These pay no heed to you, O king.* **They do not serve your gods and they do not worship the golden statue that you have set up.'**

"*Then Nebuchadnezzar in furious rage commanded that Shadrach, Meshach, and Abednego be brought in...Nebuchadnezzar said to them, 'Is it true...that you do not serve my gods and you do not worship the golden statue that I have set up? Now if you are ready...to fall down and worship the statue that I have made, well and good. But if you do not worship, you shall immediately be thrown into a furnace of blazing fire, and who is the god that will deliver you out of my hands?'*

"*Shadrach, Meshach, and Abednego answered the king, 'O Nebuchadnezzar, we have no need to present a defense to you in this matter. If our God whom we serve is able to deliver us from the furnace of blazing fire and out of your hand, O king, let him deliver us. But if not, be it known to you, O king, that we will not serve your gods and we will not worship the golden statue that you have set up.'*

"*Then Nebuchadnezzar was so filled with rage against Shadrach, Meshach, and Abednego that his face was distorted. He ordered the furnace heated up seven times more than was customary, and ordered some of the strongest guards in his army to bind Shadrach, Meshach, and Abednego and to throw them into the furnace of blazing fire. So the men were bound, still wearing their mantles, their tunics, their hats, and their other garments, and they were thrown into the furnace of blazing fire. Because the king's command was urgent and the furnace was so overheated, the raging flames killed the men who lifted*

Shadrach, Meshach, and Abednego. But the three men...fell down, bound, into the furnace of blazing fire.

"Then King Nebuchadnezzar was astonished and rose up quickly. He said to his counselors, 'Was it not three men that we threw bound into the fire?' They answered the king, 'True...' He replied, 'But I see four men unbound, walking in the middle of the fire, and they are not hurt; and the fourth has the appearance of a son of the gods.' Nebuchadnezzar then approached the door of the furnace of blazing fire and said, 'Shadrach, Meshach, and Abednego, servants of the Most High God, come out! Come here!' So Shadrach, Meshach, and Abednego came out from the fire. And the satraps...saw that the fire had not had any power over the bodies of those men...and not even the smell of fire came from them.

"Nebuchadnezzar said, 'Blessed be the God of Shadrach, Meshach, and Abednego, who has sent his <u>angel</u> and delivered his servants who trusted in him. They disobeyed the king's command and yielded up their bodies rather than serve and worship any god except their own God. Therefore I make a decree: Any people, nation, or language that utters blasphemy against the God of Shadrach, Meshach, and Abednego shall be torn limb from limb, and their houses laid in ruins; for there is not other god who is able to deliver in this way.' Then the king promoted Shadrach, Meshach, and Abednego in the province of Babylon."

Even though the angel isn't named, there is only one angel to whom this would refer, and that is Gabriel.

Daniel 4:1-3: *"King Nebuchadnezzar to all peoples, nations, and languages that live throughout the earth: May you have abundant prosperity! The signs and wonders that the Most High God has worked for me I am pleased to recount. How great are his signs, how mighty his wonders! His kingdom is an everlasting kingdom, and his sovereignty is from generation to generation."*

Okay! The king sees the truth--again--and finally understands the power of the knowledge and wisdom of Truth. Surely he won't forget again after this powerful demonstration of what Truth can accomplish. It's important to note that Daniel, Shadrach, Meshach, and Abednego, *"yielded up their bodies rather than serve and worship any god except their own God."*

One can hear the voice of Lux and the Nazarenes telling *their* story of choosing persecution and even death rather than forsaking and abandoning the knowledge that Jesus gave his life to teach to the world.

Nebuchadnezzar had another dream, and again, he calls on Daniel to interpret it:

Daniel 4:18-27: *"This is the dream that I, King Nebuchadnezzar saw. Now you, Belteshazzar (aka, Daniel), declare the interpretation, since all the wise men of my kingdom are unable to tell me the interpretation. You are able, however, for you are endowed with a spirit of the holy gods.'*

"Then Daniel...was severely distressed for a while. His thoughts terrified him. The king said, '...do not let the dream or the interpretation terrify you.' Belteshazzar answered, 'My lord, may the dream be for those who hate you, and its interpretation for your enemies! **The tree that you saw, which grew great and strong, so that its top reached to heaven and was visible to the end of the whole earth, whose foliage was beautiful and its fruit abundant, and which provided food for all, under which animals of the field lived, and in whose branches the birds of the air had nests--it is you, o king!** *You have grown great and strong. Your greatness has increased and reaches to heaven, and your sovereignty to the ends of the earth. And whereas the king saw a holy watcher coming down from heaven and saying,* **'Cut down the tree and destroy it, but leave its stump and roots in the ground**...*until seven times pass over him'--this is the interpretation, O king, and it is a decree of the* **Most High** *that has come upon my lord the king: You shall be driven away from human society...and seven times shall pass over you, until you have learned that the Most High has sovereignty over the kingdom of mortals, and gives it to whom he will.* **As it was commanded to leave the stump and roots of the tree, your kingdom shall be reestablished for you from the time that you learn that Heaven is sovereign.** *Therefore, O king, may my counsel be acceptable to you: break off your sins with righteousness, and your iniquities with mercy to the oppressed, so that your prosperity may be prolonged.'"*

Even though the King had repeatedly observed the power of Daniel's God, and even though he professed to understand,

Nebuchadnezzar is about to demonstrate, again, how easily power can corrupt rational thought and destroy knowledge and common sense. Until the king actually experiences the action of the Law, he is unable to grasp its Truth. He still believes all the wonderful things he owns have come to him because of what he has done himself. He still does not believe that "*The Most High has sovereignty over the kingdom of mortals, and gives it to whom he will.*"

Daniel 4:28-30: "*...At the end of twelve months he was walking on the roof of the royal palace of Babylon, and the king said, 'Is this not magnificent Babylon, **which I have built** as a royal capital **by my mighty power and for my glorious majesty?**'*"

Whoops! There he goes again, giving himself credit for all that he has been blessed with. Imagine what's about to happen:

Daniel 4:31-37: "*While the words were still in the king's mouth, a voice came from heaven: 'O King Nebuchadnezzar, to you it is declared: The kingdom has departed from you! You shall be driven away from human society, and your dwelling shall be with the animals of the field. You shall be made to eat grass like oxen, and seven times shall pass over you, **until you have learned that the Most High has sovereignty over the kingdom of mortals and gives it to whom he will.**' Immediately the sentence was fulfilled against Nebuchadnezzar. He was driven away from human society...until his hair grew as long as eagles' feathers and his nails became like birds' claws.*

"*'When that period was over, I, Nebuchadnezzar, lifted my eyes to heaven, and **my reason returned to me**. I blessed the Most High, and praised and honored the one who lives forever. For his sovereignty is an everlasting sovereignty, and his kingdom endures from generation to generation. All the inhabitants of the earth are accounted as nothing, as he does what he wills with the hosts of heaven and the inhabitants of the earth. There is no one who can stay his hand or say to him, 'What are you doing?'*

"*At that time my reason returned to me; and my majesty and splendor were restored to me for the glory of my kingdom. My counselors and my lords sought me out, I was reestablished over my kingdom, and still more greatness was added to me. Now I, Nebuchadnezzar, praise and extol and honor the King of heaven, for all his works are truth, and his ways are justice; and he is able to bring low those who walk in pride.'"*

So, even though it appeared that the king understood the power of the Most High, he didn't fully understand until he actually experienced the consequences of his acts. The king's experience demonstrates Jesus' admonition: *"Do unto others as you would have them do unto you, for what you do to others shall be done unto you."* In other words, the Law is sure and cannot be avoided.

But poor Daniel isn't off the hook just yet, and there are more words that apply to the events in the lives of the Nazarenes of the first and second century. Although historically, Belshazzar was the son of Nabonidus, and three kings ruled between Nebuchadnezzar and Nabonidus, the writer of Daniel tells us that Belshazzar is Nebuchadnezzar's son. I don't know the relevance of this *"error,"* or if there is any relevance, but I feel obligated to share this information.

Daniel 5:2-16: *"Belshazzar, when he tasted the wine, commanded that the vessels of gold and of silver which Nebuchadnezzar his father had taken out of the temple in Jerusalem be brought, that the king and his lords, his wives and his concubines might drink from them...They drank the wine and **praised the gods of gold and silver, bronze, iron, wood, and stone. Immediately the fingers of a human hand appeared and began writing on the plaster of the wall of the royal palace, next to the lampstand. The king was watching the hand as it wrote.** Then the king's face turned pale, and his thoughts terrified him. His limbs gave way, and his knees knocked together. The king cried aloud to bring in the enchanters, the Chaldeans, and the diviners; and the king said to the wise men of Babylon, 'Whoever can read this writing and tell me its interpretation shall be clothed in purple, have a chain of gold around his neck, and rank third in the kingdom.'"*

Another mystery for Daniel to solve!

"Then all the king's wise men came in, but they could not read the writing or tell the king the interpretation. Then King Belshazzar

became greatly terrified and his face turned pale, and his lords were perplexed.

"The queen, when she heard the discussion of the king and his lords, came into the banqueting hall. The queen said, 'O king...Do not let your thoughts terrify you or your face grow pale. There is a man in your kingdom who is endowed with a spirit of the holy gods. In the days of your father he was found to have enlightenment, understanding, and wisdom like the wisdom of the gods. Your father, King Nebuchadnezzar, made him chief of the magicians, enchanters, Chaldeans, and diviners, because an excellent spirit, knowledge, and understanding to interpret dreams, explain riddles, and solve problems were found in this Daniel, whom the king named Belteshazzar. Now let Daniel be called, and he will give the interpretation.'"

Of course, *"explaining riddles"* and *"solving problems"* is the same as *"unraveling mysteries."*

"Then Daniel was brought in before the king. The king said to Daniel...'I have heard of you that a spirit of the gods is in you and that enlightenment, understanding, and excellent wisdom are found in you. Now the wise men, the enchanters, have been brought in before me to read this writing and tell me its interpretation, but they were not able to give the interpretation of the matter. But I have heard that you can give interpretations and solve problems. Now if you are able to read the writing and tell me its interpretation, you shall be clothed in purple, have a chain of gold around your neck, and rank third in the kingdom.'"

Of course, Daniel isn't interested in the symbols of material wealth. Daniel is a detective, and his fulfillment comes from his ability to solve the puzzles and follow the clues.

Daniel 5:17-30: *"Then Daniel answered...'Let your gifts be for yourself, or give your rewards to someone else! Nevertheless I will read the writing to the king and let him know the interpretation. O king, the Most High God gave your father Nebuchadnezzar kingship, greatness, glory, and majesty. And because of the greatness that he gave him, all peoples, nations, and languages trembled and feared before him. He killed those he wanted to kill, kept alive those he wanted to keep alive, honored those he wanted to honor, and degraded* *those he wanted to degrade. But when his heart was lifted up and his spirit was hardened so that he acted proudly, he was deposed from his kingly throne, and his glory was stripped from him. He was driven from human society, and **his mind was made like that of an animal**...And you, Belshazzar his son, have not humbled your heart, even though you knew all this! You have exalted yourself against the Lord of heaven! The vessels of his temple have been brought in before you, and you and your lords, your wives and your concubines have been drinking wine from them. **You have praised the gods of silver and gold, of bronze, iron, wood, and stone, which do not see or hear or know; but the God in whose power is your very breath, and to whom belong all your ways, you have not honored.***

"So from his presence the hand was sent and this writing was inscribed. And this is the writing that was inscribed: MENE, MENE, TEKEL, and PARSIN. This is the interpretation of the matter: MENE, God has numbered the days of your kingdom and brought it to an end; TEKEL, you have been weighed on the scales and found wanting; PERSIN, your kingdom is divided and given to the Medes and Persians.'

"Then Belshazzar gave the command, and Daniel was clothed in purple, a chain of gold was put around his neck, and a proclamation was made concerning him that he should rank third in the kingdom. That very night Belshazzar, the Chaldean king, was killed. And Darius the Mede received the kingdom, being about sixty-two years old."

The message here seems to be that the sons can't learn from the lessons of their fathers. Even though one generation finally understood The Truth, a second or third generation, in spite of being aware of the earlier lessons about this new knowledge, returned to the worship of material things, false gods, false doctrines, and false idols.

Those disciples who continued to teach what Jesus taught were facing stiff opposition from the bishops and priests and other teachers of the false doctrine, as well as the Roman government. *"The King"* was in control, and the doctrine supported by the king was back to what it had been before Jesus arrived with his knowledge, wisdom, parables, and message of unconditional love. The false god was a new god, but it was still false.

The Truth that Jesus taught was quickly forgotten by the men and women of Judea. And those who tried to keep it alive were being persecuted and killed by the thousands; the knowledge was being destroyed. And instead receiving praise and thanksgiving for being a great and wonderful and wise Teacher of Truth and Universal Law, Jesus became an idol nailed to a tree and worshipped as a god. You can almost hear Lux shouting through the shadows of time: "*You fools! You did it again! Will you never learn?*"

Notice who has the wisdom to call for Daniel: the Queen. A woman, was the only person present who knew to suggest that the king call on Daniel for interpretation of the "*secret writing*" that appeared on the wall.

It's another mystery! There are words written on the wall that only Daniel can interpret, the same man who solved the mysteries of *Susanna* and *Bel.*

All the information previously provided by Lux has been repeated here. The Truth is being corrupted by the government and church leaders, people are worshipping false idols, and a woman was key to solving the riddle. And again, there is a mystery to be solved, this time in the form of a riddle written on the wall.

CHAPTER FOUR

"A stone was brought and laid on the mouth of the den..."
Daniel 6:17

"They found the stone rolled away..."
Luke 24:2

DANIEL'S DEN
AND
THE TEACHER'S TOMB

The similarities between Luke's gospel and Daniel's narratives are just too similar to be ignored. And there's more that rings of parallels with Lux:

Daniel 6:3-9: *"Soon Daniel distinguished himself above all the other presidents and satraps because an excellent spirit was in him, and the king planned to appoint him over the whole kingdom. So the presidents and the satraps **tried to find grounds for complaint against Daniel in connection with the kingdom. But they could find no grounds for complaint or any corruption, because he was faithful, and no negligence or corruption could be found in him.** The men said, 'We shall not find any ground for complaint against this Daniel unless we find it in connection with the law of his God.' So the presidents and satraps conspired and came to the king and said to him, 'O King Darius...all...are agreed that the king should establish an ordinance and enforce an interdict, that whoever prays to anyone, divine or human, for thirty days, except to you...shall be thrown into a den of lions.'"*

The king signed the document, of course, and Daniel disobeyed it. Of course!

Daniel 6:10-23: *"Although Daniel knew that the document had been signed, he continued to go to his house, which had **windows in its upper room** open toward Jerusalem, and to get down on his knees three times a day to pray to his God and praise him, just as he had done previously. The conspirators came and found Daniel praying and seeking mercy before his God. Then they approached the king and said concerning the interdict, 'O king! Did you not sign and interdict, that anyone who prays to anyone, divine or human, within thirty days except to you, O king, shall be thrown into a den of lions?' The king answered, 'The thing stands fast, according to the law of the Medes and Persians, which cannot be revoked.' Then they responded to the king, 'Daniel, one of the exiles from Judah, pays no attention to you, O king, but he is saying prayers three times a day.'*

*"When the king heard the charge, he was very much distressed. He was determined to save Daniel, and until the sun went down he made every effort to rescue him. Then the conspirators came to the king and said to him, 'Know, O king, that it is a law of the Medes and Persians that no interdict or ordinance that the king establishes can be changed.' Then the king gave the command, and Daniel was brought and thrown into the den of lions. The king said to Daniel, 'May your God, whom you faithfully serve, deliver you!' A **stone was brought and laid on the mouth of the den**, and the king sealed it with his own signet and with the signet of his lords, so that nothing might be changed concerning Daniel.*

"Then the king went to his palace and spent the night fasting; no food was brought to him, and sleep fled from him.

*"Then at **break of day**, the king got up and hurried to the den of lions. When he came near the den where Daniel was, he cried out anxiously to Daniel, 'O Daniel, servant of the living God, has your God whom you faithfully serve been able to deliver you from the lions?' Daniel then said to the king...'My God **sent his angel** and shut the lions' mouths so that they would not hurt me, because **I was found blameless** before him; and also before you, O king, I have done no wrong.' Then the king was exceedingly glad and commanded that Daniel be **taken up** out of the den. So Daniel was **taken up** out of the*

den, and no kind of harm was found on him, because he had trusted in his God."

And now King Darius *"wrote to all peoples and nations of every language throughout the whole world"*:

Daniel 6: 25-27: *"May you have abundant prosperity! I make a decree, that in all my royal dominion people should tremble and fear before the God of Daniel: For he is the living God, enduring forever. His kingdom shall never be destroyed, and his dominion has no end. He delivers and rescues, he works signs and wonders in heaven and on earth; for he has saved Daniel from the power of the lions."'*

I think it would be good to pause in order to compare the above with Luke's story about Jesus' last days. There are so many similar phrases and ideas between Daniel and Lux that the connection is impossible to miss.

For instance, Luke 22:12: *"He will show you a large room upstairs, already furnished."* Daniel prays in an upper room, knowing he is breaking the law, and Jesus goes to the upstairs room for his final Passover meal, and breaks the law in doing so. (It was Jewish law that a lamb be served at this meal, and according to Luke, Jesus served only bread and wine).

The *"official charges"* were (Luke 23:2-24): *"'We found this man perverting our nation, **forbidding us to pay taxes to the emperor**, and saying that he himself is the Messiah, a king. Then Pilate asked him, 'Are you the king of the Jews?' He answered, 'You say so.' Then Pilate said to the chief priests and the crowds, 'I find no basis for an accusation against this man.' But they were insistent and said, 'He stirs up the people by teaching throughout all Judea, from Galilee where he began even to this place.'*

"When Pilate heard this, he asked whether the man was a Galilean. And when he learned that he was under Herod's jurisdiction, he sent him off to Herod, who was himself in Jerusalem at that time. When Herod saw Jesus, he was very glad, for he had been wanting to see him for a long time, because he had heard about him and was hoping to see him perform some sign. He questioned him at some length, but Jesus gave him no answer. The chief priests and the scribes stood by, vehemently accusing him. Even Herod with his soldiers treated him with contempt and mocked him; then he put an elegant robe on him,

and sent him back to Pilate. That same day Herod and Pilate became friends with each other; before this they had been enemies.

"*Pilate then called together the chief priests, the leaders, and the people, and said to them, 'You brought me this man as one who was perverting the people; and here I have examined him in your presence and* **have not found this man guilty of any of your charges against him.** *Neither has Herod, for he sent him back to us. Indeed, he has done nothing to deserve death. I will therefore have him flogged and release him.'*

"*They all shouted out together, 'Away with this fellow! Release Barabbas for us!' (This was a man who had been put in prison for an insurrection that had taken place in the city, and for murder.) Pilate, wanting to release Jesus, addressed them again; but they kept shouting, 'Crucify him, crucify him!' A third time he said to them, 'Why, what evil has he done?* **I have found in him no grounds for the sentence of death;** *I will therefore have him flogged and release him.' But they kept urgently demanding with loud shouts that he should be crucified; and their voices prevailed. So Pilate gave his verdict that their demand should be granted.*"

Luke 24:1-4 describes an early dawn visit, the stone rolled away, "*two men in dazzling clothes,*" and no dead body.

Luke 24:15 describes a safe Jesus, walking and talking to some of the disciples.

Quite similar to the story of Daniel, huh?

After solving the riddles and interpreting the dreams for the kings, Daniel has a dream of his own that frightens him. During the dream, Daniel approaches one of the attendants and asks for help interpreting the dream:

Daniel 7:15-28: "*As for me, Daniel, my spirit was troubled within me, and the visions of my head terrified me. I approached one of the attendants to ask him the truth concerning all this.' So he said that he would disclose to me the interpretation of the matter: As for these four great beasts, four kings shall arise out of the earth.* **But the holy ones of the Most High shall receive the kingdom and possess the kingdom forever--forever and ever.'**

"'*Then I desired to know the truth concerning the fourth beast, which was different from all the rest, exceedingly terrifying, with its* teeth of iron and claws of bronze, and which devoured and broke in pieces, and stamped what was left with its feet; and concerning the ten horns that were on its head, and concerning the other horn, which came up and to make room for which three of them fell out--the horn that had eyes and a **mouth that spoke arrogantly, and that seemed greater than the others.** As I looked, this horn **made war with the holy ones and was prevailing over them,** until the Ancient One came; then judgment was given for the holy ones of the Most High, and the time arrived when the holy ones gained possession of the kingdom.

"This is what he said: 'As for the fourth beast, there shall be a fourth kingdom on earth that shall be **different from all the other kingdoms; it shall devour the whole earth, and trample it down, and break it to pieces.** As for the ten horns, out of this kingdom ten kings shall arise, and another shall arise after them. This one shall be different from the former ones, and shall put down three kings. **He shall speak words against the Most High, shall wear out the holy ones of the Most High, and shall attempt to change the sacred seasons and the law; and they shall be given into his power for a time, two times, and a half a time.** The court shall sit in judgment, and his dominion shall be taken away, to be consumed and totally destroyed. **The kingship and dominion and the greatness of the kingdoms under the whole heaven shall be given to the people of the holy ones of the Most High; their kingdom shall be an everlasting kingdom, and all dominions shall serve and obey them.'**

"Here the account ends. As for me, Daniel, my thoughts greatly terrified me and my face turned pale; but I kept the matter in my mind.'"

Daniel 8:1-27: "In the third year of the reign of King Belshazzar a vision appeared to me, Daniel, after the one that had appeared to me at first. In the vision I was looking and saw myself in Susa the capital, in the province of Elam, and I was by the river Ulai gate. I looked up and saw a ram standing beside the gate. It had two horns. Both horns were long, but one was longer than the other, and the longer one came up second. I saw the ram charging westward and northward and southward. All beasts were powerless to withstand it, **and no one could rescue from its power; it did as it pleased and became strong.**

"As I was watching, a male goat appeared from the west, coming across the face of the whole earth without touching the ground. The goat had a horn between its eyes. It came toward the ram with the two horns that I had seen standing beside the gate, and it ran at it with savage force. I saw it approaching the ram. It was enraged against it and struck the ram, breaking its two horns. The ram did not have power to withstand it; it **threw the ram down to the ground and trampled upon it, and there was no one who could rescue the ram from its power.** Then the male goat grew exceedingly great; but at the height of its power, the great horn was broken, and in its place there came up four prominent horns toward the four winds of heaven.'

"'Out of one of them came another horn, a little one, which grew exceedingly great...It threw down to the earth some of the host and some of the stars, and trampled on them. **Even against the prince of the host it acted arrogantly;** it took the regular burnt offering away from him and overthrew the place of his sanctuary. Because of wickedness, the host was given over to it together with the regular burnt offering; **it cast truth to the ground, and kept prospering in what it did.** Then I heard a holy one speaking and another holy one said to the one that spoke, 'For how long is this vision concerning the regular burnt offering, the transgression that makes desolate, and the giving over of the sanctuary and host to be trampled?' And he answered me, 'For two thousand three hundred evenings and mornings; then the sanctuary shall be restored to its rightful state.'

"'When I, Daniel, had seen the vision, I tried to understand it. Then someone appeared standing before me, having the appearance of a man, and I heard a human voice by the Ulai, calling, **'Gabriel,** help this man understand the vision.' So he came near where I stood; and when he came, I became frightened and fell prostrate. But he said to me, 'Understand, O son of man, that **the vision is for the time of the end.'**

"As he was speaking to me, I fell into a trance, face to the ground; then he touched me and set me on my feet. He said, 'Listen, and I will tell you what will take place later in the period of wrath; for it refers to the appointed time of the end...when the transgressions have reached their full measure, a king of bold countenance shall arise, skilled in intrigue. He shall grow strong in power, shall cause fearful destruction, *and shall succeed in what he does. He shall destroy the powerful and* **the people of the holy ones. By his cunning he shall make deceit prosper under his hand, and in his own mind he shall be great. Without warning he shall destroy many and shall even rise up against the Prince of princes...** *The vision of the evenings and the mornings that has been told is true. As for you, seal up the vision, for it refers to many days from now.'*

"*So I, Daniel, was overcome and lay sick for some days; then I arose and went about the king's business. But I was dismayed by the vision and did not understand it.'*"

Daniel 9:20-27: "*While I was speaking, and was praying and confessing my sin and the sin of my people Israel, and presenting my supplication before the Lord my God on behalf of the holy mountain of my God--while I was speaking in prayer, the man* **Gabriel,** *whom I had seen before in a vision, came to me in swift flight at the time of the evening sacrifice. He came and said to me, 'Daniel,* **I have now come out to give you wisdom and understanding.** *At the beginning of your supplications a word went out, and I have come to declare it, for you are greatly beloved...'*"

Daniel 10:1-21: "*In the third year of King Cyrus of Persia a word was revealed to Daniel...The word was true, and it concerned a great conflict. He understood the word, having received understanding in the vision.*

"*At that time I, Daniel, had been mourning for three weeks. I had eaten no rich food,* **no meat or wine** *had entered my mouth, and I had not anointed myself at all, for the full three weeks.... I was standing on the bank of the great river (that is, the Tigris), I looked up and saw a man clothed in linen, with a belt of gold from Uphaz around his waist. His body was like beryl, his face like lightning, his eyes like flaming torches, his arms and legs like the gleam of burnished bronze, and the sound of his words like the roar of a multitude.* **I, Daniel, alone saw the vision; the people who were with me did not see the vision, though a great trembling fell upon them,** *and they fled and hid themselves. So I was left alone to see this great vision. My strength left me, and my complexion grew deathly pale, and I retained no strength. Then I heard the sound of his words; and when I heard the sound of his words, I fell into a trance, face to the ground.'*

"*But then **a hand touched me and roused me to my hands and knees.** He said to me, 'Daniel, greatly beloved, pay attention to the words that I am going to speak to you. Stand on your feet, for I have now been sent to you.' So while he was speaking this word to me, I stood up trembling. He said to me, 'Do not fear, Daniel, for **from the first day that you set your mind to gain understanding and to humble yourself before your God, your words have been heard**, and I have come because of your words...So Michael, one of the chief princes, came to help me, and I left him there...and have come to help you understand what is to happen to your people at the end of days. For there is a further vision for those days.'*

"*While he was speaking these words to me, I turned my face toward the ground and was speechless. **Then one in human form touched my lips**, and I opened my mouth to speak, and said to the one who stood before me, 'My lord, because of the vision such pains have come upon me that I retain no strength. How can my lord's servant talk with my lord? For I am shaking, no strength remains in me, and no breath is left in me.'*

"*__Again one in human form touched me and strengthened me.__ He said, 'Do not fear, greatly beloved, you are safe. Be strong and courageous!' When he spoke to me, I was strengthened and said, 'Let my lord speak, for you have strengthened me.' Then he said, 'Do you know why I have come to you? Now I must return to fight against the prince of Persia, and when I am through with him, the prince of Greece will come. But I am to tell you what is inscribed in the book of truth. There is no one with me who contends against these princes except Michael, your prince.*"

Daniel 11:20-39: "*Then...__In his place shall arise a contemptible person__ on whom royal majesty had not been conferred; he shall come in without warning and obtain the kingdom through intrigue. Armies shall be utterly swept away and broken before him, and the prince of the covenant as well. **And after an alliance is made with him, __he shall act deceitfully and become strong with a small party__. Without warning he shall come among the richest men of the province and do what none of his predecessors had ever done, lavishing plunder, spoil, and wealth on them. He shall devise plans against strongholds, but* *only for a time...The two kings, their minds bent on evil, shall sit at one table and exchange lies. But it shall not succeed, for there remains an end at the time appointed. He shall return to this land with great wealth, but his heart shall be set against the holy covenant. He shall work his will, and return to his own land.*

"'At the time appointed he shall return and come into the south, but this time it shall not be as it was before...He shall be enraged and take action against the holy covenant. He shall turn back and pay heed to those who forsake the holy covenant. <u>Forces sent by him shall occupy and profane the temple and fortress.</u> They shall abolish the regular burnt offering and set up the abomination that makes desolate. He shall seduce with intrigue those who violate the covenant; but the people who are loyal to their God shall stand firm and take action. <u>The wise among the people shall give understanding to many; for some days, however, they shall fall by sword and flame, and suffer captivity and plunder.</u> When they fall victim, they shall receive a little help, and many shall join them insincerely. Some of the wise shall fall, so that they may be refined, purified, and cleansed, until the time of the end, for there is still an interval until the time appointed.

"'The king shall act as he pleases. He shall exalt himself and consider himself greater than any god, and shall speak horrendous things against the God of gods. He shall prosper until the period of wrath is completed, for what is determined shall be done. He shall pay no respect to the gods of his ancestors, or to the one beloved by women; he shall consider himself greater than all. He shall honor the god of fortresses instead of these; a god whom his ancestors did not know he shall honor with gold and silver, with precious stones and costly gifts. He shall deal with the strongest fortresses by the help of a foreign god. Those who acknowledge him he shall make more wealthy, and shall appoint them as rulers over many, and shall distribute the land for a price.'"

Daniel 12:1-10: *"At that time Michael, the great prince, the protector of your people, shall arise. There shall be a time of anguish, such as has never occurred since nations first came into existence. But* *at that time your people shall be delivered, everyone who is found written in the book. Many of those who sleep in the dust of the earth shall awake, some to everlasting life, and some to shame and everlasting contempt. **Those who are wise shall shine like the brightness of the sky, and those who lead many to righteousness, like the stars forever and ever. But you, Daniel, keep the word secret and the book sealed until the time of the end. Many shall be running back and forth, and knowledge shall increase.***

*"Then I, Daniel, looked, and two others appeared, one standing on this bank of the stream and one on the other. One of them said to the man clothed in linen, who was upstream, 'How long shall it be until the end of these wonders?' The man clothed in linen, who was upstream, raised his right hand and his left hand toward heaven. And I heard him swear by the one who lives forever that it would be for a time, two times, and a half time, and that when the shattering of the power of the holy people comes to an end, all these things would be accomplished. I heard but could not understand; so I said, 'My lord, what shall be the outcome of these things?' He said, 'Go your way, Daniel, for **the words are to remain secret and sealed until the time of the end. Many shall be purified, cleansed, and refined, but the wicked shall continue to act wickedly. None of the wicked shall understand, but those who are wise shall understand.'"***

So much from the book of Daniel could have applied to the people writing Luke's gospel. As I've already noted, much of the description of the king could apply to the government and religious leaders at the time Lux was writing the books addressed to Theophilus. But here's a question to consider: Is it possible that the book of Daniel also applies to modern times? There are those who would argue that "*history repeats itself.*" And there are those who believe the book of Revelation describes the end times and that the description applies to many things which are occurring now that have never occurred before. Much of Revelation comes from Daniel, and both do seem to apply to what happened to Jesus and his disciples and what's also happening right now.

The Nazarene/Essenes believed that forces and powers existed, and they called them *"angels."* They studied *The Tree of Life* in order to know how to utilize these forces for good. The branches were *"angels of the air"*; the roots were *"angels of the earth."* The Tree represented the knowledge and the secret doctrine that the Nazarene/Essenes had protected since the time of Moses. The knowledge of that Tree, and its meaning, was lost very early in the evolution of Christianity. Just as Daniel described it for the king, the *Tree of Life* was cut down, and only the stump remained. The people, again, turned to the worship of a false idol.

I encourage everyone to review the entire book of Daniel. I've selected the portions that appear to be important to the message hidden in Luke's gospel. And even though it may seem that I've quoted large sections, which I have, there is still a great deal more.

Here are a couple of phrases that could have special significance:

"...after an alliance is made with him, he shall act deceitfully and become strong with a small party.... he shall come among the richest men of the province and do what none of his predecessors had ever done, lavishing plunder, spoil, and wealth on them.

"...the horn...had eyes and a mouth that spoke arrogantly, and that seemed greater than the others.... this horn made war with the holy ones and was prevailing over them..."

This seems to me to be the description of a specific person. But who? Who was *"making war with the holy ones"* (Jesus' disciples), *"speaking arrogantly, acting deceitfully, becoming strong with a small party, coming among the richest men, doing what none of his predecessors had ever done"*?

Since Lux was writing several decades after Jesus had been killed, probably between 80 and 120 CE, the answer to this mystery has to be found in the documents written about what occurred after the crucifixion. That would be The Acts of the Apostles and Paul's letters. But that will take us away from Luke's gospel. Before we make that journey, I'd like to return to the rest of the numbers and the surprising information they contain.

Solving the mystery of "*the mouth that spoke arrogantly*" and that "*seemed greater than the others*," and who "*made war with the holy ones and was prevailing over them*," will take some work. I'm so excited about the "*secret of the numbers*" in Luke's gospel, I really want to go through the rest of them before getting down to the more difficult task of the hidden story. The numbers speak for themselves; the words require some major detective work.

CHAPTER FIVE

"But in truth, I tell you, there were many widows in Israel in the days of Elijah,
when the heaven was shut up three years and six months..."
Luke 4:25

MAAT TO MATH
AND
NUMBERS TO NAMES

With the knowledge that Luke's Gospel was prepared for us by the Nazarenes, it became easier to spot, and easier to understand, some things that the church has either ignored, glossed over, or tried to explain away. For example:

Luke 3:23: *"Jesus, when he began his ministry, was about thirty years of age, being the son (as was supposed) of Joseph, the son of **Heli**, the son of **Matthat**, the son of Levi, the son of Melchi, the son of Jan'na-i, the son of Joseph, the son of **Mattathi'as**, the son of Amos, the son of Nahum, the son of Esli, the son of Nag'ga-i, the son of **Ma'ath**, the son of **Mattathi'as**, the son of Sem'e-in, the son of Josech, the son of Joda, the son of Jo-an'an, the son of Rhesa, the son of Zerub'babel..."*

An annotation for this section in *The New Revised Standard Version of the Oxford Annotated Bible*, p. 83 reports: ***"The persons named from Heli to Zerubbabel are otherwise unknown.** For the rest of the genealogy, compare Genesis..., Ruth..., Chronicles...."*

Whoa! I'm not ready to just move on with that glossing of this text. This is far too interesting now.

First **Heli:** Helios was the Greek sun god and well-known to all philosophers. But there's something even more interesting about the word heli. Does the word *helix* mean anything to you?

Remember the prophetess, Anna, from Luke 2:36-7:

*"And there was a prophetess, Anna, the daughter of Phanuel, of the tribe of Asher; she was of a great age having lived with her husband **seven** years from her virginity, and as a widow till she was **eighty-four."***

This is the ceremony for the baby Jesus; the *newborn baby* Jesus.

Multiply 84 by pi 3.1428571 (22/7). It equals 264. But what does this number relate to? The quotation that follows is a real brain-twister. It isn't necessary to understand exactly what it means. It's quoted here just to show that the number relates to current knowledge about DNA.

Bruce Cathie, *The Energy Grid*, Adventures Unlimited Press, 1990, 1997, p. 163:

"Buckminister Fuller's geometric analysis of the DNA molecule (which is basically in accord with the Watson-Crick model) found that helical columns of tetrahedra (tetrahelix) nestle together in local clusters of five tetrahedra (ten make a helix cycle) around a transverse axis in a tetrahelix nestling column. But five tetrahedra, triple bonded to one another around a common edge axis fall short of 360 degrees by 7 degrees, 20 minutes. This gap is called the 'birth unzipping angle of the DNA/RNA behavoirs.' The unzipping occurring as the birth dichotomy, the new life breaking off from the old pattern with the perfect imprint and repeating the other's growth pattern.

7 degrees times 60 minutes times 60 seconds = 25,200 seconds;

20 minutes times 60 seconds = 1200 seconds;

*25,200 + 1,200 = **26 400 seconds**."*

The "*birth unzipping angle,*" is 26,400 seconds. Do you think Lux chose a story about the newborn baby Jesus, and inserted the number 84, in order to try to tell the theophilosophers deciphering the hidden message that the Nazarenes knew about the DNA double helix? Or is it just coincidental that this number is hidden in the chapter immediately preceding the mention of *Heli?* Of course this raises a pertinent question: Why was the word *helix* chosen to describe the DNA/RNA discovery? Is it simply another "*coincidence*"?

What about the other names, "*otherwise unknown*," except for this reference at Luke 3:23-38?

Maat, was a popular Egyptian goddess, and Maat, or some derivation of it, appears in Luke's list of Jesus' ancestors four times. One spelling, Ma'ath, is off by just one letter. In fact, Maat was also known as Ma'at. Note the spelling with the apostrophe.

Who was Maat, or Ma'at? The following description appears at David C. Scott's web site: www.touregypt.net/godsofeygyp/maat.htm:

MA'AT

"*Patron of: truth, law and universal order.*

"*Appearance: A **woman** wearing a crown surmounted by a huge ostrich feather. Her totem symbol is a stone platform or foundation, representing the stable base on which order is built.*

"*Description: Maat was the personification of the **fundamental order of the universe, without which all of creation would perish**. The primary duty of the pharaoh was to uphold this order by maintaining the law and administering justice. To reflect this, many pharaohs took the title 'Beloved of Ma'at,' emphasizing their focus on justice and truth.*

"*At any event in which something would be judged, Maat was said to be present, and her name would be invoked so that the judge involved would rule correctly and impartially. In the underworld, the heart of the deceased was weighed by Anubis against Maat's feather. If the heart was heavy with wicked deeds, it would outweigh the feather, and the soul would be fed to Ammit. But if the scales were balanced, indicating that the deceased was a just and honorable person in life, he would be welcomed by Osiris into the Blessed Land. Maat's presence in all worlds was universal, and all the gods deferred to her.*

"*Worship: Worshipped and revered widely throughout all of Egypt. Even the gods are shown praising Maat.*"

And Caroline Seawright explains at, www.touregypt.net/godsofegypt/maat2.htm:

*"Her name, literally, meant '**truth**' in Egyptian. **She was truth, order, balance and justice personified. She was harmony, she was what was right, she was what things should be. It was thought that if Ma'at didn't exist, the universe would become chaos, once again!**"*

What in the world are the Sun god, *Helios*, and the goddess of Truth, *Ma'at,* doing in a Christian gospel? One is Greek, the other Egyptian. And perhaps one could surmise that the name also refer to mathematics, or to the numbers of Luke's gospel.

Okay, back to the numbers.

Chapter 4 of Luke's gospel contains very few numbers, and they are spread so far apart, it seemed unlikely to me that that they were meant to carry a secret message. But I couldn't resist the temptation to multiply them out.

Luke 4:1: *"And Jesus, full of the Holy Spirit, returned from the Jordan, and was led by the Spirit for **forty** days in the wilderness..."*

Luke 4:25: *"But in **truth**, I tell you, there were many widows in Israel in the days of Elijah, when the heaven was shut up **three** years and **six** months..."*

40 X 3 = 120

120 X 6 = 720

So? Sun? Moon? Earth? I tried dividing the diameters of each by 720:

The sun: 864,000 miles divided by 720 = 1200

The earth: 7,920 miles divided by 720 = 11

The moon: 2,160 miles divided by 720 = 3

All are equally divisible by 720. I wondered about the speed of light. If you add a zero at the end, and divide by 720, an interesting number appears:

1866240 divided by 720 equals 2592. The *"precession of the equinoxes"* (the wobble caused by the earth's tilt on its axis) is 25,920 years in length. I guess we're still on the right track. By many accounts, this lengthy cycle will be completed in the year 2012 when the earth's axis points toward the center of the Milky Way Galaxy again and our solar system moves into another density zone within the Universe.

The year 2012 is the end of the Mayan calendar, and many

people believe the prophecies in Daniel and Revelation, also found in Tobit, refer to what will happen at the end of this cycle. It is suggested that the prophecies were made possible, and are accurate, because the cycle occurs every 25,920 years. The ancient prophets held the secret knowledge of the previous occurrences and what always must happen to the sun, earth, planets and their moons at the end of these cycles.

John Michell, *The Dimensions of Paradise*, Adventures Unlimited Press, 2001, p. 36-7, notes (referring to the dimensions of New Jerusalem): *"This is achieved by means of the Pythagorean 3, 4, 5 triangle...The sum of these three numbers, 3 + 4 + 5, is 12, their product, 3 x 4 x 5, is 60, and the numbers 12 and 60 are at the root of the numerical code which supplies all the dimensions of the New Jerusalem. Added together 12 and 60 make 72, and multiplied together they give 720.* **This is the number of Truth (because (in Greek) "the truth" has the value by gematria of 72),** *and it reveals the truth of things in providing the multiplier which raises the dimensions of the squared-circle figure, created by the 3, 4, 5 triangle, to those of the New Jerusalem."*

Interesting, then, that included in Luke 4:25 is the word *truth*, when the product of the numbers in Chapter 4 equal 720, and 72 is gematria for *"The Truth."* I'll explain gematria later for those who aren't familiar with it. And since *"The Truth"* is actually the title of something (the science of the Nazarenes), it should be capitalized, as I have done.

Just for fun I added these numbers. They total 49, and the square root of 49 is 7, one of Plato's favorite numbers, and one used frequently in the Bible.

Chapter 5 contains only one number:
Luke 5:2: *"And he saw **two** boats by the lake..."*
Chapter 6 contains only one number:
Luke 6:13: *"And when it was day, he called his disciples, and chose from them **twelve**."*
Multiple numbers don't appear again until Chapter 7:
Luke 7:19: *"And John, calling to him **two** of his disciples..."*

Luke 7:41: *"A certain creditor had **two** debtors; one owed **five hundred** denarii, and the other **fifty**."*

Not much happens when these numbers are multiplied:

2 x 2 x 500 x 50 equals 100,000.

I tried the numbers in Chapters five, six, and seven, 2, 12, 2, 2, 500, 50:

2 X 12 = 24

24 x 2 = 48

48 x 2 = 96

96 x 500 = 48 000

48 000 x 50 = 2 400 000

Means nothing to me, except that twenty-four is the number of hours in a day.

Going back one more chapter to include the numbers in Chapter 4 provides a number that is very interesting and important, and I'm comfortable it is the number we're supposed to discover. All the numbers in Chapters 4, 5, 6, and 7 are: 40, 3, 6, 2, 12, 2, 2, 500, and 50.

40 X 3 = 120

120 x 6 = 720

720 x 2 = 1440

1440 X 12 = 17 280

17 280 x 2 = 34 560

34 560 x 2 = 69 120

69 120 x 500 = 34 560 000

34 560 000 x 50 = 1 728 000 000

1.728 ft. is a measurement known as an "Egyptian Royal Cubit." There are 1750 of them in the Great Pyramid's base perimeter (Michell, p. 96).

And isn't this amusing? 1 foot contains 12 inches; 12 divided by 10 = 1.2.

Now "cube it": 1.2 x 1.2 x 1.2 = 1.728. Clever, huh? A *cubit* is what you get when you divide 12 inches by 10 and then "cube it."

Look at all the things that happen with this number:

660 ft equals 1 furlong or 1 stadia.

1.728 x 660 = 114 048. That is the diameter of the moon

measured in feet AND John Michell's solution to Plato's *World-soul* number puzzle (Michell, p. 164).

1.728 x the biblical number 144 000 = 248 832. The mean circumference of the earth through the poles is 24,883.2 miles.

Now multiply each of the numbers in chapters 4, 5, 6, and 7 by 1.728:

40 x 1.728 = 69.12; Michell, p. 96: "...This makes the... Egyptian stade 691.2 ft..."

3 x 1.728 = 5.184
6 x 1.728 = 10.368
2 x 1.728 = 3.456
12 x 1.728 = 20.736
500 x 1.728 = 864
50 x 1.728 = 86.4

Michell, p. 164, lists twelve numbers that are generally accepted as components of Plato's *World-soul* series. I've selected from that list only those that apply here. They are 864, 1728, 3456, 5184, and 10368. Lux is a student of Pythagoras and Plato, and this is information he transmits several times. "The Nazarenes of Jesus' time," he says, "were Pythagoreans."

Notice also that the numbers in the diameter of the sun, as well as a square drawn around it, are included in these products: 864 and 3456.

Chapter 8 contains multiple numbers, and three of the four are twelve's.

Luke 8:2: *"And the **twelve** were with him, and also some women who had been healed of evil spirits and infirmities: Mary, called Magdalene, from whom **seven** demons had gone out, and Joanna, the wife of Chuza, Herod's steward, and Susanna, and many others, who provided for them out of their means."*

Luke 8:42: *"...For he had an only daughter, about **twelve** years of age, and she was dying."*

Luke 8:43: *"And a woman who had had a flow of blood for **twelve** years and could not be healed by any one..."*

The numbers are: 12, 12, and 12.

$12 \times 7 = 87$

$84 \times 12 = 1008$

$1008 \times 12 = 12\ 096$

Nothing. But I did begin to notice that the word *Now* pops up at various times in Luke's gospel. It seems to begin paragraphs that contain numbers. I wondered if it was serving as a code of some sort--perhaps a break for separating the numbers for multiplication. I experimented.

What if, I wondered, those two ending twelve's are to be separated from the other numbers? Again, I combined the numbers in Chapters five, six, seven, and eight. But this time I separated them where the word *Now* appeared:

$2 \times 12 = 24$

$14 \times 2 = 48$

$48 \times 500 = 24\ 000$

$24\ 000 \times 50 = 1\ 200\ 000$

$1\ 200\ 000 \times 12 = 14\ 400\ 000$

$14\ 400\ 000 \times 7 = 100\ 800\ 000$

Dropping the ending zeroes, and multiplying by pi: $1008 \times 3.1428571 = 3168$. Recall, a square drawn around the earth equals 31,680 miles.

Then, the remaining two twelve's: $12 \times 12 = 144$. The speed of light, divided by the number of seconds in one revolution of a spherical body is .144 (186,624 divided by 1,296,000 = .144). Important to Einstein's formula for creating mass, $E=mc^2$? Maybe. Perhaps it has something to do with the energy required to spin a spherical object, such as the earth, one time, relative to the speed of light interacting with the energy creating the motion. If the creation of mass (m) is a result of Energy (E) divided by the speed of light squared (c^2), this ratio, .144, could be quite relevant. But then, I'm not a physicist or a mathematician.

I'll quote from Michell's book again, from a chapter called, "Gematria: *the names and numbers of God*," p. 62, *The Dimensions of Paradise*:

"*The first principle of Christianity, Lord Jesus Christ, (Greek letters converted to numerical values), has the number 3168, the most notable of all symbolic numbers, and the Holy Spirit, (Greek letters converted to numerical values), 1080, took on both the number and attributes of the Earth Spirit (Greek letters), of which it is an anagram."*

And on page 63, Michell states:

"Yet several of the Gnostic masters who taught it (interpreting texts by their number) *had great reputations for scholarship, and they were obviously sincere in believing that the numerical philosophy of the ancient sages was the greatest benefit that Christianity had inherited from the past. Far from controverting the truth of the new religion, it proved its legitimacy.*

"So said the Gnostics, and now that they have passed away and Gnosticism has long ceased to threaten the stability of organized religion, one is free to investigate their claims without prejudice or fear of rancour. Modern theologians agree that much of the content of the Gospels was adopted from earlier, pre-Christian religions, and Christianity is unshaken by such discoveries. Few would now think it discreditable that certain names, phrases and legends in the New Testament were based on that sacred code of number which informed the great religions and philosophies of antiquity. Indeed, after viewing the harmonious structure of ratios which was the prototype of St. John's Holy City, one may come to sympathize with the understanding of the old Gnostics, that Christianity is the richer, and the more worthy and likely to endure, for being rooted in the traditions of ancient sacred science."

What hasn't been recognized until now is that the Gnostics managed to get their *"sacred science of number"* into the gospels chosen, sanctioned, and promoted by the Church that was determined to wipe gnosticism from history completely.

CHAPTER SIX

"Then he opened their minds to understand the scriptures, and he said to them, "Thus it is written, that the messiah is to suffer and to rise from the dead on the third day, and that repentance and forgiveness... is to be proclaimed in his name to all nations..." Luke 24:45-47

THE CODES CONTINUE
LUKE'S CHAPTERS NINE THROUGH TWENTY-FOUR

(A QUICK TRIP, SKIPABLE FOR THOSE WHO HATE NUMBERS)

Luke 9:1: *"And he called the **twelve** together and gave them power and authority over all demons and to cure diseases."*

Luke 9:3: *"And he said to them, 'Take nothing for your journey, no staff, nor bag, nor bread, nor money; and do not have **two** tunics.'"*

Luke 9:12: *"Now the day began to wear away; and the **twelve** came and said to him..."*

Luke 9:13: *"But he said to them, 'You give them something to eat.' They said, 'We have no more than **five** loaves and **two** fish...'"*

Luke 9:14: *"For there were about **five thousand** men. And he said to his disciples, 'Make them sit down in companies, about **fifty** each.'"*

Luke 9:16: *"And taking the **five** loaves and the **two** fish he looked up to heaven, and blessed and broke them, and gave them to the disciples to set before the crowd."*

Luke 9:17: *"And all ate and were satisfied. And they took up what was left over, **twelve** baskets of broken pieces."*

Luke 9:22: *"...saying, 'The Son of man must suffer many things, and be rejected by the elders and chief priests and scribes, and be killed, and on the **third** day be raised.'"*

Luke 9:28: *"Now about **eight** days after these sayings..."*

Luke 9:30: *"And behold **two** men talked with him..."*

Luke 9:32: *"Now Peter and those who were with him were heavy with sleep, and when they wakened they saw his glory and the **two** men who stood with him."*

Luke 9:33 *"...'Master, it is well that we are here; let us make **three** booths, **one** for you and **one** for Moses and **one** for Elijah...'"*

As shown in the Introduction, these fifteen numbers multiplied total 24,883,200,000,000, which, if all zeros are dropped, is the circumference of the earth.

John Michell's incredible book, *The Dimensions of Paradise*, which I previously mentioned and will refer to again, proves that he is, at least in my opinion, the most knowledgeable *"numbers person"* on the planet, and I insist that my friends buy their own copy. Mine is never more than a few feet away from me. It is invaluable for anyone interested in *"The Numbers."*

Michell's numeric index lists a harmonic of that final number that shows up after multiplying the fifteen numbers in Chapter 9. That harmonic number is 248 832.

Dimensions of Paradise, p. 24: *"The difference in scale between the 12 000 furlongs and the 144 cubits of the New Jerusalem indicates that it represents both the macrocosm and the microcosm, the order of the heavens and the constitution of human nature. Both are measured by the sacred units which apply to the astronomical as well as to the human scale and thus unite the two. When the dimensions of the New Jerusalem are made commensurable as 12 furlongs and 14400 cubits the geometric groundplan of the City becomes visible, for,*

*"14400 cubits = 14400 x 1.728 = **24 883.2 ft.**, and*

"12 furlongs = 12 x 660 = 7920 ft.

"The significance of these measures is that a circle of diameter 7920 ft. has a circumference of 24 883.2 ft. *In ancient sacred or cosmological arithmetic the pi ratio between the diameter and circumference of a circle was made rational as a simple fraction, the most convenient being 22/7. For numerical reasons others were also* *used, including 864/275. This is slightly more accurate than 22/7 and it makes the above calculation exact, for 7920 x 864/275 = 24 883.2.*

"*Thus the basic plan of the New Jerusalem is a square of 12 furlongs containing a circle of circumference 14 400 cubits. Measured in miles instead of feet, the wall of the New Jerusalem forms a plan of the earth, for* **the earth's mean diameter is some 7920 miles and its circumference through the poles is 24 883.2 miles.** *The significance of this number is that 248 832 = 12 to the fifth power (12 x 12 x 12 x 12 x 12 = 248 832).*"

Another interesting fact: *Adding* 12, 2, 12, 5, 2, 5000, 50, 5, 2, 12, 3, 8, 2, 2, 3 equals 5120. Divide 248832 by 512 = **486**. Mitchell, *The Dimensions of Paradise*, p. 146:

"*The widths of the rings round the shaft (radius 720) are thus made, 3240, 2160, 4860, 1620, 4320, 1440, 1080, 6480.*"

This is in the section labeled "*The music of the heavenly wheels,*" another of Plato's puzzles. And 512 shows up on page 159 in the "*double series*" numbers for solving Plato's *World-soul* number. Whoever wrote Luke's gospel knew Plato intimately.

Chapter Ten:

Luke 10:1: "*After this the Lord appointed* **seventy-two** *others, and sent them on ahead of him,* **two by two,** *into every town and place where he himself was about to come.*" (Check your footnotes. Some sources use seventy, but the more ancient use 72, and it should be clear by now that the correct number is 72.)

Luke 10:17: "*The* **seventy-two** *returned with joy...*"

Luke 10:30: "*Jesus replied, 'A man was going down from Jerusalem to Jericho, and he fell among robbers, who stripped him and beat him, and departed, leaving him* **half** *dead.*'"

Luke 10:35: "*And the next day he took out* **two** *denarii and gave them...*"

Multiply: 72 x 2 x 2 x 72 x .5 x 2:

72 x 2 = 144
144 x 2 = 288
288 x 72 = 20 736
20 736 x .5 = 10 368

10 368 x 2 = 20 736

Remember the "Egyptian Royal Cubit"?

1.728 x 12 (inches per foot) = 20.736 inches per 1 Egyptian Royal Cubit.

John Michell provides additional information about this number, p. 99:

"The most important order of metrology in the dimensions of the Stonehenge circle is that known as Hebrew, which is referred to in Biblical accounts of the Temple at Jerusalem. The tradition was that its units represented fractions of the earth's polar axis, and for that reason it was investigated by Sir Isaac Newton during his inquiry into the dimensions of the earth as reckoned by the ancients. His researches led him to attribute a length approximating to 2.0736 ft. to the unit he called a sacred cubit which is really a double foot. This figure was made exact by John Taylor, who recognized it as equal to six-fifths of the longer Egyptian cubit of 1.728 ft. A unit of 2.0736 ft. is, however, considerably too short to represent a ten-millionth part of the earth's polar radius, so Taylor supposed the existence of a larger version. Multiplying 2.0736 ft. By the 176/175 fraction which expresses the two different versions of the other units produces a unit of 2.0854491 ft., and that unit is indeed a ten-millionth of the polar radius. The radius is thus made equal to 3949.7142 miles, which is virtually identical to modern estimates of its length."

And on pages 158-9, within the section called, *"The number of the Soul,"* Plato's puzzle reappears:

"Plato gives no apparent clues as to the numbers comprising the physical world, but its aggregate number is likely to be the same as that of the World-soul since the two were designed to fit together..."

"Of the many scholars who have offered solutions to the problem of the World-soul scarcely any two have arrived at exactly the same figures. The following analysis proceeds from firm ground, beginning with the original divisions of the Soul material which Plato specifies, into the areas where disagreements arise.

"The traditional mode of exhibiting the seven basic numbers of the World-soul, as practised in Plato's Academy, is in the form of the Greek lambda, the letter L...

"The left leg of the lambda represents the double intervals (1, 2, 4,

8) and the right the triple intervals (1, 3, 9, 27). Each of the intervals must now be filled with an arithmetical mean and a harmonic mean. The Pythagorean convention is against the use of fractions on the grounds that unity is indivisible, so in order to obtain whole numbers for the means to be inserted it is necessary to multiply the basic numbers by 6. The three intervals in both series being each filled by two means (italicized below), the result is two series of ten numbers:

"6, 8, 9, 12, 16, 18, 24, 32, 36, 48 for the double intervals;
"6, 9, 12, 18, 27, 36, 54, 81, 108, 162 for the triple intervals.

"Between the successive terms of these series there are, as Plato says, intervals of 3:4, 4:3 and 9:8. His next instruction is to divide the 4:3 intervals, which are those of a musical fourth, into intervals of 9: 8, which is the value of a musical tone. Two tones do not quite amount to a fourth; left over is the interval 256:243 which is known as the leimma. This is shown by the equation 9/8 x 9/8 x 256/243 = 4/3. For the 4:3 intervals to be divided in this way so that every term in the series remains an integer, the series must be further multiplied, and at a later stage they have to be increased again, the necessary multiple being 64. The original terms, 1, 2, 3, 4, 8, 9, 27, have thus to be multiplied by 6 x 64 or 384, so the first term in the series becomes 384 and the last is 27 x 384 = 10 368. This makes the sum of the seven original numbers, each having been multiplied by 384, equal to 20 736 or 12 to the fourth power."

That was a lot of information just to get to the number 20 736, but how else could I quote it? Do I understand it? Not really, but it doesn't matter. Lux links to it, Michell writes about it, and I accept that it relates to both the Universe and to Plato's *World-soul* puzzle.

Chapter Eleven contains only one number:
Luke 11:26: *"Then he goes and brings **seven** other spirits..."*
Chapter Twelve contains nine:
Luke 12:6: *"Are not **five** sparrows sold for **two** pennies?"*
Luke 12:38: *"If he comes in the **second** watch, or in the **third**..."*
Luke 12:52: *"for henceforth in one house there will be **five** divided, **three** against **two** and **two** against **three** .. "*
Multiplying the numbers in Chapter Twelve, 5, 2, 2, 3, 5, 3, 2, 2, 3:

5 x 2 = 10
10 x 2 = 20
20 x 3 = 60
60 x 5 = 300
300 x 3 = 900
900 x 2 = 1800
1800 x 2 = 3600
3600 x 3 = 10800

The radius of the moon is 1080 miles. Since Chapter Eleven's "*seven*" is still sitting there unused, I multiplied 1080 by 7, which equals 75 600. And yes, Michell has something to say about 756 on page 95:

"...*the average length at the base of each of the Pyramid's four sides was 755.785 ft. This is within about 2.5 inches of the length evidently intended, 756 ft., which is equal to 500 cubits of 1.512 ft. A cubit of this length has been identified from the measurements of other ancient monuments and is generally accepted by metrologists. It is the unit referred to by Agatharchides who wrote that the side of the Pyramid measured 500 cubits.*"

Out of curiosity, I multiplied 75 600 by pi (3.1428571) = 237 600. That is the distance between the earth and the moon.

❧

Chapter Thirteen contains seven numbers:

Luke 13:4: "*Or those **eighteen** upon whom the tower in Siloam fell...*"

Luke 13:7: "*And he said to the vinedresser, 'Lo, these **three** years I have come seeking fruit on this fig tree...*'"

Luke 13:11: "*And there was a woman who had had a spirit of infirmity for **eighteen** years...*"

Luke 13:14: "*...but the ruler of the synagogue, indignant because Jesus had healed on the sabbath, said to the people, 'There are **six** days on which work ought to be done...*'"

Luke 13:16: "*And ought not this woman, a daughter of Abraham whom Satan bound for **eighteen** years, be loosed from this bond on the sabbath day?*"

Luke 13:21: *"It is like leaven which a woman took and hid in three measures of flour..."*

Luke 13:32: *"And he said to them, 'Go and tell that fox, 'Behold, I cast out demons and perform cures today and tomorrow, and the **third** day I finish my course.'"*

The numbers: 18, 3, 18, 6, 18, 3, 3.

Here we go!

18 x 3 = 54
54 x 18 = 972
972 x 6 = 5832
5832 x 18 = 104 976
104 976 x 3 = 314 928
314 928 x 3 = 944 784

I don't have a clue, and for the first time, Michell has let me down as far as this specific product is concerned. But Michell, p. 160, the section on Plato's *World-soul* number, does give a clue as to what this number might be.

The number 972 above (18 x 3 x 18), is a component of the *"double series"* numbers Michell uses in trying to solve Plato's *World-Soul* puzzle. It is part of a 9:8 ratio with 864, and also a part of a 256:243 ratio with 1024. In other words, 972 falls between 864 and 1024. The number 5832 above (18 x 3 x 18 x 6), is a components of the *"triple series"* numbers. It falls between 5184 and 6561, and the ratio with 5184 is 9:8; with 6561 the ratio is also 9:8. Here's how it works mathematically:

9 times 108 = 972; 8 times 108 = 864.

The ratio between 972 and 864 is 9 to 8, written 9:8.

4 times 256 = 1024; 4 times 243 = 972.

The ratio between 1024 and 972 is 256 to 243, or 256:243.

9 times 648 = 5832; 8 times 648 = 5184.

The ratio between 5832 and 5184 is 9:8.

9 times 729 = 6561; 8 times 729 = 5832.

The ratio between 6561 and 5832 is 9:8.

Most of us are so far removed from math and ratios that this kind of stuff is almost painful. It isn't really necessary to understand them in order to recognize that the writer of Lux knew them and understood them and tried to pass on the knowledge, or gnosis. The fact that I can't find a modern explanation for the product of the numbers in Chapter 13 may simply mean that it's information that hasn't been rediscovered yet. It's worth noting that some of the numbers it links to are familiar:

864: diameter of the sun is 864,000 miles.

729 times 1296 = 944 784. The number of seconds in one revolution of a sphere is 1 296 000. (360 degrees times 60 minutes times 60 seconds = 1 296 000.)

6561 times 144 also equals 944 784. I used 144 because the ratio of the speed of light, 186,624 miles per second to one rotation of a sphere in seconds, 1 296 000 is .144. So, there is something in this number, and it relates to something in Creation. Maybe someone will recognize it, or maybe I'll find it myself in some obscure document.

Another possibility I've considered when the numbers don't work, is that they were changed in some translation. There are several footnotes in the Revised Standard Versions of the Bible that warn of additions, deletions, and alterations of texts. Since texts were destroyed after they were copied, except for those hidden in clay jars and discovered in modern times, there's really no way to know if, when, or what changes were made to the earliest texts. For this reason, I tried dropping the final three in this series of numbers. Without the final three, the sum of the numbers is 66, not 69. And the product is 314 928. Other than differing from pi 864/275 or (3.14181818) by .007461819 and pi 22/7 (or 3.1428571) by .0064229, it has no significance that I can find. But perhaps being this close to pi is enough.

✒

Chapter Fourteen contains only three numbers:

Luke 14:19: *"And another said, 'I have bought **five** yoke of oxen..."*

Luke 14:31: *"Or what king, going to encounter another king in war, will not sit down first and take counsel whether he is able with ten thousand to meet him who comes against him with twenty thousand?"*

Multiplying:

5 x 10,000 = 50,000

50,000 x 20,000 = 1 000 000 000.

Chapter Fifteen contains three numbers:

Luke 15:4: *"What man of you, having a hundred sheep, if he has lost one of them, does not leave the **ninety-nine**...and go after the one which is lost..."*

Luke 15:7: *"Just so, I tell you, there will be more joy I heaven over one sinner who repents than over **ninety-nine** righteous persons who need no repentance."*

Luke 15:11: *"And he said, 'There was a man who had **two** sons..."*

Not much here, but:

99 x 99 = 9801;

9801 x 2 = 19 602.

Combining Chapters Fourteen and Fifteen:

5 x 10,000 x 20,000 x 99 x 99 x 2 = 19 602 000 000 000.

Chapters 14 and 15 remain a puzzle that I haven't been able to decode. Perhaps one of the numbers was changed during some translation. It only takes one to ruin the formula.

Chapter Sixteen contains five numbers:

Luke 16:6: *"He said, 'A **hundred** measures of oil.' And he said to him, 'Take your bill, and sit down quickly and write **fifty**.'"*

Luke 16:7: *"Then he said to another, 'And how much do you owe?' He said, 'A **hundred** measures of wheat.' He said to him, 'Take your bill, and write **eighty**.'"*

Luke 16:28: *"...For I have **five** brothers..."*

It occurred to me that the reduction of these owed amounts might indicate fractions or ratios. I first looked for the fractions:

50 divided by 80 equals .625; 80 divided by 50 equals 1.6.

The sum of the numbers in Chapter Fifteen, 198 times 1.6 = 316.8. That was interesting. And, of course, 198 divided by .625 also equals 316.8.

99 times 1.6 = 158.4;

3168 times 5 = 15 840, also interesting. It is one-fifth the diameter of the earth, which means, if you multiply 1584 by 5 (brothers), the product is 7920, the earth's diameter in miles.

I wondered: 7920 x 5280 = 41 817 600 feet;

41 817 600 feet divided by 1584 = 26 400. Recall that number was explained by Bruce Cathie in, *The Energy Grid*, Adventures Unlimited Press, 1990, 1997, page 163:

"But five tetrahedra, triple bonded to one another around a common edge axis fall short of 360 degrees by 7 degrees, 20 minutes. This gap is called the birth unzipping angle of the DNA/RNA behaviors. The unzipping occurring as the birth dichotomy, the new life breaking off from the old pattern with the perfect imprint and repeating the other's growth pattern.

"Can we assume that this angle is arbitrary within the geometry? If Cathie is right then harmonics should be clearly evident in this natural process.

7 degrees 20 seconds = 26400 seconds of arc.

"If it is shared by each of the faces then each angle becomes 44 minutes which equals 2640 seconds. We can therefore see that 264 has clearly emerged as a primary harmonic associated with the formation of organic matter."

Above my head? Yes. But apparently Cathie has discovered something known by the Gnostics who wrote Luke's gospel. That number, 264, is not commonly known. Certainly not as well known as the diameters of the sun, earth, and moon. But it is there in the data relating to *"DNA/RNA behaviors."* And it's in two different chapters of Luke's gospel, as well.

Chapter Seventeen contains nine numbers: 7, 7, 10, 1, 10, 9, 2, 1, 2, 1.

Luke 17:4: *"...And if he sins against you **seven** times in the day,* *and turns to you **seven** times, and says, 'I repent,' you must forgive him."*

Luke 17:12: *"And as he entered a village he was met by **ten** lepers..."*

Luke 17:17: *"Then said Jesus, 'Were not **ten** cleansed? Where are the **nine**?"*

Luke 17:34: *"I tell you, in that night there will be **two** in **one** bed; **one** will be taken and the other left. There will be **two** women grinding together; **one** will be taken and the other left."*

7 x 7 = 49
49 x 10 - 490
490 x 10 = 4900
4900 x 9 = 44100
44100 x 2 = 88200
88200 x 2 = 176400

Mitchell to the rescue! *The Dimensions of Paradise*, p. 43:

*"The New Jerusalem square of 1440 acres contains a circle of area 108900 NJ (New Jersualem) units, and a circle with circumference equal to the perimeter of that square has an area of **176400** or **420** squared NJ units. In these calculations, pi is 22/7."*

Chapter Eighteen contains only three numbers:

Luke 18:10: ***"Two** men went up into the temple to pray, one a Pharisee and the other a tax collector."*

Luke 18:31: *"And taking the **twelve**, he said to them, 'Behold, we are going up to Jerusalem.'"*

Luke 18:33: *"...They will scourge him and kill him, and on the **third** day he will rise."*

2 x 12 = 24
24 x 3 = 72; the number of *"The Truth"* in gematria.

Chapter Nineteen:

Luke 19:8: *"And Zacchaeus stood and said to the Lord, 'Behold, Lord, the **half** of my goods I give to the poor...'"*

Luke 19:13: *"Calling **ten** of his servants, he gave them **ten** pounds..."*

Luke 19:16: *"The first came before him, saying, 'Lord, your pound has made **ten** pounds more...'"*

Luke 19:17: *"And he said to him, 'Well done, good servant! Because you have been faithful in a very little, you shall have authority over **ten** cities.'"*

Luke 19:18: *"And the second came, saying, 'Lord, your pound has made **five** pounds.'"*

Luke 19:19: *"And he said to him, 'And you are to be over **five** cities.'"*

Luke 19:24: *"And he said to those who stood by, 'Take the pound from him, and give it to him who has the **ten** pounds.'"*

Luke 19:25: *"(And they said to him, 'Lord, he has **ten** pounds!')"*

Luke 19:29: *"When he drew near to Bethphage and Bethany, at the mount that is called Olivet, he sent **two** of the disciples..."*

The numbers: .5, 10, 10, 10, 10, 5, 5, 10, 10, 2.

The product is 25 000 000; the sum is 72.5. Nothing. Then I wondered why verse 25 appeared in parentheses. Maybe it isn't to be used in the calculation. I tried it. The product becomes 2 500 000; and the sum 62.5.

Mitchell, page 127, in the section called *"The Measures of Atlantis"*:

"It is notable that each area is a multiple of a basic unit, which is the area of the inner circle of the ten royal lineages, 625 NJ units. This number is appropriate to Atlantis which was designed by the numbers 10 and 5, because 625 = 5 to the forth power." Now Luke's writer alludes to Atlantis, another favorite story of the ancient philosophers in Plato's Academy.

And, 2 500 000 divided by 625 equals 4 000.

Chapter Twenty:

Luke 20:12: *"And he sent yet a **third**..."*

Luke 20:29: *"Now there were **seven** brothers; the first took a wife, and died without children..."*

Luke 20:30: *"...And the **second**..."*

Luke 20:31: *"...and the **third** took her and likewise all **seven** left no children and died."*

Luke 20:33: *"In the resurrection, therefore, whose wife will the woman be? For the **seven** had her as wife."*

3 x 7 = 21
21 x 2 = 42
42 x 3 = 126
126 x 7 = 882
882 x 7 = 6174

It may be that the individual steps toward the final product carry significance. For example, in this group of numbers, multiplying pi (3.1428571) by 126 equals 396. The radius of the earth is 3960 miles. Michell addresses the number 882 on page 171, and it requires a little knowledge about gematria. I won't get into that subject in depth here. Many others have done that with great skill. And no one who reads this book and finds it remotely interesting should fail to purchase John Michell's *The Dimensions of Paradise*, and Bruce Cathie's *The Energy Grid*. Both men have spent decades researching their specialties, and I would have had no starting point were it not for them. I cannot over emphasize the importance of reading their books.

Chapter Twenty-one:
Luke 21:2: *"...And he saw a poor widow put in **two** copper coins."*

Chapter Twenty-two:
Luke 22:3: *"Then Satan entered into Judas called Iscariot, who was of the number of the **twelve**."*

Luke 22:34: *"He said, 'I tell you, Peter, the cock will not crow this day, until you **three** times deny that you know me.'"*

Luke 22:47: *"While he was still speaking, there came a crowd, and the man called Judas, one of the **twelve**, was leading them."*

Luke 22:61 *"And the Lord turned and looked at Peter. And Peter* *remembered the word of the Lord, how he had said to him, 'Before the cock crows today, you will deny me **three** times.'"*

12, 3, 12, and 3:

12 x 3 = 36

36 x 12 = 432

432 x 3 = 1296

Incorporating the 2 from Chapter 21:

1296 x 2 = 2592

Precession of the equinoxes is 25 920 years.

Chapter Twenty-three:

Luke 23:22: *"A **third** time he said to them, 'Why, what evil has he done?'"*

Luke 23:44: *"It was now about the **sixth** hour, and there was darkness over the whole **earth** until the **ninth** hour, while the **sun's light** was eclipsed."*

The reference to the sun being eclipsed puts the moon in this scene. The significance is clear: that's what this whole blessed gospel is about: The earth, the sun, and the moon, and all of Creation!

3 x 6 = 18

18 x 9 = 162 (one of Michell's numbers, p. 146, *"The Music of the Heavenly Wheels."*)

Added, the numbers total 18. 162 divided by 18 equals 9; 162 multiplied by 18 equals 2916, one of the numbers in Michell's *"double series"* group used to determine Plato's *World-soul* number.

Chapter Twenty-four presents a problem and provides an example of how the numbers in a couple of the chapters don't seem to point to anything astronomical or scientific. The numbers, as shown in the text, are:

2, 3, 11, 2, 7, 3, 11, 3

Multiplied, the product is 91 476.

Luke: 24:4: *"...Behold **two** men stood by them in dazzling apparel..."*

Luke 24:7: *"...That the Son of man must be delivered into the hands of sinful men, and be crucified, and on the **third** day rise."*

Luke 24:9: *"...And returning from the tomb they told all this to the **eleven** and to all the rest. Now it was Mary Magdalene and Joanna and Mary the mother of James and the other women with them who told this to the apostles; but these words seemed to them an idle tale, and they did not believe them."*

Luke 24:13: *"That very day **two** of them were going to a village named Emmaus, about **seven** miles from Jerusalem..."*

Luke 24:21: *"...Yes, and besides all this, it is now the **third** day since this happened."*

Luke 24:33: *"And they rose that same hour and returned to Jerusalem; and they found the **eleven** gathered together and those who were with them..."*

Luke 24:46: *"...And said to them, 'Thus it is written, that the Christ should suffer and on the **third** day rise from the dead...'"*

But a footnote provides this information regarding verse 13, *"seven miles"*: *"Greek, sixty stadia; other ancient authorities read a hundred sixty stadia."*

So, we have to try the number used in the Greek translation, sixty:

$2 \times 3 \times 11 \times 2 \times 60 \times 3 \times 11 \times 3 = 784\ 080.$

And, we have to try the number used by *"other ancient authorities,"* a hundred sixty:

$2 \times 3 \times 11 \times 2 \times 160 \times 3 \times 11 \times 3 = 2\ 090\ 880.$

But the final choice, *"a hundred sixty,"* are the numbers that are consistent with the majority of Luke's gospel:

$2 \times 3 = 6$

$6 \times 11 = 66$

$66 \times 2 = 132$

$132 \times 160 = 21\ 120$

$21\ 220 \times 3 = 63\ 360$

$63\ 360 \times 11 = 696\ 960$

$696\ 960 \times 3 = 2\ 090\ 880.$

I didn't immediately recognize that number, but I had an urge to divide it by 5280 to see if I recognized it in miles:

2 090 880 divided by 5280 = 396. The radius of the earth is 3960 miles.

What a deal! And what a man or woman, or group, it took to put this thing together for us. The numbers are a great deal of fun to play with, but considering the risks of preparing this document and presenting it to the church leaders for inclusion in the *Holy Bible*, it's far more important to try to discover the rest of the hidden message. What other *Truths* were conveyed to us?

We now know who they were: they were Nazarene Gnostics educated in Greek philosophy, Greco-Roman and Egyptian mythology, Pythagorean/Platonic numbers, and the Old Testament.

We know the conditions under which they were living and working: they were being persecuted and were unable to speak openly. Their lives and freedom were at risk.

We know why they were being persecuted: they refused to abandon the teachings of Jesus (best identified by studying the teachings of Pythagoras, since virtually all references to Jesus' true teachings have been obscured by the false doctrine).

We know some of the knowledge they managed to preserve, once scientists, astronomers, and physicists had reacquired the knowledge of the solar system and DNA/RNA behaviors. It's all there in the numbers in Lux and Acts (and, of course, the Book of Revelation, which John Michell has covered, or uncovered, completely).

I know there's much more in these numbers than I've been able to pull out with my limited knowledge of science. My goal is to provide a starting point for the real philosophers, the chemists, astronomers, physicists, geneticists, Old Testament scholars, and the Greek mythologists. There is so much more to be discovered.

The time has come to try to solve the mystery of how Jesus' ministry, and those who remained loyal to it, came to be destroyed. Was it the Roman government? Or the temple priests? The Pharisees, Sadducees, or some other predominant religious group? Can the story be pieced together by studying the numbers, obscure references to biblical, historical, and mythological characters and stories in Luke's gospel and the Acts of the Apostles? If I didn't think it could be done, this book would have to end right here. This is just the end of Part One. The best is yet to come!

PART TWO

THE AX OF THE APOSTLE

(ALSO KNOWN AS
"THE ACTS OF THE APOSTLES")

CHAPTER ONE

"Even if a tenth part remain in it, it will be burned again,
like...an oak whose stump remains standing when it is felled.
The holy seed is its stump."
Isaiah 6:13:

EXTINCTION OF ESSENES/
NAZARENES

The person, or persons, responsible for Lux Gospel also wrote the Acts of the Apostles. The opening paragraph is, again, addressed to *Theophilus*:

Acts 1:1-5: *"In the first book, Theophilus, I wrote about all that Jesus did and taught from the beginning until the day when he was taken up to heaven,* **after giving instructions through the Holy Spirit to the apostles whom he had chosen.** *After his suffering he presented himself alive to them by many convincing proofs, appearing to them during forty days and speaking about the kingdom of God. While staying with them, he ordered them not to leave Jerusalem, but to wait there for the promise of the Father. 'This,' he said, 'is what you have heard from me; for John baptized with water, but you will be baptized with the Holy Spirit not many days from now.'"*

Who were these *"apostles whom he had chosen"*? They are named:

Acts 1:13-14: *"When they had entered the city, they went to the room upstairs where they were staying, Peter, and John, and James, and Andrew, Philip and Thomas, Bartholomew and Matthew, James*

*son of Alphaeus, and Simon the Zealot, and **Judas brother of James**.
All these were constantly devoting themselves to prayer, together with
certain women, including Mary the mother of Jesus, as well as his
brothers."*

Acts 2:1-4: *"When the day of Pentecost had come, they were all
together in one place. And suddenly from heaven there came a sound
like the rush of a violent wind, and it filled the entire house where they
were sitting. Divided tongues, as of fire, appeared among them, and a
tongue rested on each of them. All of them were filled with the Holy
Spirit and began to speak in other languages, as the Spirit gave them
ability."*

I wanted to confirm that the numbers continued to send
messages. Chapter 1 contains just six: 40, 2, 120, 2, 2 and 11. They
are found at Acts 1:3, 10, 15, 23, 24, and 26.

40 x 2 = 80
80 x 120 = 9600
9600 x 2 = 19 200
19 200 x 2 = 38 400
38400 x 11 = 422 400

What is it? Michell is silent, and so is Cathie. My first
impulse, since it was such a large number, was to divide it by
5280 to see if it had something to do with feet verses miles.

422 400 divided by 5280 equals 80.

Not exactly earth shattering. Perhaps Chapters One and
Two are to be combined. Chapter 2 lists only two numbers,
and that seems to be the pattern when a chapter is short on
numbers.

Acts 2:14: *"...but Peter, standing with the **eleven**, lifted up his
voice and addressed them."*

Acts 2:15: *"For these men are not drunk, as you suppose, since it is
only the **third** hour of the day..."*

422 400 x 11 = 4 646 400
4 646 400 x 3 = 13 939 200

Now I had a bigger number, but it was still unfamiliar. I
decided to try the same procedure:

13 939 200 divided by 5280 = 2640. That's the number that's
related to DNA/RNA behaviors.

Bruce Cathie has developed a formula for the formation of matter. On page 159 of *The Energy Grid*, he writes:

"The unified equations tell us that the whole Universe is manifested by the harmonic geometric matrix of light itself. The whole of reality is light. Therefore it follows, that we as human beings must consist of nothing more than a geometric collection of the harmonic wave-forms of light--guided by intelligence."

Cathie's formula consists of three numbers:

"1703 is the Earth Mass Harmonic."

"1439 is the Speed of Light Harmonic."

"264 is a harmonic that recurs within the polar squares."

Suffice it to say that at least one modern researcher has developed a formula for the creation of matter that uses the number, 264, as part of the equation. Perhaps we can assume Lux had the same or similar knowledge and was leaving it for us to find.

Also, 264 x 3 = 792; the diameter of the earth is 7920 miles; 264 x 2 = 528; the number of feet in one mile is 5280.

Even though the numbers appear to continue delivering messages, Acts was not written to demonstrate knowledge of the numbers. Luke's gospel did that. Acts was written to tell the rest of the story of what happened to the doctrine Jesus and his followers taught. The hidden messages in Lux, combined with the hidden messages in Acts, a little knowledge of history and myths, and of course the Bible itself, shed ample light on what happened. In solving this mystery, what is missing from our Bible almost as revealing as what remains.

A review of the path Christianity and the Bible have traveled is probably warranted. This is all according to recorded history, and most of it has been covered on one TV program or another in recent years.

Many people still cling to the belief that the *Bible* is the *"Inspired Word of God."* But even the most conservative of religious leaders have begun to admit that some *"interpolations"* and *"corrections"* probably occurred during its many translations.

And most people are now aware that the reason the Protestant faiths exist at all is because the *"Reformers"* caught the Church of Rome in some deceptions, some of which had been initiated in the first century.

When the printing press made bibles available to educated men, not just the clergy, they discovered the first deceit. There was no indication in the scriptures that only priests, bishops, and Popes had access to God. But these early protesters, subsequently known as *Protestants*, had no access to the *original* texts. They had no way of knowing the route the scriptures had traveled to reach the form that had finally reached them. The conspiracy in the very early years of *"Christianity"* to destroy the real message of Jesus the Nazarene could not have been known. The priests, bishops, and Popes had done a good job in their quest to destroy all divergent texts, all texts that might have revealed the real Jesus and his real message.

Everyone now knows about the persecution and killing of *"heretics"* in the first two centuries and beyond, culminating in the fourth century when virtually all of the remaining heretic Gnostics, Nazarenes and Essenes, Pythagorean/Maneans, were slaughtered and their texts (at least most of them) destroyed. And everyone knows about the killing of heretics with increasing fervor until well into the seventeen century.

The Inquisition was conducted with the approval of the Church of Rome, for God's sake! People who accepted any other religion, or who studied any form of philosophic or scientific investigation, were tortured until they recanted and converted. If they didn't convert, they were killed. Sometimes they died even after professing conversion. It has been reported that Christopher Columbus feared for his life at the hands of the Church if it was learned that he had a map showing the earth to be a sphere.

And this torture and killing did not stop with the dismantling of the official Inquisition forces. "Heretics," such as the Salem witches, continued to be burned at the stake even into the eighteenth century.

Doesn't this raise some red flags about the kind of people

who promoted the Church's doctrine? Were their actions something Jesus would have encouraged? How can people who claim to love Jesus, and who claim to be searching for His Truth and salvation, not question the doctrine that was handed down through the bloody hands and Satanic actions of the Church leaders?

All the efforts of all the Church leaders through all the centuries began to crumble in 1945. With the discovery of texts that dispute the Church's claims that Paul spread the religion of Jesus, and that the Church would reveal that religion, the deception has now be unearthed. It has been over fifty years, and it has taken this long for the translations to begin to reach the masses. But now that we have them, plus the history of other movements before, during, and after Jesus' life on earth, the fun is about to begin.

Jesus and the Nazarene communities were surrounded by great oppression. The hand of the Roman government spread across a wide area. Excessive taxation had become an impossible burden, not only for the Roman population, but also for the average Jew living in Judea, Galilee, and elsewhere. That should have been enough to warrant cooperation among all Jews. But that wasn't the case. The Jewish hierarchy had become increasingly oppressive, as well. The temple priests were living lavishly in mosaic-tiled mansions, while the masses struggled to feed their children.

So the *"common Jew,"* the *"people,"* were living in misery, oppressed, abused, and fearful of both the Roman government and their own religious leaders, especially the High Priest, Caiaphas, and the chief priests under him. That wasn't the worst part. There were three distinct factions of Judaism, and each claimed to teach the *"Laws of Moses."* These three sects of Judaism were the *Sadducees*, the *Pharisees*, and the *Nazarene/ Essenes*.

Before Jesus decided to take *The Nazarene Way of Life* to the people of Galilee and Judea, the Nazarenes were viewed simply as outcasts. They were reviled because they were totally self-sufficient, and they lived and married within their own communities. They were, however, called on to teach the children of the privileged, and their knowledge of the healing power of herbs and plants was used to help anyone who fell ill or was seriously injured.

The King James Version, and most biblical translations taken from it, refer to Jesus as *"Jesus of Nazareth."* It appears that Matthew's gospel was used to instigated the first attempt to separate Jesus from the sect of the Nazarenes by inferring that the term *Nazarene* referred to the town from which Jesus came:

Matthew 2:21-23: *"And he rose and took the child and his mother, and went to the land of Israel. But when he heard that Archelaus reigned over Judea in place of his father Herod, he was afraid to go there, and being warned in a dream he withdrew to the district of Galilee. And he went and dwelt in a city called Nazareth, that what was spoken by the prophets might be fulfilled, 'He shall be called a Nazarene.'"*

Biblical scholars agree there is no prophecy about the Messiah being a Nazarene. Perhaps it was removed by the Jewish leaders who did not want the Messiah to come from the sect of Nazarenes.

Or maybe this verse was added when someone within the church decided to separate Jesus from the doctrine of the Nazarene/Essenes. Whatever the case, this is one piece of evidence that a deception had begun. It appears that the writer who put these words into the gospel of Matthew didn't expect anyone to ever learn that the definition of the word, *Nazar,* was *Wise Man,* or *One Above,* or that Jesus was a member of a sect of Judaism called *Nazarenes.*

The discoveries at Nag Hammadi and Quamran have forced later versions of the Bible to be modified. Jesus is now referred to in *Wesley's New Testament* translation as *"Jesus the Nazarene."* And *The New Oxford Annotated Bible, With The Apocrypha,* 1991, 1994, by Oxford University Press, Inc., has added footnotes throughout the New Testament which show *"of Nazareth"* was *"the Nazorean"* in the original Greek version.

That's what the original Greek and Hebrew said, *"Jesous o Nazoraios,"* and scholars more knowledgeable than I insist the scribes were well aware that this is *"Jesus the Nazarene,"* and not *"Jesus of Nazareth."* Why make a change like this if there wasn't something the early church leaders wanted to hide from the people?

The first place to look for an answer to that question is the origin of the word *Nazarene.* Like much of the research I've done into the life and times of Jesus, there are multiple opinions. Most sources agree that the word *Nasa* is Hebrew and means *to rise up.* The Old Testament verses refer to them as *Nazarites,* or some translations use *Nazirites.*

The best place to establish what the New Testament scribes might have known about *o Nazoraios* is the Old Testament. This was covered previously in part, but it's important, so I'll do a quick review here.

The word *Nazarite* can be found in Numbers 6:2 and 13, and also in 6:19-21, Judges 13:5-7, and Judges 16:17.

Numbers 6:1-5: *"And the Lord said to Moses, 'Say to the people of Israel, When either a man or a woman makes a special vow, the vow of a **nazirite,** to separate himself to the LORD, he shall separate himself from wine and strong drink; he shall drink no vinegar made from wine or strong drink, and shall not drink any juice of grapes or eat grapes, fresh or dried. All the days of his separation he shall eat nothing that is produced by the grapevine, not even the seeds or the skins.*

"All the days of his vow of separation no razor shall come upon his head; until the time is completed for which he separates himself to the LORD, he shall be holy; he shall let the locks of hair of his head grow long."

A footnote on page 169 of *The Oxford Annotated Bible with the Apocrypha, Revised Standard Version,* 1973, Oxford University Press, explains:

" Nazirites are holy persons who have taken the vow to separate himself to the LORD."

The King James Version uses *Nazarite* rather than *Nazirite,* but they are the same word.

This is the same sect the New Testament refers to in the few areas that the references remain as *Nazarenes.*

Some biblical scholars argue that the city of Nazareth did not exist prior to, or during, Jesus' lifetime. They base this opinion on the fact that no map nor historian of the era mentioned this city. Some say it was established around 60 ACE, others give it a date sometime in the third or fourth century ACE. Still, many scholars insist that there was a tiny village of Nazareth, too small to be on maps, located in Galilee during Jesus' lifetime. But they don't suggest it was established by a group of *Wise Men* called *Nazarenes.* Perhaps the omission of their village on maps of the time speaks to the prevailing attitude toward the Nazarenes.

What's important is that the knowledge and wisdom of *Wise Men*, or *Magi*, or *Nazars* were the precursors of Greek philosophy. The *Nazars'* involvement with the building of the Great Pyramid of Giza is quite likely, and the Greek mathematician, Pythagoras, who lived from about 580 to about 500 BCE, became a member of the Nazarene sect when he visited Egypt.

There are volumes of information available in books, TV documentaries, and of course, the Internet, about these "*Holy People*" from ancient times. It's relatively well established that the Nazars pre-date the Great Pyramid, Pythagoras, Plato, and ancient Greek philosophy. However, it also appears that, as the doctrine moved through time and through the various "*Secret Sects*" and "*Mystery Schools*" that protected their secret doctrines, it evolved to conform with the knowledge gained through time. After Pythagoras, a man obsessed with numbers, geometry, and science, the doctrine picked up some coloring from him. After Plato's description of his ideal city, which he called, "*Magnesia,*" the doctrine picked up some of Plato. The description of New Jerusalem in the book of Revelation contains the same dimensions as Magnesia, and it contains the same numbers found within the structure of the Great Pyramid of Giza. But even more important is the relationship between New Jerusalem and the sizes of the earth and moon.

Even within the Nazarenes of a specific point in time, different sects, or perhaps different members within the sects, lived their lives in different ways. Some sects or members of sects were celibate and prohibited the use of wine. Some stressed the importance of families and may have considered a little wine appropriate. Their goal was to live as healthy a lifestyle as possible and to be able to access the wisdom of the angels. Think about it: if all of them were celibate, they would soon die out!

Some anointed with oil, some did not. All opposed killing and violence of any kind, including animal sacrifices, and virtually all historians agree that they were strict vegetarians. They wore robes woven from a single piece of white linen. They educated women as well as men, and women were allowed to teach the doctrine. They were known as healers and had mastered the art of mixing herbs and plants to treat illnesses. This mixing of herbs and plants, often heated in pots over open fires, is reminiscent of the image of witches over their boiling pots. These were the women killed by the armies of the church for nearly two thousand years. It seems reasonable to draw the conclusion that these Nazarene women, seen mixing their healing herbs and plants, were demonized by the early church during their effort to separate Jesus from the Nazarene healers and teachers.

The celibate, monastic, non-drinking group of Nazarenes were probably the group within the Nazarene communities referred to as *Essenes*. This may have been, for some, an initiation or training period within the sect through which most, if not all, graduated and returned to the life which emphasized the importance of family.

They held all things in common. Acts 2:44-47 is the first information provided about this:

"And all who believed were together and had all things in common; and they sold their possessions and goods and distributed them to all, as any had need. And day by day, attending the temple together and breaking bread in their homes, they partook of food with glad and generous hearts, praising God and having favor with all the people."

An annotation addresses this practice of the Nazarene/ Essene communistic lifestyle (*The New Oxford Annotated Bible*, p. 164):

"Jerusalem Christians for a time, like the Essenes (see Mt. 3.7 n.), had everything in common (4.32-35), but 5.4 suggests that this was not a universal rule." (Acts 5:4: "While it remained unsold, did it not remain your own? And after it was sold, were not the proceeds at your disposal?")

I'm not sure I agree that Acts 5:4 indicates joint ownership was not a universal rule within the Nazarene communities. The fact that ownership was joint meant that everything was at everyone's disposal. This concept may be difficult for the capitalistic mind to comprehend. The mind says, *"If I hand it over to common ownership, I no longer own it and I no longer have it at my disposal."* To one indoctrinated in socialism, or pure communism (not Marxism!), all things are actually at the disposal of any who have need of them. Instead of owning and having at my disposal one acre of land, I own jointly, and have at my disposal equally, my one acre plus all the acres of all the people.

It must have been important to Lux that this information be clearly explained and understood, because Acts 4:32-37 repeats it:

"Now the company of those who believed were of one heart and soul, and no one said that any of the things which he possessed was his own, but they had everything in common. And with great power the apostles gave their testimony to the resurrection of the Lord Jesus, and great grace was upon them all. There was not a needy person among them, for as many as were possessors of lands or houses sold them, and brought the proceeds of what was sold and laid it at the apostles' feet; and distribution was made to each as any had need. Thus Joseph who was surnamed by the apostles Barnabas (which means 'Son of encouragement'), a Levite, a native of Cyprus, sold a field which belonged to him, and brought the money and laid it at the apostles' feet."

Another annotation, found on page 166 NT of *The New Oxford Annotated Bible with the Apocrypha,* 1994, adds:

"The sharing of goods. Christians took care of their needy (Rom. 12.8; 1 Cor. 13.3; Heb. 13.16), but it was only in Jerusalem that this type of communal living (similar to that of the Essenes) was practiced for a time."

This statement is incorrect!

The Nazarenes believed that the Old Testament books of Moses had been corrupted by the orthodox Jewish priests (that would be the Sadducees and Pharisees). They believed, and taught, that the only true books of Moses were held by them. These were the books that contained the knowledge of the *Tree of Life*.

They established communities in Egypt, as well as in Judea and Galilee, and there are various names applied to these various sects: Essenes, Osseans, Ebionites, and Jessenes. They established settlements near Qumran (celibate, monastic and male) and at Mount Carmel in Galilee, (a community of families sharing all resources and assets equally).

The Way was a term used by the Nazarenes for their secret religious teachings and their communal way of life. Was Jesus a member of the sect of the Nazarenes that Pythagoras adopted as his own religion? Or was he called a *Nazarene* because he came from the town of Nazareth? According to the documents the church has tried to sell to the public for nearly two thousand years, he was *from Nazareth*.

There is nothing in the Bible about *The Way of the Nazarenes* that is tied to Jesus and his teachings. The only reference to *"The Way"* or the *"sect of the Nazarenes,"* is in reference to Paul. It is only in Acts' description of Paul that the Bible reveals that the *Nazarenes* were a *sect* of Judaism, which taught *The Way,* studied *The Truth*, and lived *The Life*. Acts also reveals that the Nazarenes were criticized.

Acts 28:22: *"But we desire to hear from you what your views are; for with regard to this sect we know that everywhere it is spoken against."*

If the writer had connected Jesus with the *"sect of the Nazarenes,"* the translators would have removed it. But putting this information with Paul allowed them to get it included and left alone.

Some modern biblical translations, Wesley's New Testament and Holman's Christian Standard Bible, for example, now use *the Nazarene* rather than *of Nazareth* in the following verses: Matthew 2:23; 26:71; Mark 1:24; 10:47; 14:67; 16:6; Luke 4:34; 18:37; 24:19; John 18:5; 18:7; 19:19; Acts 2:22; 3:6; 4:10; 6:14; 22:8; 26:9.

But several *Bible Dictionaries* accessible on the Internet are no help in getting at the truth. Easton's Bible Dictionary (www.crosswalk.com/Dictionaries/Eastons) provides this erroneous information:

"Nazarene: This epithet (Gr. Nazaraios) is applied to Christ only once (Matthew 2:23). In all other cases the word is rendered 'of Nazareth' (Mark 1:24; 10:47; 14:67, etc.). When this Greek designation was at first applied to our Lord, it was meant simply to denote the place of his residence. In course of time the word became a term of reproach. Thus the word 'Nazarene' carries with it an allusion to those prophecies which speak of Christ as 'despised of men' (Isaiah 53:3). Some, however, think that in this name there is an allusion to the Hebrew netser, which signifies a branch or sprout. It is also applied to the Messiah (Isaiah 11: 1), i.e., he whom the prophets called the Netse, the 'Branch.'"

"The followers of Christ were called 'the sect of Nazarenes' (Acts 24:5). All over Palestine and Syria this name is still given to Christians."

Wrong! It was applied to Christ over fifteen times in the original Greek, but the translators removed this reference to Jesus' religious background and doctrines and replaced it with a word that inferred he came from a place called Nazareth.

And from Smith's Bible Dictionary, www.crosswalk.com/ Dictionaries/Smiths:

*"An inhabitant of Nazareth. This appellative is applied to Jesus in many passages in the New Testament. This name, made striking in so many ways, and which, if first given to scorn, was adopted and gloried in by the disciples, we are told in (Matthew 2:23) possesses a prophetic significance. Its application to Jesus, in consequence of the providential arrangements **by which his Parents were led to take up their***

abode in Nazareth, was the filling out of the predictions in which the promised Messiah is described as a netser, i.e., a shoot, sprout, of Jesse, a humble and despised descendant of the decayed royal family. Once, (Acts 24:5) the term Nazarenes is applied to the followers of Jesus by way of contempt. The name still exists in Arabic as the ordinary designation of Christians."

Wrong again! Interesting, though, that both these references reveal that in certain parts of the world today, *"Christians"* are referred to as *"Nazarenes"?* That's because Jesus and his true disciples were Nazarenes!

Baker's Evangelical Dictionary of Biblical Theology, found at web site (www.crosswalk.com/Dictionaries/BakersEv angelicalDictionary) doesn't even list the word *Nazarene* in its alphabetical index.

So how much help are these resources if they don't know, or choose not to reveal, that Jesus was actually referred to as *"The Nazarene"* in virtually all cases where the translations passed down through the centuries used *"of Nazareth"*? Easton's would even indicate that the Greek *Nazaraios* was used only once, when in fact, the oldest available Greek translation used it many times, and the latest translations that attempt to provide the most accurate renderings of the oldest texts provide this information, at the very least, in footnotes.

I'll ask the question again, because it is of utmost importance. Why wasn't the word translated as it was originally written? What was it about Jesus being *"A Nazarene"* that the early Church leaders in the first and second centuries wanted to hide? Why, in about fifteen different verses in the New Testament, were the words *"Jesus the Nazarene"* changed to *"Jesus of Nazareth?"* Is it just me? Doesn't that raise a red flag telling us that there's something here the early Church leaders were compelled to hide?

I think there's a smoking gun here. Maybe it should be called a *"smoking canon,"* pun intended! And I think it can be found even within translations that perpetuate the error in all of the above verses by inferring that Jesus was *"from Nazareth,"* rather than *"a Nazarene."*

From *The New Oxford Annotated Bible, copyright 1994:*

Acts 24:5: *"For we have found this man (Paul) a petilent fellow, an agitator among all the Jews throughout the world, and a ringleader of the **sect of the Nazarenes**."*

A annotation on page 197 NT:

"Sect, the word is usually used in a bad sense (24.14; 28.22). Nazarenes, Christians as followers of Jesus of Nazareth (2.22); a meaning not found elsewhere in early Christian literature."

Perhaps the *"early Christian literature"* was written by people familiar with the sect of the Nazarenes, of which Jesus was a member. Perhaps they were fully aware that a *Nazarene* was not a citizen of Nazareth, as alluded to in this footnote, but rather a member of a sect of Judaism whose secret teachings included Greek philosophy and the influence of Pythagorean numerology. Perhaps they knew the meaning of *Nazarene* and had no reason to hide that meaning. Only the later Church leaders, in their determination to change the meaning of Jesus and his message, sought to hide the meaning of the word *Nazarene.*

Paul's response is found in Acts 24:14: *"But this I admit to you, that **according to the Way, which they call a sect,** I worship the God of our fathers, believing everything laid down by the law or written in the prophets..."*

Acts 24:22: *"But Felix, having a rather accurate **knowledge of the Way**, put them off, saying, 'When Lysians the tribune comes down, I will decide your case."*

Notice that this translation capitalized the word *Way,* acknowledging that it signifies a title of something--in this case, the doctrine of the Nazarenes.

Another footnote provided by the editors of *The New Oxford Annotated Bible,* copyright 1994, page 197 NT, *"clarifies"* the meaning of *"the Way":*

"The Way, i.e. The true way of the Lord, was one of the earliest names for Christianity."

This explanation has served as the cover story for those whose agenda is to perpetuate the deception. Indeed, in the first century, both during and after Jesus' departure from his disciples, *The Way* was the doctrine of the sect of Nazarenes. Paul never actually claimed that he had converted to *The Way* or that he had become a Nazarene. He didn't deny it, but his answer to the charge was evasive at best, according to Acts 24:14. Look at it again: *"But this I admit to you, that according to the Way, which they call a sect, I worship the God of our ancestors, believing everything laid down according to the law or written in the prophets."*

What Paul actually affirms is his dedication to the teachings of the Pharisees, not to the teachings of *The Way of the Nazarenes.* The doctrine of the Nazarenes bore little resemblance to the doctrine called *"Christianity"* taught by Paul, modified and adopted by the early church leaders and later by Constantine, and eventually spread throughout the world.

Even the translations that acknowledge that *The Way* was a title placed on the doctrine of the Nazarenes ignore the error in their translations which indicate that Jesus claimed that he was *"the way."*

Acts 9:1-2: *"Meanwhile Saul, still breathing threats **and murder** against the disciples of the Lord, went to the high priest and asked him for letters to the synagogues at Damascus, so that **if he found any belonging to the Way, men or women, he might bring them bound to Jerusalem."***

The Way is, indeed, what Jesus was teaching. It is the religion that Paul persecuted, but it is not the religion that Paul promoted.

This definition of *The Way* raises another question. What about John 14:6? We all know from English assignments how dramatically the meaning of a sentence can change by just the change of punctuation. Personally, I would prefer that the translations of biblical texts be presented as they appeared in the original language without quotation marks based on an individual's *"best guess."* Often, *"best guess"* is synonymous with *"guess that best serves my agenda."*

John 14:6 has traditionally been translated as: *"I am the way, the truth and the life."* That has a drastically different meaning than, *"I Am--The Way, The Truth and The Life."* The first claims to *be* the way, truth, and life, the second says "*I AM*" is the Way, Truth, and Life.

Exodus 3:14: "*And God said unto Moses, 'I AM THAT I AM': and he said, 'Thus shalt thou say unto the children of Israel, 'I AM hath sent me unto you.'*"

Sounds to me as if "*I AM*" is the name for God, according to what Moses said God told him.

Based on Exodus 3:14, is it possible, even highly likely, that Jesus did not claim to be "*the way, the truth and the life*," but rather taught that *God*, or the *I AM*, is *The Way*; *God, I AM*, is *The Truth*; and *God, I AM*, is "*The Life*"?

I AM was used by the Hebrews as a synonym for God. And if you change the punctuation traditionally used in John 14:6, *I AM* describes that invisible, intangible, spiritual center of our being, our connection to the Big *I AM* that encompasses all of us and everything. It is the Oneness that is everything, because everything is actually One.

But John 14:6, "*I Am--The Way, The Truth, and The Life,*" was translated by early Christians and passed through to today's *Revised Versions* as, "*I am the way, the truth and the life.*" Now, the editors of *The New Oxford Annotated Bible with Apocrypha, New Standard Version, 1973*, provide a footnote that tells us that *The Way* referred to "*one of the earliest names for Christianity.*" Rather than accepting these editors' claim that *The Way* was an early name for Christianity, I think it's clear that *The Way* was the name the Nazarenes used to describe their doctrine, and it was the message Jesus taught during his lifetime. And *The Way* was what James the Just, Jesus' brother, Mary Magdalene, and Levi taught after Jesus died. It was the Gnostic doctrine of the knowledge of the Universe that Luke's gospel and the Acts of the Apostles attempted to preserve.

It becomes clear that at the time the scriptures were first recorded, it was common knowledge that *The Way*, was the Nazarene doctrine. What's most revealing is that the King James Version of these passages changed the Greek from "*The Way*" to "*this way.*" Some translators, professing to provide modern and more correct translations, do even more. All of them describe Paul as a *ringleader* or *leader* of a **SECT** of the Nazarenes. But Acts 24:14 and Acts 24:22 demonstrate the deception. Here are some telling comparisons:

Acts 24:14:

King James Version: *"...that after the way which they call heresy..."*

God's Word Translation: *"...'I'm a follower of the way (of Christ), which they call a sect.'"*

New Revised Standard Version: *"...that according to the Way, which they call a sect,..."*

Holman Christian Standard: *"...that according to the Way, which they call a sect..."*

Acts 24:22:

King James Version: *"Felix...having more perfect knowledge of that way,..."*

God's Word Translation: *"Felix knew the way (of Christ) rather well..."*

New Revised Standard Version: *"Felix...who was...well informed about the Way..."*

Holman Christian Standard Version: *"...Felix was accurately informed about the Way..."*

Even though the Greek from which all were taken used *The Way* to refer to the teachings of *"the sect of the Nazarenes,"* the King James translation initiates the deception, and *God's Word Translation*, and many others, continue it. *God's Word* overtly attempts to improve the cover-up of the fact that Jesus belonged to the sect of the Nazarenes by inserting (of Christ) after *"the way."*

Some biblical transcribers, and many church leaders, for some reason, don't believe the average person reading the Bible should know that Jesus and his followers belonged to a sect called the *Nazarenes*. Every effort was made to separate Jesus from this *sect* whose doctrine was called *The Way*, whose knowledge of Science was called *The Truth*, and whose communal sharing of assets was called *The Life*.

Why? Are they afraid that some Christians might be curious about what the doctrine of *The Way* contained? Are they afraid that people might wonder just what the Nazarene teachings were? If Jesus was a leader within the sect of the Nazarenes, it stands to reason that he was bringing their teachings to the public. But the Church leaders did not want that knowledge disseminated. Why? I'll make a guess: They did not want the public to know what Jesus taught! They wanted the public to know only what the Church taught *about* Jesus.

"Christianity" in the *"fundamentalist"* form practiced today came from the teachings of Paul. Some may claim that the foundation of their religion is based on Paul's interpretation of Jesus' teachings. But is that true? Is Paul's doctrine actually based on Jesus' teachings?

"I have lived as a Pharisee," Paul says (Acts 26:5). He was not raised as a Nazarene, but as a Pharisee. He never met Jesus; he was never taught by Jesus. He met Peter and John and some of that particular group of disciples, and according to Paul's letters, they disagreed with each other about the doctrine. And Peter and his brother, Andrew, according to ancient texts circulated by Mary Magdalene, Matthew, and Jesus' brother James, as well as the Bible itself, were those who appeared not to get it!

But Paul! Paul isn't even mentioned by the gospel writers accepted into the canon nor the gospels rejected by the Nicean Council. Only in Acts does anyone write about him, and only from his letters can we know what he taught. But the *real story* of Paul--*the truth*--is told in the secret language of Lux and Acts, and Acts Chapter 20 gives some of the best non-numeric clues.

CHAPTER TWO

"And when the crowds saw what Paul had done,
they said...'The gods have come to us in the likeness of men!'
Barnabas they called Zeus,
and Paul...they called Hermes."
Acts 13:11

GODDESSES
AND
GREEK TRAGEDIES

It's unfortunate that the study of Greek tragedies and myths has become almost extinct in our country. It's a good thing we have the Internet to simplify reviewing these subjects. If I hadn't been forced to read some of them in high school and college decades ago, the names and locations would have gone right over my head.

Acts 20:4-6: *"He (Paul) was accompanied by Sopater the son of **Pyrrhus** from Beroea, by **Aristarchus** and **Secundus** from Thessalonica, by **Gaius** from Derbe, and by Timothy, as well as by Tychiucus and **Trophimus** from Asia. They went ahead and were waiting for us at **Troas,** but we sailed from Philippi after the days of Unleavened Bread, and in five days we joined them at **Troas**, where we stayed for seven days."*

Troas, although not built over it, is very near the ancient city of Troy and was considered the modern Troy at the time Acts was written.

Several of these names Lux/Acts lists as Paul's companions

caught my eye. Pyrrhus, Gaius, Secundus, and Aristarchus rang a distant bell in my head. My first thought was to try to find them using my Internet search engine. When I typed in *Gaius*, one of the first choices was *Gaius Plinius Secundus*, better known as *Pliny the Elder*, born 23 ACE died 79 ACE.

Gaius Plinius Secundus was a Roman writer and was considered to be an important scientist. He lived in Rome under the rule of Nero and was very likely a contemporary of the writer of Luke's gospel. He wrote *Naturalis Historia* and a twenty-volume set of books of the history of the German Wars. He also wrote a thirty-one volume work on the history of his times, which covered the period from Nero to Vespasian. It is quoted by Tacitus, and is one of the authorities used in the works of Suetonius and Plutarch.

Web site, www.wikipedia.org/wiki/Pliny_the_Elder:

*"He was also influenced by the Epicurean and the Academic and the revived **Pythagorean schools**. But his view of nature and of God is essentially Stoic. It was only (he declares) the weakness of humanity that had embodied the Being of God in many human forms endued with human faults and vices (ii. 148). The Godhead was really one; it was the soul of the eternal world, displaying its beneficence on earth, as well as in the sun and stars (ii.12 seq., 154 seq.)."*

Makes one think of Plato's *World-soul* puzzle, doesn't it? And this interesting note: *"At the conclusion of his literary labours, as the only Roman who had ever taken for his theme the whole realm of nature, **he prays for the blessing of the universal mother on his completed work.***

"In literature he assigns the highest place to Homer and to Cicero (xvii. 37 seq.); and the next to Virgil.

"He takes a keen interest in nature, and in the natural sciences, studying them in a way that was then new in Rome, while the small esteem in which studies of this kind were held does not deter him from endeavouring to be of service to his fellow countrymen (xxii.15).

"The scheme of his great work is vast and comprehensive, being nothing short of an encyclopaedia of learning and of art so far as they are connected with nature or draw their materials from it."

The Nazarenes placed great importance on the *Universal*

Earth Mother and the *Universal Spirit Father*. These form the trunk of the *Tree of Life* so important to the Nazarene/Essene studies.

Acts 20:4 deserves another look. The word order of the 1973 edition of *The New Oxford Annotated Bible* differs from the 1994 edition quoted above:

"Sopater of Borea, the son of Pyrrhus, accompanied him; and the Tessalonians, Aristarchus and Secundus; and Gaius of Derbe, and Timothy and the Asians, Tychicus and Trophimus."

Note the close proximity of *Secundus* and *Gaius*, in light of the fact that *Pliny the Elder's* full name was *Gaius Plinius Secundus*. Another clue?

Aristarchus, 310 to 230 BCE, a Greek, was another scientist, and astronomer.

From www-gap.dcs.st-and.ac.uk/-history/Mathematicians/ Aristarchus.htm.:

*"Aristarchus was certainly both a mathematician and astronomer and he is most celebrated as the **first to propose a sun centered universe**. He is also famed for his pioneering attempt to determine the **sizes and distances of the sun and moon**.*

*"Aristarchus was a student of Strato of Lampsacus, who was head of **Aristotle's Lyceum**. However, it is not thought that Aristarchus studied with Strato in Athens but rather that he studied with him in Alexandria. Strato became head of the Lyceum at Alexandria in 287 BCE and it is thought that Aristarchus studied with him there starting his studies shortly after that date.*

*"There is little existing evidence concerning the origin of Aristarchus's belief in a **heliocentric system**. We know of no earlier hypothesis of this type but in fact the theory was not accepted by the Greeks so apparently never had any popularity.*

*"Plutarch gives us a little extra information, for he reports that Aristarchus followed **Heraclides of Pontus** in believing that the apparent daily rotation of the fixed stars was due to the rotation of the earth on its axis."*

Interesting that we have the names of two scientists who would have been well known by the educated person living at the time Luke's gospel was written. Both these names appear in some of Paul's letters to the churches and to his disciples, but the insertion of the names are usually at the very end. And wherever they might appear, no one disputes the use of interpolations by the early church leaders to solve some of the problems of texts that did not conform and/or agree with each other. One name that is not mentioned by Paul or any of his disciples writing on his behalf is Pyrrhus. (Most biblical scholars agree Paul didn't write all of his letters but had help during his travels and after he died. And even a generation or more after his death people were still using his name in Christian letters.) And the King James translators did a strange thing with this name, *Pyrrhus*: they omitted it!

Who was Pyrrhus? This is a most fascinating character, and his importance becomes evident a little later:

Pyrrhus, The Fool of Hope, (319-272 BCE) by Plutarch (probably written in 75 ACE.

Some excerpts from www.e-classics.com/pyrrhus.htm:

*"...Pyrrhus joined up with **Demetrius**, the husband of his sister..."*

*"Demetrius came with an army and installed himself as King of **Macedonia**."*

*"The older Macedonians who had seen **Pyrrhus** in combat remarked that he looked and fought just like **Alexander**."*

*"Pyrrhus also sent some **agents, who pretended to be Macedonians. These spies** spread the suggestion that now the time had come to be liberated from the harsh rule of Demetrius by joining Pyrrhus, who was a **gracious friend of soldiers**."*

*"And so **without fighting, Pyrrhus became King of Macedonia** (286 BC)."*

More interesting information is found in the last few verses of Acts 19 and the first few verses of Acts 20. Note the use of the same names found in the story of Pyrrhus:

Acts 19:24: *"A man named **Demetrius**, a silversmith who made silver shrines of Artemis..."*

Acts 19:33: *"Some of the crowd gave instructions to **Alexander**, whom the Jews had pushed forward. And Alexander motioned for silence and tried to make a defense before the people."*

Acts: 19:38: *"If therefore **Demetrius** and the artisans with him have a complaint against anyone, the courts are open, and there are proconsuls; let them bring charge there against one another."*

Three short verses complete Chapter 19 and then Chapter 20 opens with:

*"After the uproar had ceased, Paul sent for the disciples; and after encouraging them and saying farewell, he left for **Macedonia**."*

Acts 20:2-3: *"When he had gone through those regions and had given the believers much encouragement, he came to Greece, where he stayed for three months. He was **about to set sail for Syria when a plot was made against him by the Jews**, and so he decided to return through **Macedonia**."*

Again, Acts 20:4-6: *"He was accompanied by Sopater of Beroea, the son of **Pyrrhus**,... These went ahead and were waiting for us at **Troas**; but we sailed from Philippi after the days of Unleavened Bread, and in five days we joined them in **Troas**, where we stayed for seven days."*

A note about Pyrrhus follows the information on the previously mentioned web site: *"The kings there (Epirus) were descended from that Pyrrhus (a.k.a. Neoptolemus) who was the son of Achilles, the famous Greek warrior of the Trojan War. Both Pyrrhus and Alexander were worthy descendants of Achilles, who like them, was a fiery warrior whose restless soul could never be at peace."*

Pyrrhus was one of the soldiers who hid inside the Trojan horse. Was the name *Pyrrhus* inserted here in Luke's gospel in the same sentence as *Troas* to direct the reader to the legend of the Trojan Horse? And is his relationship to Achilles (as in, *Achilles Heel*) another clever insertion to describe Paul? Are these more clues from our mysterious mystery writer of Lux/Acts? The number of words used in Acts that matched the words used in the web site's description of Pyrrhus, in addition to the name *Pyrrhus*, is four. They are *Alexander, Demetrius, Macedonia*, and *Troas*.

Plutarch wrote *Pyrrhus, The **Fool of Hope**.* Acts was written after Paul's letters to the churches. Could this section be linked to 2 Corinthians 13:11:

*"**I have been a fool!** You forced me to it, for I ought to have been*

commended by you. For I was not at all inferior to these superlative apostles, even though I am nothing."

Paul also refers to himself as *"a fool"* at 2 Corinthians 11: 16-29:

*"I repeat, let no one think that **I am a fool**; but if you do, then **accept me as a fool**, so that I too may boast a little. What I am saying in regard to this boastful confidence, I am saying not with the Lord's authority, **but as a fool**; since many boast according to human standards, I will also boast. For you gladly **put up with fools**, being wise yourselves! For you put up with it when someone makes slaves of you, or preys upon you, or takes advantage of you, or puts on airs, or gives you a slap in the face. To my shame, I must say, we were too weak for that!*

*"But whatever any dares to boast of--**I am speaking as a fool**--I also dare to boast of that. Are they Hebrews? So am I. Are they Israelites? So am I. Are they descendants of Abraham? So am I. Are they ministers of Christ? **I am talking like a madman**--I am a better one: with far greater labors, far more imprisonments, with countless floggings, and often near death. Five times I have received from the Jews the forty lashes minus one. Three times I was beaten with rods. Once I received a stoning. Three times I was shipwrecked; for a night and a day I was adrift at sea; on frequent journeys, in danger from rivers, danger from bandits, danger from my own people, danger from Gentiles, danger in the city, danger in the wilderness, danger at sea, danger from false brothers and sisters; in toil and hardship through many a sleepless night, hungry and thirsty, often without food, cold and naked. And, besides other things, I am under daily pressure because of my anxiety for all the churches. Who is weak, and I am not weak? Who is made to stumble, and I am not indignant?"*

Luke has Paul say, Acts 23:6: *"...I am on trial concerning **the hope** of the resurrection of the dead."*

Paul speaks again, Acts 24:15: *"I have **a hope** in God--**a hope** that they themselves also accept..."*

Paul again, Acts 26:6-7: *"...I stand here on trial on account of **my hope** in the promise made by God to our ancestors, a promise that our twelve tribes **hope** to attain, as they earnestly worship day and night. It is for this **hope**, your Excellency, that I am accused by Jews!"*

And again, Acts 28:20:...*it is for the sake of **the hope** of Israel...*"

Quite a lot of effort seems to have gone into connecting Paul to Pyrrhus. Paul called himself *a fool* in a ranting essay to the Corinthians that sounds as if it came from the mind of a mad man. Luke then has Paul speak of "*hope*" repeatedly in a relatively small space in Acts. More than any other of the coded messages, Luke wants us to know that learning about Pyrrhus will tell us the truth about Paul.

He couldn't write an essay called *Paul: The Spy Who Pretended to be an Apostle of Jesus Who Infiltrated the Movement and Destroyed It from Inside.* That essay would have been destroyed by the early church. So he did the next best thing. He linked Paul with Pyrrhus in such a way that the connection could not be missed. No wonder King James removed *Pyrrhus* from the most utilized translation of the *Bible* ever circulated among the masses. Any fool could pick up on the message because virtually everyone knew that Pyrrhus hid inside the Trojan Horse!

Paul's letters to the various churches contain the word *hope* over *forty* times; fifteen times in the letter to the Romans alone; ten times in the two letters to the Corinthians. That must have caught Luke's eye and imagination. Combined with the tirade of *the fool* in the letter to the Corinthians, he must have believed that *Pyrrhus: The Fool of Hope* would be an obvious clue for any decent detective looking for the truth about the early church and Paul's role in it.

According to Luke, Paul seemed to have a great deal of protection during his travels, a fact he doesn't mention in this speech. His imprisonments were more like house arrests, and a good argument can be made that they were actually for his protection from those he had angered. More on this topic a little later.

There are other references to names which link to myths being circulated at the time Lux was written:

Acts 20:9-12 : *"There were many lights in the upper chamber where we were gathered. And a young man named* **Eutychus** *was sitting in the window. He sank into a deep sleep as Paul talked still longer; and being overcome by sleep, he fell down from the third story and was taken up dead. But Paul went down and bent over him, and embracing him said, 'Do not be alarmed, for his life is in him.' And when Paul had gone up and had broken bread and eaten, he conversed with them a long while, until daybreak, and so departed. And they took the lad away alive, and were not a little comforted."*

Although it seems notable that Paul leaves this young man lying on the ground stunned, if not dead, and goes back upstairs to eat and converse "*a long while*"--until daybreak, there's more here than just a strange reaction on by Paul. Many students of Homer have noticed a similarity between Luke's Eutychus and Homer's Elpenor. A web site that can be found at www.depts.drew.edu/jhc/macdonald.html presents an argument by Dennis R. MacDonald, Hiff School of Theology, that supports my proposal that Lux used stories and myths that would have been well known by the people of the time. MacDonald writes:

"*I propose a more economical solution to the peculiarities in Acts 20:7-12, but one apparently never before advanced; namely, that Luke attempted, somewhat infelicitously, to recast the story of Elpenor found in Books 10-12 of The Odyssey. Elpenor, the youngest of Odysseus's crew, asleep on a roof, fell to his death in the middle of the night. Odysseus was unaware of the tragedy until Elpenor's soul came to meet him from the netherworld. Later, Odysseus gave Elpenor's corpse the requisite lamentation and burial. Because of the popularity of Odysseus's visit to the netherworld in Odysseus Book 11, the famous nekyia,* **Luke could assume that his more educated readers would have recognized the similarities between the stories.** *Luke apparently recast Homer's story in order to contrast Elpenor's lethal fall from Circe's roof with Eutychus's good fortune at having died in the presence of a wonder-working apostle. Here at last we have a reason for the lamps, the fall, the delay of the revivication.*

"*After having spent a year with the goddess Circe on her island home of Aeaea, Odysseus insisted on continuing his journey back to Ithaca. Circe provided a lavish dinner prior to the disembarkation, and Odysseus spent the night with her, learning the magic he would need to summon from the dead* **the blind seer** *Tiresias who could tell him how to find his way home. At break of day, Odysseus woke his crew from their deep, dinner-induced sleep in order to sail at once for their rendezvous with the dead. All sailed off but Elpenor. Odysseus speaks:*

"'There was one, Elpenor, the youngest of all, not over valiant in war nor sound of understanding, who had laid him down apart from his comrades in the sacred house of Circe, seeking the cool air, for he was heavy with wine. He heard the noise and the bustle of his comrades as they moved about, and suddenly sprang up, and forgot to go to the long ladder that he might come down again, but fell headlong from the roof, and his neck was broken away from the spine, and his spirit went down to the house of Hades.' (Odyssey 10.552-60).

"Odysseus's ship took him to the edge of the world, where, in near total darkness, he performed bloody necromantic rites in order to attract the souls of the dead, especially that of Tiresias. To Odysseus's horror, the first soul to meet him was that of Elpenor, who told the hero how he had died and begged him to burn his corpse in full armor and to bury his ashes with due rites.

"Leave me not behind thee unwept and unburied as thou goest thence, and turn not away from me, lest haply I bring the wrath of the gods upon thee. Nay, burn me with my armour, all that is mine, and heap up a mound for me on the shore of the grey sea, in memory of an unhappy man, **that men yet to be may learn of me.** *Fulfil this my prayer, and fix upon the mound my oar wherewith I rowed in life when I was among my comrades.'"* *(11.72-78)* (Gott note: emphasis added.)

"Odysseus promised.

"Indeed, after he had won his traveling instructions from Tiresias, had seen a host of the dead--including his mother, Achilles, Agamemnon, and Heracles--and had witnessed the punishments of the wicked, Odysseus returned to Aeaea where he beached the ship at night. Odysseus tells king Alcinous of the Phaeacians what happened next.

"As soon as early Dawn appeared, the rosy-fingered, then I sent forth my comrades to the house of Circe to fetch the body of the dead Elpenor. Straightway then we cut billets of wood and gave him burial

where the headland runs furthest out to sea, sorrowing and shedding big tears. But when the dead man was burned, and the armour of the dead, we heaped up a mound and dragged on to it a pillar, and on the top of the mound we planted his shapely oar.' (12.8-15).

"Because of his strategic location immediately prior to, at the beginning of, and immediately following one of Homer's most memorable and controversial episodes, Elpenor **became an ancient household word, even in Christian households**. *Clement of Alexandria, writing at the end of the second century cited the example of Elpenor's fall in order to discourage drunkenness and assumed that his readers would recognize the tale: 'just as Elpenor 'broke his neck' (Odyssey 10.560) when he fell down because he was drunk.'"* (Gott note: Emphasis added.)

A bit further into his essay MacDonald compares the two stories point by point:

"Both here and in Acts 20:11-12 the resolution of the victim's plight does not occur until dawn. Odysseus can only mourn and bury his dead comrade; Paul's God raises Elpenor's counterpart back to life. Furthermore, Odysseus himself did not fetch Elpenor's corpse, his comrades did, 'sorrowing and shedding big tears' (12.12). Similarly, Paul did not revive Eutychus's corpse, his converts did, 'and were not a little relieved.' Compare the following lines:

"*Odyssey 12.10:* 'to fetch the body of the dead Elpenor';

"*Acts 20:12:* 'they fetched the lad, living.'

"*Odyssey 10-12:* Odysseus and crew leave Troy and sail back to Achaea;

"*Acts: 20:7-12* 'Paul and crew stop at Troy, having left Achaea to sail back to Jerusalem.

"*Odyssey: First person plural (most of book 10)*

"*Acts: First person plural (10:1-8)*

"*Odyssey: After a sojourn, a meal (10.466-77)*

"*Acts: After a sojourn, a meal (20:6,7,11)*

"*Odyssey: Circe's 'dark halls' (10.479)*

"*Acts: There were plenty of lamps in the upper room. (20:8)*

"*Odyssey: 'sweet sleep' (10.548)*

"*Acts: 'deep sleep' (20:9)*

"*Odyssey: Switch to third person (10.552)*

"Acts: Switch to third person (20:9)
"Odyssey: Elpenor fell from a roof (10.559-11.64)
"Acts: Eutychus fell from the third story (20:9)
"Odyssey: Elpenor's soul goes to Hades (10.560-11.65)
"Acts: Eutychus's soul stays in him (20:10)
"Odyssey: Delay in burying Elpenor until dawn of the next day (12.1-15)
"Acts: Delay in raising Eutychus until dawn of the next day (20:10)

"Odyssey: Associates fetch the body (12.10)
"Acts: Associates revive the body (20:12)

"Troas, of course, is ancient Troy. To be sure, the city of Troy during Luke's day was not precisely on the location of the ancient city, but it was nearby, and the two were repeatedly identified with each other. **No educated ancient would have been numb to the Troy's rich mythological and Homeric associations, including the nostos of Odysseus and Elpenor back to Achaea from the Troad. By placing the story of Eutychus in Troy,** <u>**Luke seems to be hinting that one should read it in light of Troy's legacy.**</u>*"*

That's my point regarding all Lux/Acts allusions to ancient known texts! Lux was trying to say **"Go read them! What are they about? That's what we're trying to say is going on here! The Nazarene/Essene message is being destroyed by these 'wolves in sheep's clothing!' The Tree of Life is being cut down again! The world must someday know what happened!"**

MacDonald's essay continues: *"The most important hypertextual clue, however, is the name Eutychus. Homer repeatedly emphasizes Elpenor's bad fortune. He simply forgot that he was sleeping on a roof, died, and was not missed by the crew: 'we had left his corpse behind us in the hall of Circe, unwept and unburied' (11.53-54). The young soldier survived the Trojan war, Lawstrygonian cannibals, and Polyphemus, only to step off Circe's roof to his doom. Elpenor himself states that he was the victim of 'an evil fate', (11.61) and calls himself 'an unhappy man' (10.76). Odysseus too addresses him as 'unfortunate' (11.80). When Ovid referred this story, his single adjective for the lad was miser, 'wretched,' 'unhappy.' Eutychus, on the other hand, means 'lucky.' Although usually one must avoid putting too much stock in the meanings of personal names used in Acts, such onomastics were commonplace in Greek literature, as early as Homer himself...*

"In light of the other similarities between the two stories, the selection of the name Eutychus hardly seems accidental."

Here's the clincher that supports my proposal. Read it a couple of times, and note the word *encode***:**

"If the hypothesis advanced here is correct--namely, that the story in Acts 20:7-12 is a hypertextual transvaluation of Homer's Elpenor--it bears weighty implications for our understanding of Acts as a whole. First, **Luke apparently expected his primary audience (Theophilus, say) to have been sufficiently aware of The Odyssey in order to** decode **the Eutychus story as a clever transformation of a classical tale. Luke was writing for a sophisticated reader.**

"Second, **other passages of Acts, especially other we-passages, may also play off against the Homeric epics or other Greek mythology.** *For example, the story of Paul and Silas dragged off to prison for exorcising a slave girl and their subsequent prison break has parallels in 'The Bacchae' of Euripides. Tiresias' prophecy to Odysseus concerning his death might compare with Agabus's prophecy to Paul about his death. One also must not overlook the famous shipwreck scene in Acts 27-28 and the story of the serpent at Malta. Odysseus too faces dreadful monsters on islands and outlives them.*

"Third, if the story of Elpenor lies behind that of Eutychus, it would add support to those who suggest that Acts ought not be read as an historical record but as an **historical novel***. One misses the point in the Eutychus tale if one insists that Luke intended the reader to view it as an historical event. Rather, Luke's 'Lucky' in Troas is an alternative to Homer's unlucky Elpenor on his way home from Troy."*

Hold it! The third implication is where in my humble opinion everyone has gone wrong regarding Lux/Acts. The fundamental Christians believe it is a completely historical record of events during the early days of Christianity; the educated, agnostic-leaning scholars claim it is completely fictional in content.

I propose a third option: The stories are a blend of history, popular myths, and famous classical literature. These stories were used to convey the *"historical truth"* about what had happened to Jesus and his message about *The Nazarene Way*. They are about what was happening to the descendants of Jesus' faithful disciples at the time these two books addressed to *Theophilus* were written. Not only are they historical novels, they are also mystery novels! And both the history and the mystery were written in such a way that they could be linked to what was happening at the time.

That the writer was educated has not been disputed. It's the purpose of the content that has been overlooked. Within the various stories, most of which can be easily linked to a historical account, a mythical or fictional character, location, or event, is a coded message. It says, *"The stories being told by other Christian narratives are not true. The doctrine being taught is not Jesus' doctrine. Herein lies the truth. Read the story of Daniel in the Old Testament; read the stories of Pyrrhus and the Trojan horse; read about Aristarchus, and Gaius Plinius Secundus and the other mathematicians, historians, and scientists. Read about what they knew and what they taught. For Jesus' sake! Read between the lines! Why would I direct you to Daniel and the 'contemptible, arrogant man?' Why would I direct you to the 'vow of the Nazirites?' Why would I direct you to the agents and spies, the soldier who defeated the enemy by hiding inside a gigantic wooden horse? Why would I disclose the horrible things Paul did to those who taught 'The Nazarene Way?' And why would so many women be given such prominent positions when women were viewed in total contempt by Paul and his disciples?"*

MacDonald's reference to similarities between stories in Acts and *The Bacchae* by Euripides' piqued my curiosity. I looked it up on the Internet: www.4literature.net/Euripides/Bacchae/. I also checked out the autobiographical information on Euripides:

Euripides lived between 480 and 406 BCE. He was a Greek poet, and at the time Lux/Acts was written, his plays were well known in the *"educated circles."* Anaxagoras had a profound impact on Euripides. Anaxagoras took exception with the mythological stories about the movement of the *"chariot sun"* across the skies. He proposed that the sun was actually a *"fiery mass of earth or stone.*" Euripides' religion did not conform to the norms of his day, and the State murdered some of his closest friends for their liberal views. Euripides wrote to expose the evils of his time. He also wrote plays and stories about Artemis, Apollo, Dionysus, and Demeter, all names used in Acts that appeared in *Bacchae*, written by Euripides in 406 BCE.

His "*unorthodox religion*" is expressed in these brief words form Theatre History.com, www.theatrehistory.com/ancient/euripides009.html:

"And is thy faith so much to give?
Is it so hard a thing to see,
That the spirit of God, whate'er it be,
The Law that abides and falters not, ages long,
The Eternal and Nature-born--these things be strong?"

There were a couple of other things that jumped out at me as I read *Bacchae*: The main character is *Dionysus*, son of *Zeus*. *Zeus* is actually named in Acts, as well as *Dionysus*.

Acts 13:11: *"And when the crowds saw what Paul had done, they lifted up their voices saying in Lycao'nian, 'The gods have come down to us in the likeness of men!'* **Barnabas they called Zeus, and Paul, because he was the chief speaker, they called Hermes.**"

Acts 17:34: *"But some of them joined him (Paul) and became believers, including* **Dionysius** *the Areopagite and a woman named Damaris, and others with them.*"

First Barnabas, Paul's companion, is called *Zeus*. Then *Dionysius* becomes another of Paul's companions. Twice Acts refers the educated reader to myths about Zeus, and specifically to the story of *Dionysus* in *Bacchae* by Euripides. What can it tell us about Paul?

The play opens with a speech by Dionysus during in which he says:

"**Lydia's** *glebes, where gold abounds, and* **Phyrgia** *have I left behind...*"

Luke 16:6: *"And they went through the region of* **Phrygia**..."

Luke 16:14: *"One who heard us was a woman named* **Lydia**...*of Thyatira, a seller of purple goods.*"

Bacchae's Cadmus speaks some interesting words which are of great importance:

"Even though he is no god, as you assert, still say he is; be guilty of a splendid fraud, declaring him the son of Semele, that she may be thought the mother of a god and we and all our race gain honor."

In the very early years of Christianity, there was a great debate and a great division between two opposing factions fighting for dominance. One side, Nazarene/Essene/Pythagorean Gnostics, said Jesus was a spiritually evolved teacher, the other side, Paul's disciples, claimed that Jesus was a god--the God, in fact.

Later in Euripides' play, Pentheus asks: *"What special feature stamps your rites?"*

Dionysus replies: *"That is a secret to be hidden from the uninitiated."*

Compare the following words and phrases from *Bacchae* and Luke's gospel:

When Pentheus threatens to cut Dionysus' hair, he protests:

"My locks are sacred; for the god I let them grow."

Luke 18:18: *"After this Paul...sailed for Syria...At Cenchreae...he cut his hair, for he had a vow."*

Dionysus is bound and thrown into a stall; he describes the events:

Dionysus: *"Meantime came the Bacchic god and made the house quake..."*

Luke 16:26: *"...and suddenly there was a great earthquake..."*

Dionysus: *"...and thinking maybe that I had escaped, rushed into the palace with his murderous sword unsheathed."*

Luke 16:27: *"...he drew his sword and was about to kill himself, supposing that the prisoners had escaped..."*

Later Dionysus speaks to Pentheus: *"...you are so eager to see what is forbidden, and **to show your zeal in an unworthy cause,** come before the palace, let me see you clad as a woman...**to spy upon your own mother** and her company."*

Dionysus, again to Pentheus: *"You shall hide in the place that fate appoints, **coming by stealth to spy** upon the Bacchanals."*

Pentheus: *"Take me through the very heart of Thebes, for **I am the only man among them bold enough to do this deed."***

And then this interesting dissertation is found in the chorus:

*"To the hills! to the hills! fleet hounds of madness, where the daughters of Cadmus hold their revels, **goad** them into **wild fury against the man** disguised in woman's dress, **a frenzied spy** upon the Maenads. First shall his mother mark him as he peers from some smooth rock or **riven tree**, and thus to the Maenads she will call, 'Who is this of Cadmus' sons comes hasting to the mount, to the mountain away, **to spy on us**, my Bacchanals? Whose child can he be? For he was never born of woman's blood; but from some lioness maybe or Libyan Gorgon is he sprung.' **Let justice appear and show herself, sword in hand, to plunge it through and through the throat of the godless, lawless, impious son of Echion, earth's monstrous child! who with wicked heart and lawless rage, with mad intent and frantic purpose, sets out to meddle with thy holy rites,** and with thy mother's, Bacchic god, thinking with his weak arm to master might as masterless as thine. This is the life that saves all pain, if a man confine his thoughts to human themes, as is his mortal nature, making no pretence where heaven is concerned. I envy not deep subtleties; far from other joys have I, in tracking out great truths writ clear from all eternity, that a man should live his life by day and night in purity and holiness, striving toward a noble goal, and should honour the gods by casting from him each ordinance that lies outside the pale of right. **Let justice show herself, advancing sword in hand to plunge it through and through the throat of Echion's son, that godless, lawless, and abandoned child of earth!** Appear, O Bacchus, to our eyes as a bull or serpent with a hundred heads, or take the shape of a lion breathing flame! Oh! come, and with a mocking smile cast the deadly noose about the hunter of thy Bacchanals, e'en as he swoops upon the Maenads gathered yonder."*

The play ends with this song from the chorus:

*"Many are the forms the heavenly will assumes, and many a thing the gods fulfil contrary to all hope; **that which was expected is not***

brought to pass, while for the unlooked-for Heaven finds out a way. E'en such hath been the issue here."

The discovery of the word *goad* in *Bacchae* reminded me of this strange verse, Acts 25:14: *"Saul...why are you persecuting me? It hurts you to kick **against the goads**."*

Once again Luke's gospel parallels a piece of classical literature which tells the story of a spy, not in sheep's clothing or hiding in a wooden horse or dressed as a Nazarene apostle, but dressed as a woman in order to spy on the women as they practiced their religion. Lux cleverly links Saul/Paul to *"a frenzied spy"* by inserting a strange phrase and a word that grabs the attention of anyone looking for clues to solving a mystery. Their voices can be heard from that distant past, begging someone, anyone, everyone, to hear their story and know the truth about the spy Saul, the false prophet and false apostle Paul.

And here's another clue in Acts 19:29: *"So the city was filled with the confusion; and they* **rushed together into the** theater, dragging with them Gaius and Aristarchus, Macedonians who were Paul's companions in travel."* (*"*They*" included **Demetrius and Alexander**.)

Plutarch, in *Demetrius*, written in 75 ACE, describes the following:

*"In this condition was the city when Demetrius made his entrance and issued a proclamation that **all the inhabitants should assemble in the** theatre..."*

Shortly after this scene *"in the theatre,"* **Alexander** also appears in Plutarch's story about Demetrius. With both Demetrius and Alexander leading a large crowd into the theatres, the hidden message is still on track.

Acts 28:1:4: *"After we had reached safety, we then learned that the island was called Malta. The natives showed us unusual kindness. Since it had begun to rain and was cold, they kindled a fire and welcomed all of us around it. Paul had gathered a bundle of brushwood and was putting it on the fire, when a viper, driven out by the heat, fastened itself on his hand. When the natives saw the creature hanging from his hand, they said to one another, 'This man must be a murderer;*

though he has escaped from the sea, justice has not allowed him to live.'''

Lux takes this opportunity to again call Paul a murderer.

Acts 28:5-8: *"He, however, shook off the creature into the fire and suffered no harm. They were expecting him to swell up or drop dead, but after they had waited a long time and saw that nothing unusual had happened to him, they changed their minds and began to say that he was a god."*

Lux describes here exactly what happened to Jesus and his teachings. Paul's doctrine, based on his Pharisee training, was gaining in popularity. Jesus' Nazarene/Essene/Pythagorean message was falling on deaf ears. Paul portrayed himself has having the truth; he portrayed Jesus' disciples as being ignorant of that truth.

Acts 28:11: *"Now in the neighborhood of that place were lands belonging to the leading man of the island, named **Publius**, who received us and entertained us hospitably for three days. It so happened that the father of Publius lay sick in bed with fever and dysentery. Paul visited him and cured him by praying and putting his hands on him. After this happened, the rest of the people on the island who had diseases also came and were cured. They bestowed many honors on us, and when we were about to sail, they put on board all the provisions we needed."*

Who is *Publius*? I suspected Plutarch might answer that question, and an Internet search turned up a website: http://en.wikipedia.org/wiki/Publius_Clodius_Pulcher:

*"...according to Plutarch (Cicero, 29), he (Publius) rendered Cicero every assistance and acted as one of his body-guards. The affair of the mysteries of the Bona Dea, however, caused a breach between Clodius and Cicero in December 62. **Clodius, dressed as a woman (men were not admitted to the mysteries), entered the house of Caesar (then pontifex maximus), where the mysteries were being celebrated,** in order to carry on an intrigue with Pompeia Sulla, Caesar's wife. He was detected and brought to trial, but escaped condemnation by bribing the jury."*

Son of a gun! Publius, like Bacchae's Pentheus, is another spy dressed as a woman and sneaking into the religious ceremonies of women! Paul certainly encounters interesting characters, doesn't he?

I really felt as if I were on a roll at this point. Even though I knew from the numbers that someone was trying to reveal something terribly important, I still had reservations about the rest of the purpose, which I suspected had something to do with information they wanted to pass on about Paul. After all, nearly half of Acts is about Paul. But now I had to go back and look for other names and references to Greek mythology and historical characters. The results of that task are described in the chapter which follows.

Lux/Acts ends with these words:

Acts 28:16-22: *"When we came into Rome, **Paul was allowed to live by himself**, with the soldier who was guarding him. Three days later he called together the local leaders of the Jews. When they assembled, he said to them, 'Brothers, though I had done nothing against our people or the customs of our ancestors, yet I was arrested in Jerusalem and handed over to the Romans. When they had examined me, the Romans wanted to release me, because there was no reason for the death penalty in my case. But when the Jews objected, I was compelled to appeal to the emperor--even though I had no charge to bring against my nation. For this reason therefore I have asked to see you and speak with you, since it is for the sake of the **hope** of Israel that I am bound with this chain.' They replied, 'We have received no letters from Judea about you, and none of the brothers coming here has reported or spoken anything evil about you. But we would like to hear from what you think, for with regard to this sect we know that everywhere it is spoken against.'"*

Acts 28:23-31: *"After they had set a day to meet with him, they came to him at his lodgings in great numbers. From morning until evening he explained the matter to them, testifying to the kingdom of God and trying to convince them about Jesus both from the law of Moses and from the prophets. Some were convinced by what he had said, while others refused to believe. So they disagreed with each other; and as they were leaving, Paul made one further statement: 'The Holy Spirit was right in saying to your ancestors through the prophet Isaiah, 'Go to this people and say, You will indeed listen, but never understand,*

and you will indeed look, but never perceive. For this people's heart has grown dull, and their ears are hard of hearing, and they have shut their eyes; so that they might not look with their eyes, and listen with their ears, and understand with their heart and turn--and I would heal them.'

"'Let it be known to you then that this salvation of God has been sent to the Gentiles; they will listen.'

"He lived there two whole years at his own expense and welcomed all who came to him, proclaiming the kingdom of God and teaching about the Lord Jesus Christ with all boldness and <u>without hindrance</u>."

The *"boldness"* in these closing words is what the writers say about those who were persecuting them and trying to destroy Jesus' message. Lux/Acts put the words in front of their oppressors--in plain view. They invited the church leaders to investigate and to study these stories and determine if they followed the *"Christian doctrine"* Paul and his disciples were teaching. It was to these church leaders that they said *"with all boldness"*:

"You listened, but you didn't understand; you looked, but you didn't perceive; your heart is dull and you are unable to hear the message of truth which we place before you. You didn't hear; you didn't see the Truth before your very eyes. You have missed your chance to receive Jesus' knowledge and to experience his forgiving Love."

And they also missed the hidden messages which transmitted the truth about what was happening to the Nazarenes.

The complete text from Isaiah is worth repeating now that it can be seen in context.

Isaiah 6:9-13: *"And he said, 'Go and say to this people: 'Keep listening, but do not comprehend; keep looking, but do not understand. Make the mind of this people dull, and stop their ears, and shut their eyes, so that they may not look with their eyes, and listen with their ears, and comprehend with their minds, and turn and be healed.' Then I said, 'How long, O Lord?' And he said: 'Until cities lie waste without inhabitant, and houses without people, and the land is utterly desolate; until the Lord sends everyone far away, and vast is the emptiness in the midst of the land. Even if a tenth part remain in it, it will be burned again, like a terebinth or an oak whose stump remains standing when it is felled.'* **The holy seed is its stump.***"*

Lux/Acts has now taken us full circle. Lux opened with Gabriel who led us to Daniel, 4:14:

*"Cut down the tree and cut off its branches...**But leave the stump of its roots in the earth.***"*

Daniel ends at Chapter 12:9-10: *"He said, 'Go your way, Daniel, for the words are shut up and sealed until the time of the end. Many shall purify themselves, and make themselves white, and be refined; but **the wicked shall do wickedly; and none of the wicked shall understand; but those who are wise shall understand.***"'*

Acts ends with Paul and Isaiah: **"The holy seed is its stump."**

A parallel exists within the Bible itself. The *Tree of Life* is described very early in the Bible:

Genesis 2:9: *"Out of the ground the Lord God made to grow every tree that is pleasant to the sight and good for food, **the tree of life** also in the midst of the garden, and the tree of the knowledge of good and evil."*

Revelation ends with a reference to this same *Tree of Life*:

Revelation 22:10: *"And he said to me, 'Do not seal up the words of the prophecy of this book, for the time is near. **Let the evildoer still do evil, and the filthy still be filthy, and the righteous still do right, and the holy still be holy.***"'*

Notice the similarity between these words, attributed to Jesus in Revelation, and Daniel's words: *"...the wicked shall do wickedly,"* etc. highlighted above.

Revelation 22:11-12: *"See, I am coming soon; my reward is with me, to repay **according to everyone's work.** I AM, the Alpha and the Omega, the first and the last, the beginning and the end.'*

*"Blessed are those **who do his commandments, so that they will have the right to the** tree of life **and may enter the city by the gates.** Outside are the dogs and sorcerers and fornicators and murderers and idolaters, and every one who loves and practices falsehood.*

*"It is I, Jesus, who **sent my angel to you** with this testimony for*

the churches. **I am the root** and the descendant of David, the bright morning star.'"

Alpha/Omega; first/last; beginning/end: all mean the same thing. And what is at the beginning and end of the Bible? *The Tree of Life*. What is at the beginning and end of Lux/Acts? *The Tree of Life*. The emphasis seems to be on this tree, its remaining stump, its roots, and its seed.

And to stress this fact, Jesus himself has now sent his own *coded* message. I'll translate the words quoted above that my ears hear:

*"I AM (Jehovah) is found at the **beginning** and the **end** of the Holy Bible. If you want to know The Truth about "God" find the one thing that is in the **first** Book and in the **last** Book. YHVH, Jehovah, God, is described in that Alpha and Omega. Know the Tree of Life and what it symbolizes and you will know God."*

CHAPTER THREE

"Three months later we set sail on a ship that had wintered at the island,
an Alexandrian ship with the Twin Brothers as its figurehead."
Acts 28:11

THE LEGEND OF CASTOR AND POLLUX

Once I discovered that Lux had inserted names from Greek mythology popular at the time into the stories about the Apostles and Jesus, I had to go back to the beginning of Acts and pay more attention to the names. I quickly realized that the names might not be exactly the same as the mythological characters, but they were close enough that any person of the time would recognize the connection. That became clear with the first name I was able to identify.

Acts 18:24-28: *"Now there came to **Ephesus** a Jew named **Apollos**, a native of **Alexandria**. He was an eloquent man, well-versed in the scriptures. **He had been instructed in <u>The Way</u> of the Lord; and he spoke with burning enthusiasm and <u>taught accurately</u> the things concerning Jesus**, though he knew only the baptism of John. He began to speak boldly in the synagogue; but when Priscilla and Aquila heard him, they took him aside and explained **<u>The Way</u> of God** to him more accurately. And when he wished to cross over into Achaia, the believers encouraged him and wrote to the disciples to welcome him. On his arrival he greatly helped those who through grace had become believers, for he powerfully refuted the Jews in public, showing by the scriptures that the Messiah is Jesus."*

Acts 19:1-7: "*While **Apollos** was in Corinth, Paul passed through the interior regions and came to **Ephesus**, where found some disciples. He said to them, 'Did you receive the Holy Spirit when you became believers?' They replied, '**No, we have not even heard that there is a Holy Spirit.**' Then he said, 'Into what then were you baptized?' They answered, 'Into John's baptism.' Paul said, 'John baptized with the baptism of repentance, telling the people to believe in the one who was to come after him, that is, in Jesus.' On hearing this, they were baptized in the name of the Lord Jesus. When Paul had laid his hands on them, the Holy Spirit came upon them, and they spoke in tongues and prophesied--altogether there were about twelve of them.*"

There is an interesting annotation, page 189NT, *The New Oxford Annotated*, 1993, that attempts to explain why the disciples might have claimed that "*we have not even heard that there is a Holy Spirit.*":

"*All who read the Old Testament would know of a Holy Spirit. The reference may be to outward signs of the Spirit's presence.*"

But this recognition of a statement that could not have been true simply provides another example of how Lux inserted information known to be wrong by any serious student of the Bible and other Greek literature in order to attract attention.

Acts 19:34: "*But when they recognized that he was a Jew, for about two hours all of them shouted in unison, 'Great is **Artemis** of the **Ephesians**!' But when the town clerk had quieted the crowd, he said, 'Citizens of Ephesus, who is there that does not know that the city of the **Ephesians** is the temple keeper of the great **Artemis** and of the statue that fell from heaven?*'"

An Internet search for *Apollo* brought up several options, but *Apollonius of Tyana* caught my eye. At www.apollonius.net/bernard 1 e.html, is an essay entitled, "*Apollonius the Nazarene*," by Dr. R. W. Bernard, B.A., M.A., Ph.D. (1964). It provides very curious information. Some quotes form Part 2, "*Similarities Between Apollonius and Jesus*":

"*Before his birth, the coming of Apollonius was preceded by an Annunciation, his coming being announced to his mother by an Archangel. He was born in the same mysterious manner in the same year when Jesus is supposed to have been born (the year 4 BC). Like the latter, in his childhood he displayed wonderful precocity in religious matters; then he went through a period of preparation; then came a period of public and positive activity; then a passion; then a kind of resurrection; and finally an ascension.*

"The messengers of Apollo sang at his birth as the angels did at that of Jesus. He also was exposed to the attacks of enemies, though always engaged in doing good. He similarly went from place to place carrying out the work of reform, being accompanied by his favorite disciples, amongst whom disaffection, discouragement and even treachery made their appearance. And when the hour of danger was at hand, in spite of the prudent advice of friends, and the abandonment of his disciples, he went straight to Rome, where Domitian, the cruel emperor, was seeking to kill him, just as Jesus went up to Jerusalem and to certain death. And before this event, he had been a victim of Domitian's no less cruel predecessor, Nero, as Jesus had been exposed to the machinations of Herod Antipas. Like Jesus, he is accused of working miracles of mercy by the aid of magic and unlawful arts, whereas he only succeeded in working them because he was a friend of the gods and worthy to be esteemed as such. Like Jesus on the road to Damascus, he fills an avowed enemy with wondering dismay by an apparition several years after his resurrection and ascension.

"His miraculous appearance to his friends--Damis and Demetrius--who thought at first that he was a spirit, remind us at once, in the way this was related, of the resurrection of Jesus after his death."

This seems a good time to quote from Acts:

Acts 17:34: *"But some of them joined him and became believers, including Dionysius the Areopagite and a woman named **Damaris** and others with them.."*

Acts 19:23-24: *"About that time no little disturbance broke out concerning the Way. A man named **Demetrius**, a silversmith who made silver shrines of Artemis, brought no little business to the craftsmen."*

We now know Lux is sending coded information, and the fact that *Damaris and Demetrius* are placed with Paul, and *Damis and Demetrius* were friends of Apollonius is probably no coincidence. Perhaps the best way to support this assumption is to list the names Lux uses that relate to Greek Gods, Goddesses, myths, historical figures, and scientists and mathematicians. Most of these names are given to people who accompany Paul in his travels to preach his gospel. They are listed in order of appearance; a brief description of the myths and characters will be provided when we attempt to solve the mystery of their presence.

Acts 14:12: Zeus; Hermes:;

Acts 17:34: Dionysius (a.k.a. Bacchus and Iacchus);

Acts 19:29: Gaius, Aristarchus;

Acts 18:1: Aquila; Pontus; Priscilla (Prisca);

Acts 18:24: Apollos. (Apollo);

Acts 19:9: Tyrannus (Oedipus Tyrannus);

Acts 19:24: Artemis; Demetrius;

Acts 20:4 Pyrrhus, Aristarchus, Secundus Gaius (a.k.a. Pliny the Elder);

Acts 28:11: The Twin Brothers (a.k.a. Castor and Pollux).

There are several additional names that qualify as being "*close*" to mythological characters. I include these names because I learned, and shared in Part One, that some of the numbers in Luke's gospel were changed or manipulated; it's fair to assume that some of the names might have been changed, as well:

Acts 16:24: Lydia; similar to the Greek Goddess Leda:

Acts 18:7: Titius Justus; similar to a Greek myth about Tydeus, son of Oeonus and Calydon.

Acts 18:8: Crispus; similar to Greek myth character, Acrisius, a son of Abas and the twin brother of Proteus. There is also *Chrysippus*, known as "*the greatest of the Greek Stoic philosophers*" and co-founder, with Zeno, of Stocism. He was considered to be equal to Aristotle, especially in the area of logic. Plutarch wrote about Chrysippus.

Acts 20:4: Trophimus; similar to a Greek myth character, Trophonius, a stone mason.

It becomes even more interesting when the myths which correspond to these names chosen by the writer of Acts are investigated:

Acts 14:12: Zeus and Hermes: (Unlike most of the names

used, Zeus and Hermes are not disguised as companions or friends of Paul. Paul and Barnabas are called by these names after they heal a man who had been crippled from birth.)

Zeus: the third king of the Greek gods; disguised as a swan he seduced Leda and became the father of two eggs from which came Pollux, Castor, and Helen of Troy.

Hermes:: Greek god of oratory, son of Zeus and Maia.

Acts 17:34: Dionysius: Greek god of happiness, a.k.a. Bacchus and Iacchus. Also the main character in a play by Plutarch.

Acts 19:29:

Gaius: Greek goddess of earth; she formed the earth and with Oranos, the Sky, gave birth to children which were the rivers, plains, trees and other features of earth. (from www.prob ertencyclopaedia.com).

Aristarchus: famous scientist and mathematician; wrote about Pythagoras;

Acts 18:1:

Aquila: in Greek mythology, a magnificent eagle that was always by the side of Zeus. According to www.winshop.com: *"The myth and history: Aquila, the Eagle, lies south of the Cygnus, the Swan, next to and westwards from Delphinus, the Dolphin...";*

Pontus: ancient sea-god, son of Gaia and Aether; Heraclides of Pontus wrote about Pythagoras;

Priscilla (Prisca): *prisca theologia* is an ancient myth that said all of civilization (theology, philosophy, mathematics, writing, etc.) were passed down from ancient times though all of history by a series of prophets, the *prisci theologi*. The names frequently mentioned as members of this lineage are Thoth/Hermes, Orpheus, Pythagoras, Plato, Krishna, Buddha, and Zoraster.

Acts 18:24: Apollos. (Apollo: important Greek God; child of Zeus and Leto, twin brother of Artemis, Greek goddess of the moon.)

Acts 19:9: Tyrannus (Oedipus Tyrannus: Greek myth: Left to die, Oedipus Tyrannus is saved and raised by a king; years later while traveling through the countryside, he accidentally kills the man who was his biological father and marries the woman who was his biological mother. When they discover the horrific sin they have unknowingly committed, his mother kills herself and Oedipus blinds himself by cutting out his eyes.)

Acts 19:24:

Artemis: (Apollo's twin sister); Greek goddess of the moon. The Virgin Goddess of fertility, vegetation, the wilderness, wild animal life and the chase (www.probertencyclopaedia.com)

Demetrius: The name and principle character of one of Plutarch's plays. This play was written in 75 ACE, making it contemporary with most of the gospels and Paul's letters. Demetrius is also the name of one of Paul's companions and the name of a friend of Apollonius of Tyana.

Acts 19:33: Alexander; Plutarch wrote *Life of Alexander* and *The Fortune and Virtue of Alexander;* Alexander wrote about Pythagoras and pythagorean symbols;

Acts 20:4

Pyrrhus: the birth name of Achilles' son who was renamed *Neoptolemus* when he went to Troy. He was one of the soldiers who hid inside the Trojan Horse.

Secundus Gaius: Also known as *Pliny the Elder*, historian and scientist. Wrote about Pythagoras;

Acts 28:11: The Twin Brothers (Castor and Pollux: twins born to Zeus and Leda)

Additional names that qualify as being "close enough":

Acts 16:24: Lydia; Greek Goddess Leda was the mother of Pollux and Castor;

Acts 18:7: Titius Justus; Greek myth Tydeus, son of Oeonus and Calydon;

Acts 18:8: Crispus; Greek myth: Acrisius, a son of Abas and the twin brother of Proteus.

Acts 20:4: Trophimus; Greek myth: Trophonius, a legendary architect of antiquity who was the first to use stone to construct monuments. He and his brother, Agamedes, built the temple of Apollo in Delphi, and Trophonius alone built the temple of Apollo at Pagassae.

The quantity of names from Greek mythology that appear in just a few chapters of Luke's descriptions of Paul, his friends and traveling companions and their destinations, simply cannot be due to mere "*coincidence*." It is clear that Lux wants us to review the myths and history that relate to these names. Aristarachus, Alexander, and Secudnus Gaius wrote books about Pythagoras, and the early Nazarenes were students of Pythagoras and Plato.

It is also worthy of mentioning that Plutarch's works show up repeatedly in Lux and Acts. An excellent biography is found at www.livius.org/pi-pm/plutarch/plutarch, and the following material is excerpted from that web site:

Plutarch was born around 46 ACE and died between 99 and 125. He was a "*Greek of high standing*" during the time of greatest upheaval in early Christianity. He was the son of wealthy parents and **studied philosophy, rhetoric, and mathematics at the platonic Academy of Athens.** But it is said that he remained open to influences from other philosophical schools, such as the Stoa and the school of Aristotle.

He was one of the leading citizens of Chaeronea and is known to have represented this town on several occasions. He is known to have visited the governor of Achaea, and he traveled to Alexandria and Rome several times. Lucius Mestrius Florus, a consul during the reign of Vespasian, was Plutarch's friend and guide during his visit to Bedriacum, where two important battles had been fought in 69 ACE, and he was also responsible for getting Roman citizenship for Plutarch.

He occupied an office in the holy city Delphi and is known to have become one of the two permanent priests responsible for the interpretation of the words of Pythia, the prophetess of Delphi.

He is said to have written between 200 and 300 books. He was often visited by Greeks and Romans, and the emperor Trajan may have been one of the visitors.

With that necessary interruption after the discovery of *Apollos*, and the probability that Lux is leading Theophilus to *Apollonius of Tyana*, the next question is, why?

Luke's description of Apollos makes it clear that he is a Nazarene:

Acts 18:24: *"...there came to Ephesus...a Jew named Apollos, a native of Alexandria...well-versed in the scriptures...instructed in* **The Way***..."*

Historians, including Bernard, report that *Apollonius of Tyana* spent a great deal of time in Ephesus, the same place Luke's *Apollos* first appears.

Bernard reports that: *"The first discourse of Apollonius given at Ephesus was from the porch of the* **temple of Diana** *(a.k.a. Artemis), after the manner of the Stoics, exhorting them to spend their time in study and philosophy (spirituality) and to abandon their dissipations and cruel sports. He also preached on 'Community of Goods' ('communism') illustrating his discourse with the parable of the sparrows."*

Acts 18:26: *"He (Apollos) began to speak boldly in* **the synagogue***; but when Priscilla and Aquila heard him, they took him aside and explained* **The Way** *of God to him more accurately."*

Lux describes Apollos as being knowledgeable about *The Way,* which would include the *"Community of Goods"* or communal life, yet whatever he was speaking about in this scene, Paul's disciples *"corrected"* him.

Bernard provides additional historical accounts of *Apollos,* or *Apollonious,* that could also describe Jesus as we've come to know him through reading the four gospels:

"The following inspiring description of the Christ-like figure of Apollonius is given by Campbell in his book Apollonius of Tyana." (Gott notes: F.A. Campbell is the full name of the author.)

"A strange distinctive figure, clad in white linen and not in garments wrought of skins; with feet unsandaled and with locks unshorn; austere, reserved, and of meagre mien; with eyes cast upon the ground as was his manner, Apollonius of Tyana drew to him with something of a saint's attraction all simple folk, and yet won as intimates the Emperors of Rome.

"Through his love for all life and swift appreciation of the beauty of the human form, he drew high to the sufferings of the body and became acquainted with the sufferings of the soul. He sought to heal,

or at least to soothe, some of the distresses, physical and spiritual, of his day, that even the sacred oracles of Aegae and of Delphi pronounced him more than mortal, referred the distempered body and the smitten soul to him, for relief, knowing that from his very presence proceeded a peculiar virtue, a benign influence, an almost theurgic power.

"By years of silence and contemplation, by extensive travel and by a continuous spiritual and worldly experience, he deepened to no minute measure, an originally powerful and intense personality, and so it was that at length he became the admiration not only of all countries through which he passed, but of the whole Roman and Hellenic world."

"Another writer gives the following description of Apollonius: 'He had a Zeus-like head, long beard and hair descending to his shoulders, bound with a deep fillet. Damis describes Apollonius as ever mild, gentle and modest, and in this manner, more like an Indian than a Greek, though, when witnessing some special enormity, he would burst out indignantly against it. (Gott note: sounds something like Jesus' reaction toward the money changers in the temple.) *His mood was often pensive, and when not speaking he would remain for long with eyes cast down, plunged in deep thought.'"*

"From Philostratus' biography, we gather the following facts about the life and character of Apollonius of Tyana. He was born in the year 4 BC. At the age of twelve he was sent to Tarsus in Cilicia, the alleged birthplace and home of 'St. Paul.' There he studied every system of philosophy, and perfected himself in rhetoric and general literature. He took up residence in the temple of Aesculapius, famed for its marvelous cures, and was initiated by its priests into their mysteries, after which he performed cures that astonished not only the people but those masters of the art of healing. **He then finally decided to adopt the philosophy of Pythagoras, and rigorously observed the trying discipline instituted by the Samian sage. He abstained from animal food, wine and women--and lived upon fruits and herbs, dressed only in white linen garments of the plainest construction, went barefooted and with uncovered head, and wore his hair and beard uncut.** *He was especially distinguished for his beauty, his genial bearing, his uniform love and kindness, and his imperturbable equanimity of temper."*

"*Determined to devote himself to the pursuit of knowledge and the teaching of philosophy, he gave away his large patrimony to his poor relatives and went to Antioch, then a center of learning but little less noted than Athens or Alexandria. There he began his great mission by teaching philosophy to a number of disciples and to the people. He then entered the temple of Apollo Daphne at Antioch and learned the mysteries of its priests. Later he traveled to India in search of wisdom and visited the Gymnosophist philosophers of Egypt. He then returned to Greece to restore the Mysteries and to teach the doctrines of Krishna and Buddha, which he learned at the feet of his Himalayan teacher Iarchas. (These Teachings, embodying the Buddhist gospels that Apollonius carried westward, became the origin of the Christian religion).*

"*It was claimed for Apollonius by his followers that he was the son of a god (Proteus), a claim which he repudiated. Nevertheless it was believed by people that Apollonius was of divine parentage and that messengers of Apollo sang at his birth.*"

"*The miracles said to have been performed in India by the Hindu savior Krishna, during his mission being almost identical with those attributed to Apollonius, were all well known and discussed in Alexandria at this time; and although Apollonius never encouraged the propagation of his divine nature, yet he never emphatically repudiated it, knowing that but little respect attached to the person or teachings of any philosophy with the vulgar multitudes unless founded on evidence of divine inspiration, the demonstrations of which were in the form of 'miracles'; and he appears to have allowed the vulgar populace to believe this. Thus arose the belief that he was the son of God, and was a second Krishna, or a Christ.*"

"*At Ephesus, he was worshipped under the title of Hercules, the warder-off of evil. Reville says that 'after his death, the city of Tyana paid him divine honours; and the universal respect in which he was held by the whole of the pagan world testified to the deep impression which caused one of his contemporaries to exclaim, 'we had a god living among us.'*'"

"*Concerning Apollonius' universal renown during the first century, W.B. Wallace writes: 'His noble countenance, his winning presence, his pure doctrine, his unsullied life, his ardent advocacy of the immortality of the soul, as well as his miracles--led men to believe, wherever he went, that he was more than mortal. He consorted and corresponded with the mighty ones of the earth.'"*

"J.A. Froude writes: 'According to Philostratus he was a heathen saviour, who claimed a commission from heaven to teach a pure and reformed religion, and in attestation of his authority went about healing the sick, curing the blind, raising the dead men to life, casting out demons, stilling tempests, and prophesying future events--which came afterwards to pass.'"

"There is reason to think that the followers of Apollonius were Essenes or Therapeuts, of which sects he was undoubtedly the leader. *According to Reville, 'Apollonius and his followers, like Pythagoras and his disciples, constituted a regular order of Pagan monks.'"*

"According to Phillimore, Apollonius founded a church and a community, composed of his disciples--who were undoubtedly the branch of Essenes known as Nazarenes or Therapeuts. *Phillimore says, 'Apollonius may be said to have founded a 'church'; but there was nothing commercial in the institution; he was not salaried by his admiring disciples.'"*

I've provided quite a bit of information about *Apollonius of Tyana* because this background is important before proceeding with what Lux appears to be trying to tell us by bringing in the information about *Apollos* and the other names from Greek mythology. It's at this point that the hidden message gets really interesting.

From *"Apollonius the Nazarene, Part 4, Events in the Life of Apollonius of Tyana: Birth and Youth of Apollonius, as recorded in 'The Life of Apollonius of Tyana' by his biographer, Philostratus"* by R.W. Bernard:

*"The country people said that he was the son of **Zeus**; others called him a son of **Apollo**; while still others considered him as an incarnation of **Proteus**, the God of Wisdom, who prior to his birth, appeared to his mother and told her that she would bear a child who would be an incarnation of himself."*

"Apollonius was born in the year 4 BC, the acknowledged year of the birth of Christ. His birth, like his conception, was miraculous. Just

before his nativity, his mother was walking in a meadow, where she lay down on the grass and went to sleep. Some wild **swans**, *at the end of a long flight approached her and by their cries and the beatings of their wings, awakened her so suddenly that her child was born before its time. The swans, apparently, had foreseen and marked by their presence the fact that on that day was to be born a being whose soul would be as white as their own plumage and who, like them, would be a glorious wanderer."*

Between Acts Chapter 14 and Chapter 28, Lux uses approximately fifteen names that can be linked to Greek mythological characters and/or Pythagoras. One of those names is Zeus, and another name, Lydia, is very similar to *Leda. Leda,* according to Greek mythology, was seduced by Zeus, disguised as a swan, and gave birth to two eggs. From these eggs came her daughter Helen, and sons, **Pollux and Castor**.

Pollux and Castor were referred to, though not by name, at Acts 28:11: *"Three months later we set sail on a ship that had wintered at the island, an Alexandrian ship with the* **Twin Brothers** *as its figurehead."* An annotation explains: *"The Twin Brothers, Castor and Pollux, were worshiped by sailors."*

Apollonius' biographer also tells us that some *"considered him as an incarnation of Proteus."* Proteus was the twin brother of Acrisius (similar to *Cripsus,* Acts 18:8).

Apollo is described at www.probertencyclopaedia.com:

"In Greek and Roman mythology, Apollo was the god of the sun, music, poetry, prophecy, agriculture, and pastoral life, and leader of the Muses. **He was the twin child of Zeus and Leto**. *Ancient statues show Apollo as the embodiment of the Greek ideal of male beauty. Apollo epitomized the transition between adolescence and manhood in Greek male society."*

Lux refers to the twins, Castor and Pollux, by reporting that the ship's figurehead was the *"Twin Brothers."* Lux names *Crispus,* similar to *Acrisius,* who has a twin brother, Proteus. And Apollonius' biographer reports some believed him to be the incarnation of Proteus, in which case he would have a twin brother. Now who might that twin brother be?

One of the ancient texts the early church rejected,

discovered at Nag Hammadi along with some partial works of Plato, was the gospel of Thomas. It opens with these words:

"These are the secret sayings that the living Jesus spoke and Didymos Judas Thomas recorded."

Didymos is Greek for *twin*; *Thomas* is the Semetic words for *twin*. There are several web sites that provide the text from the Gnostic gospel of Thomas that suggest that Jesus had a twin brother. Most report that in the Syriac tradition, based on the *Acts of Judas Thomas*, Judas is Jesus' twin. Mark 6:3 and Matthew 13:55 name *Judas* as one of Jesus' brothers, but not a twin brother. And of course there is the infamous and mysterious *Judas Iscariot.*

Pollux and Castor were also known as *Dioscuri*, which means *"sons of Jove."* *Jove* was another name for *Zeus*, who was also known as *Jupiter*. Notice the similarity between *Iscariot* and *Dioscuri*: *scario* versus *scuri* may be more than mere coincidence. This seems particularly curious considering the doubt about the meaning of the word *Iscariot.* It seems reasonable to suggest that the original might have been *Jesus and Judas Dioscuri*: Jesus and Judas, sons of the God, Zeus, Jove, Jupiter, or Jehovah (take your pick).

Jesus and Apollonius were born in the same year under similar circumstances and lived their lives in such a way as to have historians, both ancient and modern, draw comparisons between them. Some argue that Jesus never actually existed and was simply made up, plagiarized from the historical Apollonius. Opponents to that theory are usually willing to acknowledge that Apollonius lived during the same time as Jesus, but argue that Jesus' teachings and miracles were attached to Apollonius to discredit the early Christian movement.

Dr. R.W. Bernard, *"Apollonius the Nazarene Part 1: The Historical Apollonius Versus the Mythical Jesus"*:

"Furthermore, the main events of the lives of both men were so closely parallel that the reader cannot help but conclude that if Jesus is not a fictitious imitation of Apollonius, then Apollonius must be an imitation of him, since it would be highly improbable for two such similar men to have been born the same year and to have such similar biographies."

Here's another idea, and I present it as a possible solution based on the code Lux gives in this section of Acts. Jesus and Apollonius were not only born in the same year, but they were born on the same day, at approximately the same time. They were identical twins. They were separated shortly after birth, probably after the circumcision ceremony directed by the prophetess Anna. Looking back at the description of the ceremony, we find that Luke 2:24 quoted Numbers 6:10, but one change was made, and it is now clear why:

Numbers 6:10: "...__*two*__ *turtledoves or two young pigeons.*"

Luke 2:24: "...__*a pair*__ *of turtledoves, or two young pigeons.*"

Webster defines *pair* as: "*Two things that are similar in function or form.*" This "*minor*" change by someone trying to send a coded message becomes very major. There's more:

Luke 2:32: "...*a light for revelation to the Gentiles* (Apollonius), and *for glory to the people of Israel* (Yeshua)."

Luke 3:4-6 quotes Isaiah 40:3-5, but the words that immediately precede verse 3 carry the coded message:

Isaiah 40:1-2: "...*O comfort my people, says your God. Speak tenderly to Jerusalem, and cry to her that she has served her term, that her penalty is paid, that **she has received from the Lord's hand __double__** for all her sins.*"

The ceremony was to consecrate a **pair** of Messiahs, one for the Gentiles and one for the Jews. Apollonius was raised by a wealthy Greek family, followers of Pythagorean/Nazarenes in the cities of Tyana and Tarsus; Jeshua was raised a Nazarene/Essene near Mount Carmel in Galilee.

The biography of Apollonius includes several clues that he was a twin:

The first clue is his name; the Greek god, Apollo, was a twin.

A second clue is the belief by some that he was a reincarnation of Proteus, also a twin.

The third clue is the story of the presence of swans at his birth; recall Luke's reference to Castor and Pollux, and the Greek myth of these twins: *"Pollux was twin brother of Castor.*

He was a son of Zeus and Leda. He was born from an egg after Zeus visited Leda disguised as a swan."

"Castor was the twin brother of Pollux. He was a son of Zeus and Leda. He, like his brother was born from an egg after Zeus visited Leda disguised as a swan." (Both descriptions come from www.probert encyclopaedia.com.)

So Apollonius' biographer hints that he is a twin, and Lux, Jesus' biographer who promised to tell the truth about his life, leaves clues that he, too, is a twin. And that suggestion is supported by gospels discarded by the early church but circulated throughout the region, especially in Syria.

If there were two of them, this might explain the silence about Jesus' childhood. We really know nothing of his life until he appears at the river Jordan at the reported age of thirty. Although he appears knowledgeable of Judaism, his message is anything but. His message is Pythagorean, as demonstrated by the numbers. It is Buddhism, as demonstrated by his pacifism. It is exactly the same message that Apollonius was delivering to the wealthy, educated Greeks and Romans. Both of them taught a mixture of Pythagorus, Plato, Zoraster, and Buddha.

Perhaps Jesus was taken to India or Egypt during his childhood to be educated in Pythagorean philosophy. There are no gaps in Apollonius' life; he studied Pythagorean philosophy at the school in Tarsus in his early years, studied at the healing temple of Aegae in his teens, and visited the Brahman masters in India as an adult.

To summarize what appears to be the hidden message in Acts Chapters 14 through 28:

A Nazarene woman, probably a High Priestess named Miriam, gave birth to twin boys, destined to be described as *Gods* or *sons of God*. They were named *Yeshua* and *Yudas*. Yudas was sent to live with a wealthy and powerful family in a Pythagorean/Nazarene community in the city of Tyana. There he became known as *Apollonius*. Jeshua was perhaps sent to the Nazarene community in Alexandria, Egypt, to be schooled in philosophy.

Both were trained by the Pythagorean Priesthood

to become leaders of the Nazarene/Essene/Pythagorean movement. Both were exceptional in looks, wisdom, education, knowledge of the healing arts, science, and mathematics. They were great teachers, great leaders, and lived exceptionally pure lives according to all the tenets of Pythagoreanism.

They may or may not have known of the existence of the other during their childhood. They probably knew of each other and worked together once they took the movement to all the people. Judas, as Apollonius, taught the wealthy Greeks, men and women alike, while Jesus taught the poor and oppressed, both men and women.

The existence of two identical figures traveling throughout the known world must have presented something of a problem to the early church when it decided to make the Galilean a personification of the Jewish God, Jehovah. Since Judaism was monotheistic, two *Gods* sort of screwed up the whole charade. So, they tried to remove all references to *The Twin*.

Lux foresaw Paul's support by the Roman government, the Pharisees, and the Sadducees. Any gospel that overtly told the story of the twins, Jesus and Judas, would eventually be declared a heresy and destroyed. Lux and Ax were written to lead a good detective to Pollux and Castor, twin sons of a God and Goddess, and to Oedipus Tyrannus, born to a king but raised by another powerful family in a distant country. The existence of gospels that told of the twins was undoubtedly known, and perhaps Lux/Ax was written to provide support for those gospels. But most were later destroyed by the men in power in order to hide, among other things, the existence of the twin Messiahs of the Nazarenes.

What I find interesting and fascinating is this:

The official church condemned the Nazarene/Gnostics as heretics. The *gnosis* that was heretical included the following:

1. A sun-centered solar system;

2. A spherical earth;

3. Creation explainable mathematically (*"Number is all"*);

4. The Creator as a Duality: positive/negative energy; feminine/masculine energies;

God/Goddess Energies;

5. Sizes and distances of the sun, the moon, the earth, and the existence of other planets.

Anyone who taught or believed any of this knowledge was subject to torture and death, beginning in the second century and continuing until well into the seventeenth century. Other *"heresies"* included vegetarianism and the use of herbs and plants for healing, possessing works of Pythagoras, Plato, Socrates, Buddha, Zoraster, etc.

The *"science"* of the western world was the science of the church: a flat earth which was the center of the universe, Male Creator/God, God as healer, etc. In fact, all of the *"Science of Western Religion"* is now known to have been erroneous. Tough luck for the millions of men, women, and children who refused to accept it over the past two thousand years and died as a result of their doubts.

Shortly after the turn of the twentieth century, new and startling information began to come to light (pun intended): Einstein proposed that *"Creation"* or *"mass"* was the result of the interaction of energy and light. By then, most people, including the fanatical religious, had been convinced that the earth was not flat nor the center of the Universe. But Einstein's work wasn't well known or supported until just a few decades ago, just about the same time that most of the hidden Nazarene/Gnostic texts were discovered.

"Coincidentally," the scientific knowledge that confirms the accuracy of the *gnosis*, condemned by the church as heresy, wasn't available until the last century, just about the same time the hidden Gnostic/Nazarene texts that preserved the proof of their knowledge and doctrines was found.

And now, thanks to those two coinciding discoveries, plus the miracle of Internet search engines, Lux and Ax can be decoded and verified by modern science and technology and the texts the Nazarene/Gnostics preserved! Don't you just love it!!

CHAPTER FOUR

"At the same time he hoped that money would be given him by Paul, and for that reason he used to send for him very often and converse with him."
Acts 24:26

RANSOM FOR A ROMAN
OF
HIGH STANDING

According to Acts, Paul, whose Jewish name was Saul, did some *"contemptible"* things. The first of these *"contemptible acts"* occurs in Acts 6:

Acts 6:8: *"And Stephen, full of grace and power, did great wonders and signs among the people. Then some of those who belonged to the synagogue of the Freedmen (as it was called), and of the Cyrenians, and of the Alexandrians, and of those from Cilicia and Asia, arose and disputed with Stephen. But they could not withstand the wisdom and the Spirit with which he spoke. Then they secretly instigated men, who said, 'We have heard him speak blasphemous words against Moses and God.' And they stirred up the people and the elders and the scribes, and they came upon him and seized him and brought him before the council, and set up false witnesses who said, 'This man never ceases to speak words against this holy place and the law; for we have heard him say that this Jesus of Nazareth will destroy this place, and will change the customs which Moses delivered to us.' And gazing at him, all who sat in the council saw that his face was like the face of an angel.'"*

Stephen, accused by an angry crowd and about to be stoned to death, tells the story of Joseph being sold into Egypt, of Moses becoming an exile in the land of Midian, his forty years in the wilderness of Mount Sinai, and other stories from the Old Testament. He closes by saying,

Acts 7:51-60: *"You **stiff-necked people**, uncircumcised in heart and ears, you always resist the Holy Spirit. **As your fathers did**, so do you. Which of the prophets did not your fathers persecute? And they killed those who announced beforehand the coming of the Righteous One, whom you have now betrayed and murdered, **you who received the <u>law as delivered by angels</u> and did not keep it.***

"Now when they heard these things they were enraged, and they ground their teeth against him. But he, full of the Holy Spirit, gazed into heaven and saw the glory of God, and Jesus standing at the right hand of God; and he said, 'Behold, I see the heavens opened, and the Son of man standing at the right hand of God.'

*"But they cried out with a loud voice and stopped their ears and rushed together upon him. Then they cast him out of the city and stoned him; **and the witnesses laid down their garments at the feet of a young man named Saul**. And as they were stoning Stephen, he prayed, 'Lord Jesus, receive my spirit.' And he knelt down and cried with a loud voice, 'Lord, do not hold this sin against them.' And when he had said this he fell asleep."*

Acts 8:1-3: ***"And Saul was consenting to his death. And on that day a great persecution arose against the church in Jerusalem;*** *and they were all scattered throughout the region of Judea and Samaria, except the apostles. Devout men buried Stephen, and made great lamentation over him.* ***But Saul was ravaging the church, and entering house after house, he dragged off men and women and committed them to prison."***

This story about the death of Stephen introduces Saul to the world. This is a powerful scene in which to find Saul for the first time. But before investigating Saul's participation in the stoning of Stephen, I'd like to point out some things I think Lux wanted us to notice.

Some of the words Lux put into Stephen's mouth come from the Old Testament. For instance, *"You stiff-necked people"* is used five times there; four of those references are in Exodus: 32: 9-10, 33:3, 33:5, and 34:9.

But Stephen's words are most closely paralleled at 2 Chronicles 30:7-8:

*"Do not be like your **ancestors** and your kindred, who were faithless to the Lord God of their ancestors, so that he made them a desolation, as you see. Do not now be **stiff-necked as your ancestors were**, but yield yourselves to the Lord and come to his sanctuary, which he has sanctified forever, and serve the Lord your God, so that his fierce anger may turn away from you."*

There must be something described in Chronicles that Lux wants to report; perhaps more about what they were dealing with in Jerusalem after Saul arrived. I had the urge to look at the chapters which both precede and follow Chapter 30. Here are some of the highlights from 2 Chronicles 29, 30, and 31:

2 Chronicles 29: *"For our ancestors have been unfaithful and have done what was evil in the sight of the Lord our God; they have forsaken him, and have turned away their faces from the dwelling of the Lord, and turned their backs."*

"They have also shut the doors...and put out the lamps..."

"Our fathers have fallen by the sword and our sons and our daughters and our wives are in captivity..."

2 Chronicles 30: *"...Many people came together in Jerusalem to keep the festival of unleavened bread...a very large assembly..."*

"...They set to work and removed the altars that were in Jerusalem and all the altars for offering incense they took away and threw into the Wadi Kidron."

"...There were many in the assembly who had not sanctified themselves..."

2 Chronicles 31:1: *"Now when all this was finished, all Israel who were present went out to the cities of Judah and broke down the pillars, hewed down the sacred poles, and pulled down the high places and the alters throughout all Judah and Benjamin, and in Ephraim and Manasseh, until they had destroyed them all. Then all the people of Israel returned to their cities, all to their individual properties."*

Indeed it sounds very similar to the historical accounts of what was done to Jesus' disciples. And notice how this description of what was happening in Jerusalem and Judah coincides with Saul's arrival on the scene. This is something that will occur again.

Saul's participation in Stephen's stoning seems rather strange. There must be some significance to "*the witnesses*" laying down their garments "*at the feet of a young man named Saul.*" This indicates to me that Saul was a young man of some importance. It was tradition that the witnesses to a crime would cast the first stones, but this laying down of coats at the foot of Saul is curious and no doubt meaningful.

Stephen's speech draws attention because of its length and apparent rambling. There must be something here that is quite important. Stephen is about to be killed and it seems strange that he starts talking about Abraham in Mesopotamia with such detail:

Acts 7:8-9: "*...And so Abraham became the father of Isaac, and circumcised him on the eighth day; and Isaac became the father of Jacob, and Jacob of the twelve patriarchs. And the patriarchs, jealous of Joseph, sold him into Egypt...*"

Acts 7:12-13: "*But when Jacob heard that there was grain in Egypt, he sent forth our fathers the first time. And at the second visit Joseph made himself known to his brothers, and Joseph's family became known to Pharoh.*"

Acts 7:14-16: "*Then Joseph sent and invited his father Jacob and all his relatives to come to him, seventy-five in all; so Jacob went down to Egypt. He himself died there as well as our ancestors, and their bodies were brought back to Shechem and laid in the tomb that Abraham had bought for a sum of silver from the sons of Hamor in Shechem.*"

An annotation makes this section stand out even more (*New Annotated*, 1994 page 170 NT):

"*Shechem; but according to Gen 50:13 Jacob was buried at Hebron. Abraham; but according to Gen 33:19 and Josh 24:32 it was Jacob who bought the tomb at Shechem.*"

That's a pretty big mistake for Lux to make. *Jacob* seems to become confused with *Abraham* and their burial tombs are reversed.

Josephus, the first century historian, wrote about the

stoning of "*James, brother of Jesus.*" Present at that stoning, wrote Josephus, was a man named *Saulus*. What an interesting "*coincidence.*" Could Lux be trying to send the message that James has been confused with Stephen? The name *James* in Hebrew is *Jacob*. I looked up the meaning of *Stephen*. It is a Greek word for *crown*.. If Jesus' brother James had become the High Priest of the Nazarene/Essene movement, perhaps "*crown*" would be a good code word for him.

Something else became obvious as I read and reread the story of Stephen, which stretches from Acts 6:8 through Acts 7:60, a total of sixty-seven verses. The name *Jacob* is used eight times between Acts 7:8 and 7:46, the word *Egypt* is used thirteen times between Acts 7:9 and 7:40, and the name *Joseph* is used five times between Acts 7:9 and 7:18 . Stephen's speech, therefore, is primarily about James, Joseph, and Egypt.

The Nazarene/Essenes would have known of James' stoning and that a Herodian named Saulus was in charge of it. But with Paul's letters becoming more and more the accepted authority for the new religion, could they have expected the story to survive if they told it as it was? We're lucky Josephus' *Antiquities of the Jews* remained intact enough to tell the story of James' stoning and that a *Saulus* was present. With this information from a reputable historian of the time, and knowing Lux had to code the message, it becomes obvious that *Stephen* was actually James, brother of Jesus and in charge of the Nazarene/Essene movement after Jesus' crucifixion.

There was a Nazarene/Essene community located in Alexandria, Egypt. Recall baby Jesus was said to have been hidden in Egypt in order to save him from Herod's slaughter of infant boys. Is Lux trying to report something of tremendous importance by these thirteen references to Egypt from the mouth of James, Jesus' brother, just before he is stoned to death by a crowd, under the supervision of a Herodian named *Saulus*?

What does Stephen/James/Lux tell us about Egypt?

Acts 7:9: "*The patriarchs, jealous of Joseph, sold him into Egypt...*"

Acts 7:10: Joseph was *"...appointed...ruler over Egypt and over all his household."*

Acts 7:11: *"...there came a famine throughout Egypt..."*

Acts 7:12: *"...when Jacob heard there was grain in Egypt, he sent our ancestors there on their first visit."*

Acts 7:15: *"Jacob went down to Egypt. He himself died there as well as our ancestors."*

Acts 7:17: *"But as the time drew near for the fulfillment of the promise that God had made to Abraham, **our people in Egypt increased and multiplied**..."*

Acts 7:18: *"...until another king who had not known Joseph ruled over Egypt."*

Acts 7:34: *"I have surely seen the mistreatment of my people who are in Egypt and have heard their groaning, and I have come down to rescue them. Come now, I will send you to Egypt."*

Acts 7:39 *"Our ancestors were unwilling to obey him; instead, they pushed him aside, and in their hearts they turned back to Egypt."*

Acts 7:40: *"...saying to Aaron, 'Make gods for us who will lead **the way** for us; as for this Moses who led us out from the land of Egypt, we do not know what has happened to him.'"*

(Gott note: I have to believe the use of the words, *"the way,"* is not accidental here.)

Acts 7:29: *"When he heard this, Moses fled and became a resident alien in the land of Midian. **There he became the father of two sons.**"*

That last sentence is a perfect example of *"too much information,"* one of the hallmarks of Luke's methods of attracting attention and passing on information. If this speech was written to give important information about Jesus, what could be more important than that he had two sons?

If, as Laurence Gardner contends (*Bloodline of the Holy Grail, Element Books, Ltd, 1997-1999*), *Joseph* and *Jacob* are Nazarene/Essene patriarchal titles, with *Joseph* being first and *Jacob* second in lineage order, it would appear that Lux is reporting that Stephen/James/Jacob's older brother, Joseph/Jesus, had gone into Egypt, and Jacob/James (after the stoning, brother Judas would become second in command and given the title "*Jacob/James*") followed later, and the family "*increased and multiplied*" while in Egypt--Jesus became the father of two sons.

Clement of Alexandria was a leader of the Gnostic branch of the early church. His version of Jesus' message contained a great deal of the Nazarene/Essene/Pythagorean flavor. Alexandria was known for the great wealth of knowledge in its famous library. The fact that an ancient community of Nazarene/Essene/Pythagoreans resided there would make it an ideal place to hide a fleeing Savior/Teacher/High Priest that the Pharisees, Sadducees, and Roman government had attempted to crucify. And in the Nazarene/Essene religious structure, it would have been extremely important for the High Priest, Jesus, to father children in order to continue the bloodline of High Priests and Priestesses. It appears that Lux wanted the Nazarene/Essene community, now forced underground, to know that the "*holy seed*" had been successfully planted and nurtured and had produced twofold.

It seems that *The Acts of the Apostles* which were the most important to record, were the brutal "*acts*" of the "*apostle Paul*" and the part he played in James' death. This day was of the utmost significance, for the scripture says, "*...on that day a great persecution arose against the church in Jerusalem.*" The "church in Jerusalem" to which this reference is made was the new church of the Nazarenes under the leadership of Jesus' brother, James. And this moment, this introduction of Saul was the "*beginning of the great persecution.*" This is information they wanted us to know.

Historians recorded the stoning of James as the beginning of the great upheaval in Jerusalem. Lux had to change some names to protect both the innocent and the guilty, but they got the story told, and perhaps they revealed where Jesus went after the crucifixion. Whether he died and was resurrected, as the gospels report, or was saved from death by Joseph of Arimathea, as some theorists claim, is irrelevant to his fleeing to Alexandria. Both sides of the argument agree he was seen occupying a body after being placed in the tomb. Therefore, he could have gone to Egypt for the duration of his time on earth. That's what Lux reports through Stephen's speech prior to the stoning.

Elmar R. Gruber has written a book, *The Jesus Conspiracy: The Turin Shroud and the Secrets About the Resurrection.*. An excerpt from this book can be found at www.apollonius.net/golgotha.html. Gruber has investigated the gospel of John in much the same way I've looked at Lux and Ax. He recognized coded messages in that gospel and provides the best evidence I've ever seen that Jesus was miraculously saved by the medicinal cures known to his Nazarene/Essene brothers and sisters.

"*Saul breathed threats AND murder against the disciples.*" The murder of James/Jacob was just one episode. It was happening everywhere and to many who remained loyal to The Nazarene Way.

Stephen/James' words just before he died, heard by Saul and important to the mystery, bear repeating:

"*They (your ancestors) killed those who foretold the coming of the **Righteous One, and now you have become his betrayers and murders.** You are the ones that received the **Law as <u>ordained by angels</u>**, and yet you have not kept it.*"

Saul wrote as Paul to the Galatians, 3:19-26: "*Why then the law? It was added because of transgressions, until the seed would come to whom the promise had been made; and it was **ordained through angels by a mediator**. Now a mediator involves more than one party; but God is one. Is the law then opposed to the promises of God? Certainly not! For if a law had been given that could make alive, then righteousness would indeed come through the law. But the scripture has imprisoned all things under the power of sin, so that what was promised through the faith of Jesus Christ might be given to those who believe.*

"*Now before faith came, **we were imprisoned and guarded under the law until faith would be revealed**. Therefore the law* *was our disciplinarian until Christ came, so that we might be justified by faith. But now that faith has come, we are no longer subject to a disciplinarian, for in Christ Jesus you are all children of God through faith."*

Another interesting annotation appears on page 171 NT, *New Oxford Annotated*, 1994:

"The law being ordained by angels, is considered valid; but Paul used this Jewish tradition to argue that the law is secondary (Gal 3.19)."

Remember Acts was written after Paul's letters. Acts, like Lux, was written to inform Theophilus of *"...the truth concerning the things about which you have been instructed."* And at the time Lux and Acts were written, the instructions were coming from Paul's letters, including this one to the Galatians. Lux tells us, again, that Paul's religion was not the religion of Jesus, James, and the Nazarenes.

This message in Acts is much more than a mere clue to Paul's opposition to Jesus' message. This scene puts Paul in front of a man named Stephen, hearing his words in person, first hand. He stands there and is accused of being one of the very people who betrayed and murdered Jesus. *"You received the Law..."* This is the Law Jesus taught; the Law that was *"ordained by angels..." "...and you have not kept it."*

Paul's doctrine taught that the *"law"* didn't apply to the believers. Paul didn't have a clue that the *"Law ordained by angels"* was not the *"law and the prophets,"* which had become nothing more than the rituals and traditions of men. These rituals included the incessant and required purification bathing and the animal sacrifices, both of which produced income for the High Priest and chief priests of the temple. Indeed, Jesus taught that the *"law and the prophet,"* the *"laws of men,"* were useless. But not the Law ordained by angels:

Luke 16:16: Jesus said: *"'The law and the prophets were in effect until John came; since then the good news of the kingdom of God is proclaimed, and everyone tries to enter it by force. But it is easier for heaven and earth to pass away than for one stroke of a letter in the Law to be dropped.'"*

The *"good news of the kingdom of God"* was the *"Law ordained by angels"* about which Stephen spoke. And that Law, taught by Jesus and based on the *Tree of Life* and its angels of the earth and angels of the sky, was the Law of Equal and Balanced Interchange. It was the Law of Balance between masculine and feminine energies; it is the Law of Creation And it is supported by modern physics. Between people, it is the Law of Cause and Effect: *"Do as you would have it done to you."* This is the knowledge which Jesus and all other Great Mystics taught. And until it is recognized and resurrected, no true and lasting equality and peace can come to the people on earth.

All Nazarene/Essenes knew about the *Tree of Life*, its angels, and its relationship to the Creator and to Creation. Why didn't Paul know about it?

Acts 21:37-39: *"Just as Paul was about to be brought into the barracks, he said to the tribune, 'May I say something to you?' The tribune replied, 'Do you know Greek? Then you are not the Egyptian who recently stirred up a revolt and led the four thousand men of the Assassins out into the wilderness?' Paul replied, '**I am a Jew, from Tarsus in Cilicia, a citizen of an important city; I beg you, let me speak to the people.**'"*

Acts 22:1-5: *"'Bothers and fathers, listen to the defense that I now make before you.' When they heard him **addressing them in Hebrew**, they became even more quiet. Then he said: '**I am a Jew, born at Tarsus in Cilicia, but brought up in this city at the feet of Gamaliel, educated strictly according to our ancestral law**, being zealous for God, just as all of you are today. **I persecuted 'The Way' up to the point of death, binding both men and women and putting them in prison, as the high priest and the whole council of elders can testify about me**. From them I also received letters to the brothers in Damascus, and I went there in order to bind those who were there and to bring them back to Jerusalem for punishment.'"*

Acts 22:17-21: *"'After I had returned to Jerusalem and while **I was praying in the temple**, I fell into a trance and saw Jesus saying to me, 'Hurry and get out of Jerusalem quickly, because they will not accept your testimony about me.' And I said, 'Lord, they themselves know that in every synagogue **I imprisoned and beat those who**"* *believed in you. And while the blood of your witness Stephen was shed, I myself was standing by, approving and* <u>*keeping the coats of those who killed him.'*</u> *Then he said to me, 'Go for I will send you far away to the Gentiles.'"*

Acts 22:22-29: *"Up to this point they listened to him, but then they shouted, 'Away with such a fellow from the earth! For he should not be allowed to live.' And while they were shouting, throwing off their cloaks, and tossing dust into the air, the tribune directed that he was to be brought into the barracks, and ordered him to be examined by flogging, to find out the reason for this outcry against him.*

"But when they had tied him up for the lashes, Paul said to the centurion who was standing by, 'Is it legal for you to flog a Roman citizen who is uncondemned?' When the centurion heard that, he went to the tribune and said to him, 'What are you about to do? This man is a Roman citizen.' **The tribune came and asked Paul, 'Tell me, are you a Roman citizen?' And he said, 'Yes.'** *The tribune answered, 'It cost me a large sum of money to get my citizenship.' Paul said,* **'But I was born a citizen.'** *Immediately those who were about to examine him drew back from him; and* **the tribune also was afraid, for he realized that Paul was a Roman citizen and the he had bound him**.

"Since he wanted to find out what Paul was being accused of by the Jews, the next day he released him and ordered the chief priests and the entire council to meet. He brought Paul down and had him stand before them."

Acts 23:1-11: *"While Paul was looking intently at the council he said, 'Brothers, up to this day* **I have lived my life with a clear conscience before God.'** *Then the high priest Ananias ordered those standing near him to strike him on the mouth. At this Paul said to him, 'God will strike you, you whitewashed wall! Are you sitting there to judge me according to the law, and yet in violation of the law you order me to be struck? Those standing nearby said, 'Do you dare to insult God's high priest?' And Paul said,* **'I did not realize, brothers, that he was high priest,** *for it is written, 'You shall not speak evil of a leader of your people.'"*

"When Paul noticed that some were Sadducees and others were Pharisees, he called out in the council, 'Brothers, **I am a Pharisee,**

a son of Pharisees. I am on trial concerning <u>the hope</u> of the resurrection of the dead.' When he said this, a dissension began between the Pharisees and the Sadducees, and the assembly was divided. (The Sadducees say that there is no resurrection, or angel, or spirit; but the Pharisees acknowledge all three.)'

*"Then a great clamor arose, and certain **scribes of the Pharisees' group stood up and contended, 'We find nothing wrong with this man**. What if a spirit or an angel has spoken to him?' When the dissension became violent, the tribune, fearing that they would tear Paul to pieces, ordered the soldiers to go down, take him by force, and bring him into the barracks.*

"That night the Lord stood near him and said, 'Keep up your courage! For just as you have testified for me in Jerusalem, so you must bear witness also in Rome.'"

What was Paul's testimony *for Jesus* in Jerusalem? That's the testimony Acts just recorded: Did he say he was on trial because he loved Jesus and was teaching the Nazarene Way of love and peaceful communal living? Did he say anything about Jesus at all? Did he say anything against the Pharisees or Sadducees? Is this Luke's way of telling the theophilosophers that Paul never ceased being a Pharisee? That he never ceased hating the Nazarenes? Rather than describing a man willing to die for his faith in Jesus' teachings, Paul reminded the gathering that he was a Pharisee, a son of a Pharisee, educated by a respected Pharisee priest and that he was a Roman citizen from an important city. He tells about his involvement in Stephen's stoning, persecuting and killing those of *The Way*, and then he says, *"up to this day **I have lived my life with a clear conscience before God**."*! It seems to me that Lux was trying to send several messages here:

First, Paul was an important citizen of Rome, from a powerful Roman family. Why else would the tribune be fearful when he discovered Paul's citizenship? Paul reminded them that he *"held the coats"* of those who stoned Stephen. Lux seems to say that Paul was actually in charge of the stoning.

Second, Paul was not Jesus' disciple. Every word Lux puts into Paul's mouth is a denial of Jesus and a message that he was actually a Pharisee. According to Acts this scene occurs after Paul's conversion. Where, I ask again, is the testimony FOR Jesus?

These *"Acts of the Apostle Paul,"* are horrendous. This was information they wanted us to know. The stories are repeated several times in several ways. Plus this information gives the reader a better idea of who Paul actually was--not just what he did.

Acts 23:12-13: *"In the morning the Jews joined in a conspiracy and bound themselves by an oath neither to eat nor drink until they had killed Paul. There were more than forty who joined in this conspiracy."*

Acts 23:14-21 reports that Paul's nephew (his sister's son) heard about the ambush, visited Paul in the barracks, and warned him. Paul called one of the centurians and told him to take his nephew to the Tribune, which he did.

Acts 23:22: *"So the tribune dismissed the young man, ordering him, 'Tell no one that you have informed me of this.'"*

Acts 23:23-30: *"Then he summoned two of the centurions and said, 'Get ready to leave by nine o'clock tonight for Caesarea with **two hundred soldiers, seventy horsemen, and two hundred spearmen**. Also provide **mounts for Paul to ride, and take him safely to Felix the governor.'** He wrote a letter to this effect: 'Claudius Lysias to his Excellency the governor Felix, greetings. This man was seized by the Jews and was about to be killed by them, but when I had learned that he was a Roman citizen, I came with the guard and rescued him. Since I wanted to know the charge for which they accused him, I had him brought to their council. I found that he was accused concerning questions of their law, but was charged with nothing deserving death or imprisonment. When I was informed that there would be a plot against the man, I sent him to you at once, ordering his accusers also to state before you what they have against him.'"*

How important a Roman was Paul to be given horses (plural), two hundred soldiers, seventy horsemen, and two hundred spear men? That's an army of 470 men! What did Claudius Lysias know about Paul's position in Rome? What might that position have been? Even if Lux knew, could they get by with revealing it in this document? If Paul was, for instance, the head of the Pharisee temple in Rome, or Herod Agrippa's nephew, could that have been written openly and still accepted as a Christian gospel by the later "*Christian*" church of Rome? I don't think so.

Acts 23:31: "*So the soldiers, according to their instructions, took Paul and brought him during the night to Antipatris. The next day they let the horsemen go on with him (there were seventy), while they returned to the barracks. When they came to Caesarea and delivered the letter to the governor, they presented Paul also before him. On reading the letter, he asked what province he belonged to, and when he learned that he was from Cilicia, he said, 'I will give you a hearing when your accusers arrive.' Then he ordered that he be kept under guard in Herod's headquarters.*" (Herod's headquarters at Caesarea was formerly Herod's palace.)

Acts 24:1-16: "*Five days later the high priest Ananias came down with some elders and an attorney, a certain Tertullus, and they reported their case against Paul to the governor. When Paul had been summoned, Tertullus began to accuse him, saying:*

'*Your Excellency, because of you we have long enjoyed peace, and reforms have been made for this people because of your foresight. We welcome this in every way and everywhere with utmost gratitude. But, to detain you no further, I beg you to hear us briefly with your customary graciousness. We have, in fact, found this man a pestilent fellow, an agitator among all the Jews throughout the world, and a ringleader of* **the sect of the Nazarenes**. *He even tried to profane the temple, and so we seized him. By examining him yourself you will be able to learn from him concerning everything of which we accuse him.*'

"*The Jews also joined in the charge by asserting that all this was true.*

"*When the governor motioned him to speak, Paul replied:*

"'*I cheerfully make my defense, knowing that for many years you have been a judge over this nation. As you can find out, it is not more than twelve days since I went up to worship in Jerusalem. They did not find me disputing with anyone in the temple or stirring up a crowd either in the synagogues or throughout the city. Neither can they prove* *to you the charge that they now bring against me. But this I admit to you, that **according to the Way, which they call a sect, I worship the God of our ancestors, believing everything laid down according to the law or written in the prophets.** I have a **hope** in God--a **hope** that they themselves also accept--that there will be a resurrection of both the righteous and the unrighteous. Therefore I do my best always to have a clear conscience toward God and all people."*

Notice Lux does not have Paul reply that he is a Nazarene. In fact his response is exactly what a Pharisee would have said if asked the same question: "*I believe...everything laid down according to the law or written in the prophets...*" Paul did **not** respond "*I am a Nazarene, and I believe everything taught by our Lord Jesus Christ.*"

Acts 24:17-27: "*Now after some years I came to bring alms to my nation and to offer sacrifices. While I was doing this, they found me in the temple, completing the rite of purification, without any crowd or disturbance. But there were some Jews from Asia--they ought to be here before you to make an accusation, if they have anything against me. Or let these men here tell what crime they had found when I stood before the council, unless it was this one sentence that I called out while standing before them, 'It is about the resurrection of the dead that I am on trial before you today.'*"

"*But Felix, who was rather well informed about the Way, adjourned the hearing with the comment, 'When Lysias the tribune comes down, I will decide your case.' Then he ordered the centurion to keep him in custody, but to **let him have some liberty and not to prevent any of his friends from taking care of his needs.***

"*Some days later when Felix came with his wife Drusilla, who was Jewish, he sent for Paul and heard him speak concerning faith in Christ Jesus. And as he discussed justice, self-control, and the coming judgment, Felix became frightened and said, 'Go away for the present; when I have an opportunity, I will send for you.' **At the same time he hoped that money would be given him by Paul, and for that reason he used to <u>send for him very often</u> and converse with him.***"

"*After two years had passed, Felix was succeeded by Porcius*

Festus; and since he wanted to grant the Jews a favor, Felix left Paul in prison."

Hold it!! What's this about Felix hoping Paul would give him money, since it was *"for that reason he used to send for him very often and converse with him."*

RED FLAG, RED FLAG, RED FLAG!!!

Paul and Felix had "met often" to *"converse"* in the past? And when he came to *"converse often,"* Paul gave Felix money? And Felix is hoping that Paul will give him money now? Hmmmm.

This *"prison"* where Paul is kept for two years is called *"Herod's headquarters."* Paul is required to remain there, but he has *"some liberty"* (I assume that means he can travel about the city), and his friends can visit any time and bring him anything he needs. He has freedom to travel about, freedom to have friends visit, and free room and board. Not exactly what prison meant for the poor Nazarene men and women Paul had gathered up and delivered to the authorities in Jerusalem.

I wondered if there was something about Paul that this situation alluded to; something that a historian would record that might shed light on this strange *"prison"* arrangement for Paul and this nearly obscure mention of frequent conversations and exchanges of money with Felix.

Robert Eisenman looked at the same issue and wrote, *"Paul as Herodian,"* which appeared in the *Journal of Higher Criticism* (Spring 1996, 110-122). The complete text is at www.depts.drew.edu/jhc/eisenman.html, and it's well worth reading. Some highlights which may shed light on this flying red flag:

"There are materials in the New Testament, early Church literature, Rabbinic literature, and Josephus which point to some connection between Paul and so-called 'Herodians.' These materials provide valuable insight into problems related to Paul's origins, his Roman citizenship, the power he conspicuously wields in Jerusalem when still a young man, and the 'Herodian' thrust of his doctrines (and as a consequence those of the New Testament) envisioning a community in which both Greeks and Jews would enjoy equal promises and privileges.

*"Where the consistency of the Antioch group is concerned, Acts (13:1) adds the name of 'Saulos' directly after describing the relationship between 'Manaen' and Herod the Tetrarch. Not only is it possible that Acts has garbled its material and that by 'Herod the Tetrarch' it means 'Herod of Chalcis,' who succeeded his brother/foster brother Agrippa I in 44 ACE (the time of the death of Theudas and the arrest of 'Simon Peter'), it is tempting to turn the positioning around and consider the notice about fosterage relates to 'Saulos,' not Manaen. 'Manaen' anyhow is defective. Josephus/Josipon tradition knows a 'Mannaeus' the son or nephew of Lazarus of Seruk who deserted with Josephus to Titus, and Acts 21:16 knows a 'Mnason,' who accompanies Paul on his last trip to Jerusalem because he had lodging facilities there, even though Acts considers him 'Cypriot.' However, the most plausible identification from among Paul's close associates is the quasi-anagram 'Ananias,' whom Acts portrays as welcoming Paul to 'Damascus' and who is not included in the Antioch group. It is noteworthy that **Josephus, too, knows a propagandist named 'Ananias' active in the 'East' in this period. He gets in among the women of Adiabene and converts Helen, while taking a patently Pauline line on the issue of the circumcision of her son. In this episode, Josephus also mentions a colleague of Ananias following the same approach, but declines to name him.** While these points are not in themselves particularly relevant, they are nevertheless worth remarking."*

The writer of Lux/Acts was working during the time of Josephus and Plutarch, after Mark and Matthew, after Paul's genuine letters, probably after James, Peter and all the other gospels, except perhaps John and Revelation. In order for these two books to be accepted by the Church leaders, they had to be supportive of Paul's letters. But they could give clues: name clues, location clues, history and myth clues, to lead theophilosophers to *"The Truth"* promised in the opening paragraph of Lux. Eisenman picked up on this but failed to recognize that it was *intentionally "garbled"* and *intentionally* reversed in some cases. What was important to get into the document were the names, or close proximity's, without them being noticed as coded information.

I reached my conclusion that Lux/Acts contained secret

information when I discovered the numbers. Had Eisenman been working from the premise that Lux/Acts was coded, he might have reached the conclusion that Saul's name was *carefully and intentionally* placed immediately following "*a member of the court of Herod the ruler*" in order to pass on the information that Saul WAS a member of the court of Herod.

And it seems obvious that the name *Ananias* is another code. This name is used in Acts ten times, and the first *Ananias* was a liar:

Acts 5:3: *"'Ananias,' Peter asked, 'why has **Satan filled your heart to lie to the Holy Spirit** and to keep back part of the proceeds of the land? While it remained unsold, did it not remain your own? And after it was sold, were not the proceeds at your disposal? How is it that you have contrived this deed in your heart? You did not lie to us but to **God!'** Now when Ananias heard the words, he fell down and died. And great fear seized all who heard of it. The young men came and wrapped up his body, then carried him out and buried him."*

This story is totally out of place here. It serves no purpose but to portray this Ananias as the worst possible liar. His heart is filled with evil (Satan), and he lied to the Holy Spirit and to God! Lux even used the exclamation point to stress the severity of the lie.

Shortly thereafter Lux uses the same name, Ananias, and presents version one of Paul's conversion:

Acts 9:3-9: *"Now as he was going along and approaching Damascus, suddenly a light from heaven flashed around him. **He fell to the ground** and heard a voice saying to him, 'Saul, Saul, why do you persecute me?' He asked, 'Who are you, Lord?' The reply came, 'I am Jesus, whom you are persecuting. But get up and enter the city, and you will be told what you are to do.' **The men who were traveling with him stood speechless because they heard the voice but saw no one**. Saul got up from the ground, and though his eyes were open, he could see nothing; so **they led him by the hand and brought him into Damascus. For three days he was without sight, and neither ate nor drank."***

Then Ananais enters the scene and Paul's sight is restored:

Acts 9:10-17: *"Now there was **a certain disciple at Damascus*** named **Ananias**; *and to him the Lord said in a vision, 'Ananias.' And he said, 'Here I am, Lord.'"*

"The Lord said to him, 'Get up and go to the street called **Straight,** *and at the house of* **Judas** *look for a man of Tarsus named Saul. At this moment he is praying, and he has seen in a vision a man named Ananias come in and lay his hands on him so that he might regain his sight.'*

"Then Ananias answered, 'Lord, I have heard from many about this man, **how much harm he has done to Your saints in Jerusalem; and here he has authority from the chief priests to bind all who invoke your name.'** *But the Lord said to him, 'Go, for he is an instrument whom I have chosen to bring my name before Gentiles and kings and before the people of Israel; I myself will show him how much he must suffer for the sake of my name.' So* **Ananias went and entered the house. He laid his hands on Saul and said, 'Brother Saul, the Lord Jesus, who appeared to you on your way here, has sent me so that you may regain your sight** *and be filled with the Holy Spirit.'"*

But the events are noticeably different when Lux reports it in version two, putting the words into Paul's mouth:

Acts 22:6-21: *"While I was on my way and approaching Damascus, about noon a great light from heaven suddenly shone about me.* **I fell to the ground** *and heard a voice saying to me, 'Saul, Saul, why are you persecuting me?' I answered, 'Who are you, Lord?' Then he said to me, 'I am Jesus the Nazarene whom you are persecuting.'* **Now those who were with me saw the light but did not hear the voice of the one who was speaking to me.** *I asked, 'What am I to do, Lord?' The Lord said to me, 'Get up and go to Damascus; there you will be told everything that has been assigned to you to do.' Since I could not see because of the brightness of that light, those who were with me took my hand and led me to Damascus.*

"A certain **Ananias, who was a devout man according to the law and well spoken of by all the Jews living there,** *came to me; and standing beside me, he said,* **'Brother Saul, regain your sight!'** **In that very hour I regained my sight** *and saw him. Then he said, 'The God of our ancestors has chosen you to know his will, to see the Righteous One and to hear his own voice; for you will be his witness to all the world of what you have seen and heard. And now why do*

you delay? **Get up, be baptized, and have your sins washed away, calling on his name.'**

"*After I had* **returned to Jerusalem** *and while I was praying in the temple, I fell into a trance and saw Jesus saying to me, 'Hurry and get out of Jerusalem quickly, because they will not accept your testimony about me.' And I said, 'Lord, they themselves know that in every synagogue I imprisoned and beat those who believed in you. And while the blood of your witness Stephen was shed, I myself was standing by, approving and keeping the coats of those who killed him.' Then he said to me, 'Go, for I will send you far away to the Gentiles.'*"

In this version Lux reports the people with Paul saw the light but heard nothing, exactly the opposite from the first report that they heard but did not see. Ananias is not described as "*a disciple*" but as a "*devout man according to the law*" who is "*well spoken of by the Jews*," and there is no mention of a three-day period of blindness

Luke's third version differs in obvious and important ways from the first two, and again the words are put into Paul's mouth:

Acts 26:12-18: "*With this in mind, I was traveling to Damascus with the authority and commission of the chief priests, when at midday along the road, your Excellency, I saw a light from heaven, brighter than the sun,* **shining around me and my companions. When we had all fallen to the ground, I heard a voice saying to me in the Hebrew language,** *'Saul, Saul, why are you persecuting me?* **It hurts you to kick against the goads.'** *I asked, 'Who are you, Lord?' The Lord answered, 'I am Jesus whom you are persecuting.* **But get up and stand on your feet;** *for I have appeared to you for this purpose, to appoint you to serve and testify to the things in which you have seen me and to those in which I will appear to you. I will rescue you from your people and from the Gentiles--to whom I am sending you to open their eyes so that they may turn from darkness to light and from the power of Satan to God, so that they may receive forgiveness of sins and a place among those who are sanctified by faith in me.'*"

In this version there is no Ananias, no blindness, everyone fell to the ground, and Jesus told Paul to stand up immediately. Some of the most important information seems to have been left out. Remember, all three versions were written by Lux with the purpose of *"telling the truth about what had happened."* Either Lux was a brainless idiot or he wanted to slip through a message. The first two versions of this story are linked to Acts 5:3 by Ananias, the name of a man whose heart was *"filled with Satan"* and who *"lied to the Holy Spirit and God."* The most important moment of Paul's life, his conversion and baptism, is full of contradictions. And in no way do they agree with Paul's version when he wrote to the church at Galatia. Paul doesn't mention the three days of blindness or Ananias' very important role in restoring his vision and apparently baptizing him:

Galatians 1:11-17: *"For I want you to know, brothers and sisters, that the gospel that was proclaimed by me is not of human origin; for I did not receive it from a human source, nor was I taught it, but **I received it through a revelation of Jesus Christ**. You have heard, no doubt, of my earlier life in Judaism. I was violently persecuting the church of God and was trying to destroy it. I advanced in Judaism beyond many among my people of the same age, for I was far more zealous for the traditions of my ancestors. But when **God, who had set me apart before I was born** and called me through his grace, was pleased to reveal his Son to me, so that I might proclaim him among the Gentiles, **I did not confer with any human being, nor did I go up to Jerusalem to those who were already apostles before me, but I went away at once into Arabia, and afterwards I returned to Damascus.**"*

Lux reports this event three times; there's surely a reason. It must be very, very important information. Not only does Lux report it three times, but each version is different and all are much different than Paul's version.

The use of the phrase *"against the goads"* links to Euripide's play about Dionysius: *"goad them into wild fury against the man disguised in woman's dress, a frenzied spy..."*

And the vision links to Daniel Chapter 10: *"I, Daniel, alone saw the vision; the people who were with me did not see the vision..."*

Lux uses the opportunity in all three versions to repeat Paul's evil deeds and attacks against Jesus' disciples, and he even uses the name *Judas* in version one. In this brief passage we're reminded of a horrific liar, Ananias, a horrific traitor, Judas, and the contemptible things Paul as Saul did to the disciples. Placing all three versions side by side, one is left totally confused. And that's the message. There is no truth in Paul's letters. Lux wanted to tell the story of his conversion in a way that raised immediate questions: Only Paul saw the light? Only Paul heard the voice? Blind or not? Baptized by Ananias or not? All versions can't be true, so one or all must be lies. These stories are Luke's attempts to get out the truth about Paul's lies.

Eisenmen's Essay provides more information about Paul and the politics and important people of the time:

"Herod of Chalcis' son Aristobulus, who like Agrippa I proudly proclaimed his pro-Roman sentiments on his coinage, made himself very useful to the Romans in helping to suppress this revolt. Many of these areas, too, are the scenes of Paul's most aggressive early missionary work.

"Aristobulus must be seen as one of the inner circle around Titus (along with Tiberius Alexander, Josephus, Bernice, Agrippa II and others). He is married to Herodias' daughter Salome (whose picture with his own he proudly displays on his coinage). While this is not strictly speaking an instance of marriage with a niece so frowned upon at Qumran and widely practiced by Herodians, it is very close to it. It is also interesting to consider this family's links with the Helenized Alabarch in Alexandria. The latter's family controlled the all-important Egyptian granaries and was instrumental in Vespasian's rise to power. One of its scions, Tiberius Alexander, who became procurator in Palestine after the death of Herod of Chalcis, was Titus' military commandant at Jerusalem. Josephus, who understood these matters well, specifically called attention to Tiberius' defection from Judaism, as he did to that of Bernice, Titus' mistress. Bernice's second sister Mariamne divorced her first husband in order to marry another son of the Alabarch, presumable the first husband's brother (if he was not of this family, it is another case of Gentile marriage).

"Agrippa I's third daughter, Drusilla, after contemplating marriage to the son of King Antiochus, married King Azizus of Emesa because he had agreed to circumcise himself (as Antiochus' son had not). Displaying that cynical opportunism so typical of Herodians, Drusilla

divorced him on her own initiative to marry Felix, a marriage connived at in Caesarea by someone who can be none other than the infamous Simon Magus (like its anagram 'Mnason' above, he too is a 'Cypriot'). Simon's singular service to Felix was to convince Drusilla to divorce her previous husband. In this episode many themes emerge which are of the utmost importance for dating Qumran documents and understanding the true gist of their critique of the establishment. Even Josephus, who is usually so accommodating on such matters (later finding Herodian practices congenial, he too divorces a wife), describes Drusilla's self-divorce from the King of Emesa as contrary to the 'laws of her forefathers.' He makes a similar comment about an earlier such divorce by Herodias, which is at the root of problems relating to the death of John in both Josephus and the New Testament. These divorces are anticipated by the divorce of Herod's sister Salome from the Idumaean Costobarus, so important in all our genealogies and paralleled by similar ones by Mariamne (mentioned above) and Bernice from Polemos of Cilicia to take up with Titus (which would involve her in a two-fold denunciation at Qumran, not to mention her 'riches' and the rumor of her illicit connection with Agrippa II which Josephus also mentions relative to the Polemos affair). Paul, too, shows his knowledge of this kind of divorce in discussing James' 'Jerusalem Council' 'fornication' directives in I Cor 7:10f., but importantly he does not condemn them. Instead, he gently slaps the wrist of the offending woman by recommending that she abstain from further marriage and specifies no further punitive procedures."

Eisenman also noticed the special treatment Paul received from the authorities that Acts described:

"It is not very likely that Paul could have made the miraculous escapes he does without the involvement of some combination of these powerful Herodian/Roman forces. Nothing less is conceivable under the circumstances of the attack on Paul in the Temple and his rescue by Roman soldiers witnessing these events from the Fortress of Antonia (Acts 21:31f). This episode, too, makes mention of a nephew and possibly a sister of Paul (identities otherwise unknown) resident in Jerusalem, but also presumably carrying Roman citizenship. It is they who warn him of a plot by 'zealots for the Law' or others interested in Nazirite oath procedures to kill him. Without this kind of intervention,

Paul could never have enjoyed the security to Rome (where Felix and Drusilla precede him). He arrives with funds gathered in overseas fund-raising from many of the areas into which Herodians have expanded and, in part because of this, those areas where circumcision had become such an issue because of the marital practices of Herodian princesses.

"But where Paul is concerned, one can go even further. Paul speaks in an unguarded moment in Romans 16:11 of his 'kinsman Herodian.' Though the name could refer to any person by this name anywhere, still names like Herod and its derivatives (n.b. The parallel with the name of Caesar's son 'Caesarion') are not common. Nor is there any indication that the passage is an interpolation. If it were indicative of actual familial relationships with Herodians, which in my view it is, then by itself it explains the hint of Herodian membership and/or activity in the early Christian community in Antioch. It also very easily explains the matter of Paul's Roman citizenship, which is such an important element in these escapes."

Romans 16:10-11 do seem to inadvertently reveal Paul's connection to some of the characters about whom Josephus wrote:

"Greet Apelles, who is approved in Christ. Greet those who belong to the family of Aristobulus. Greet my relative, Herodion."

This could certainly explain why Paul received special treatment while he was "imprisoned."

Eisenman:

"But Paul's Herodian links even explain how such a comparatively young man could have wielded such powers when he first came to Jerusalem and how he could have been empowered by 'the high priest' to search out 'Christians' in areas even as far afield as 'Damascus' (whether we are dealing with the 'Damascus' settlement of Qumran allusion or an actual 'Jewish Settlement in Damascus' is impossible to tell from the sources). They readily explain his easy entrance into Jerusalem ruling circles--all matters which have never been explained. The reference immediately preceding the one to Herodion in Romans 16:10, i.e., to a certain 'household of Aristobulus,' consolidates these suspicions even further. Though Aristobulus may have been a common name, still it is most prominent among Herodians, there being two or *three Aristobuluses from different lines living at the same time, the most interesting of them being Herod of Chalcis' son Aristobulus noted above."*

"So far our evidence is circumstantial; however, there is a surprising notice from another quarter which straightforwardly makes the charge we have been sketching. Epiphanius, who conserves many traditions found in rabbinic literature including the famous 'ben Panthera' nickname for Jesus, conserves a tradition about Paul (Pan 30.16.1). In its view Paul was a non-Jew who came up to Jerusalem and converted to Judaism because he wanted to marry the 'priest's' (i.e., the high priest's) daughter. (As in Pan 30.16.9, 'the priest' is usually used at Qumran and in rabbinic tradition as denotative of the 'high priest'). When disappointed in this design, he defected from Judaism and turned against 'circumcision' and 'the Law.' Epiphanius attributes this notice to the Anabathmoi Jacobou ('Ascents of James'), a lost work about the debates of James with the high priests and the Pharisees (also finding refraction in the Pseudoclementine Recognitions) over matters relating to Temple service (including in our view problems bearing on Gentiles or Gentile sacrifice/gifts in the Temple). We have no way of knowing if the tradition is true. While the Anabathmoi Jacobou would appear to have been Jewish Christian or Ebionite, and therefore hostile to Paul, this is not cause for a priori dismissing the tradition it conserves via Epiphanius; on the contrary, when one comes upon a tradition of such surprising content, it is often worthwhile paying attention to it. One famous convert of sorts did aspire to marry the high priest's daughter--in fact he married two: Herod himself. It is not impossible that this tradition conserves an echo of valuable historical data, not necessarily about Paul, but about Paul's family backgrounds; that is, not that Paul was a convert (which he may have been) or that he personally wanted to marry the high priest's daughter (which again he might have), but that he was descended from someone who was a convert and had aspired to marry the high priest's daughter, i.e., that he was an Herodian.

"In our view, it is just these Herodian origins where Paul is concerned that explain his very peculiar view of Judaism, what we perceive to be his inferiority complex and defensiveness where Jews are concerned, his jealousy of Jews, in fact his anti-Semitism generally,

and finally his extremely lax and, from the Jewish viewpoint, utterly unconscionable view of the Law. It is hard to consider that a native-born Jew, comfortable in his identity, could have indulged in the kind of insults Paul gratuitously makes concerning circumcision, circumcisers, and those keeping dietary regulations, or adopted the curious approach towards the possibility of simultaneously being a Law-keeper to those who keep the Law and a Law-breaker to those who did not in order, as he puts it, 'to win, not beat the air,' or that by avoiding circumcision, one could avoid the demands of the Law, which in some manner he saw as 'a curse.'

"This theme of a Gentile/foreigner/outsider with ambitions relating to the high priesthood undergoes a curious transformation in Talmudic traditions concerning a celebrated episode involving Hillel and Shammai, where a presumptuous outsider wishes to know the whole of the Torah 'while standing on one foot.' Shammai dismisses the interloper with a blow, but Hillel is willing to quote the 'all righteousness' commandment, 'love your neighbor as yourself.' This last, in turn, is alluded to with similar import, not only in the Gospels, the Letter of James, and the Zadokite Document, but also in Paul. Paul actually quotes the commandment in the context of allusion to 'darkness and light,' salvation, fornication, jealousy, etc., as verification of his anti-Zealot philosophy in Romans 13 above (n.b. That following this in 14:1f. Paul characterizes as 'weak' people--like James--who 'eat only vegetables'). In succeeding material relating to this presumptuous outsider, it is stated he actually wished to become a high priest.

"When viewed in the context of Paul's own reported insistence that he was a student of Hillel's grandson, Gamaliel, the tradition takes on additional resonances. One is not unjustified in considering that the individual in question is a type of Pauline outsider, and that the theme of wishing to become a high priest relates to that of wishing to marry 'the priest's' (high priest's) daughter in Epiphanius, itself relating to Paul's non-Jewish (or quasi-Jewish/Herodian) origins."

I've quoted this entire section of Eisenman's essay, lengthy as it is, because the author of Lux probably would have also had access to *Anabathmoi Jacobou* and may have assumed later scholars would know of it as well. Inserting *"Gamaliel"* into the story would have led to Hillel, and one step further to this story.

More hidden information about Paul and his real mission and message? Highly likely, I believe.

According to Acts 24:27 Paul spent the next two years under Herod's protection at his former palace, the praetorium, and then Felix *"was succeeded by Porcius Festus"* who went to Jerusalem *"where the chief priests and the leaders of the Jews gave him a report against Paul."*

The Jews asked that Paul be delivered to Jerusalem where they were planning another ambush to kill him along the way. Festus invited the Jews to return to Caesarea with him to question Paul.

Acts 25:7-27: *"When he arrived, the Jews who had gone down from Jerusalem surrounded him, bringing many serious charges against him, which they could not prove. Paul said in his defense, 'I have in no way committed an offense against the law of the Jews, or against the temple, or against the emperor.' But Festus, wishing to do the Jews a favor, asked Paul, 'Do you wish to go up to Jerusalem and be tried there before me on these charges?' Paul said, 'I am appealing to the emperor's tribunal; this is where I should be tried. I have done no wrong to the Jews, as you very well know. Now if I am in the wrong and deserve to die, I am not trying to escape death; but if there is nothing to their charges against me, no one can turn me over to them. I appeal to the emperor.' Then Festus, after he had conferred with his council, replied, 'You have appealed to the emperor; to the emperor you will go.'*

"After several days had passed, King Agrippa and Bernice arrived at Caesarea to welcome Festus. Since they were staying several days, Festus laid Paul's case before the king, saying, 'There is a man here who was left in prison by Felix. When I was in Jerusalem, the chief priests and the elders of the Jews informed me about him and asked for a sentence against him. I told them that it was not the custom of the Romans to hand over anyone before the accused had met the accusers face to face and had been given an opportunity to make a defense against the charge. So when they met here, I lost no time, but on the next day took my seat on the tribunal and ordered the man to be brought. When the accusers stood up, they did not charge him with any of the crimes that I was expecting. Instead they had certain points of disagreement with him about their own religion and about a certain Jesus, who had

died, but whom Paul asserted to be alive. Since I was at a loss how to investigate the questions, I asked whether he wished to go to Jerusalem and be tried there on these charges. But when Paul had appealed to be kept in custody for the decision of his Imperial Majesty, I ordered him to be held until I could send him to the emperor.' Agrippa said to Festus, 'I would like to hear the man myself.'

'Tomorrow,' he said, 'you will hear him.'

"*So on the next day Agrippa and Bernice came with great pomp, and they entered the audience hall* **with the military tribunes and the prominent men of the city**. *Then Festus gave the order and Paul was brought in. And Festus said, 'King Agrippa and all here present with us, you see this man about whom the whole Jewish community petitioned me, both in Jerusalem and here, shouting that he ought not to live any longer. But I found that he had done nothing deserving death; and when he appealed to his Imperial Majesty, I decided to send him.*

"*But I have nothing definite to write to our sovereign about him. Therefore I have brought him before all of you, and especially before you, King Agrippa, so that, after we have examined him, I may have something to write--for it seems to me unreasonable to send a prisoner without indicating the charges against him.'*"

Acts 26:1-11: "*Agrippa said to Paul, 'You have permission to speak for yourself.' Then Paul stretched out his hand and began to defend himself:*

"*I consider myself fortunate that it is before you, King Agrippa, I am to make my defense today against all the accusations of the Jews, because you are especially familiar with all the customs and controversies of the Jews; therefore I beg of you to listen to me patiently.'*

"*All the Jews know my way of life from my youth, a life spent from the beginning among my own people and in Jerusalem. They have known for a long time, if they are willing to testify, that* **I have belonged to the strictest sect of our religion and lived as a Pharisee**. *And now I stand here on trial on account of* **my hope** *in the promise made by God to our ancestors, a promise that our twelve tribes hope to attain, as they earnestly worship day and night.* **It is for this hope**, *your Excellency, that I am accused by Jews! Why is it thought incredible by any of you that God raises the dead?'*"

"*Indeed, I myself was convinced that I ought to do many things against the name of Jesus of Nazareth.* **And that is what I did in Jerusalem; with authority received from the chief priests, I not only locked up many of the saints in prison, but I also cast my vote against them when they were being condemned to death. By punishing them often in all the synagogues I tried to force them to blaspheme; and since I was so furiously enraged at them, I pursued them even to foreign cities.'"**

Paul then tells the story of his trip to Damascus and his conversion and appointment by Jesus, who appeared to him in a vision, to "*testify to the things which you have seen.*"

Acts 26:19-29: "*'After that, King Agrippa, I was not disobedient to the heavenly vision, but declared to those in Damascus, then in Jerusalem and throughout the countryside of Judea, and also to the Gentiles, that they should repent and turn to God and do deeds consistent with repentance. For this reason the Jews seized me in the temple and tried to kill me. To this day I have had help from God, and so I stand here, testifying to both small and great, saying nothing but what the prophets and Moses said would take place: that the Messiah must suffer, and that, by being the first to rise from the dead, he would proclaim light both to our people and to the Gentiles.'*

"*While he was making this defense, Festus exclaimed, 'You are out of your mind, Paul! Too much learning is driving you insane!' But Paul said, 'I am not out of my mind, most excellent Festus, but I am speaking the sober truth. Indeed the king knows about these things, and to him I speak freely; for I am certain that none of these things has escaped his notice, for this was not done in a corner. King Agrippa, do you believe the prophets? I know that you believe.' Agrippa said to Paul, 'Are you so quickly persuading me* **to become a Christian?**' *Paul replied, 'Whether quickly or not, I pray to God that not only you but also all who are listening to me today* **might become such as I am**--except for these chains.'*"

This verse doesn't tell us that Paul replied, "*I pray that all will become Christians.*" Paul doesn't say "*I pray that all will become seekers of 'The Truth'*" or "*followers of 'The Way'*" or "*Faithful followers of the Lord Jesus Christ.*" Lux reports that Paul said <u>**"I pray that all might become such as I am**</u>." IS THAT ARROGANCE OR WHAT?! And exactly what was Paul? He said, according to Lux/Acts, "*I am a Pharisee!*" It seems highly likely after consulting Josephus via Eisenman that he was a Herodian as well.

Perhaps Luke's repeated references to "*spies*" in myth, art, and history have greater importance now.

CHAPTER FIVE

*"Paul replied, 'Whether quickly or not, I pray to God
that not only you but also all who are listening to me today
might become such as I am--except for these chains.'"*
Acts 26:29

PRINCE OF PEACE
OR CONTEMPTIBLE CON

The number of suspects who fit Daniel's description of *"the arrogant man"* has narrowed substantially. But the case is probably not yet prosecutable beyond a reasonable doubt. One thing I think I can predict. You can never read Luke/Acts in the same light again. Even the die-hard fundamentalists and the agnostic scientists will have to struggle to ignore the numbers and their relationship to astronomical and scientific facts and figures. And the stories and names will always trigger those *"other stories"* and the message they openly delivered on behalf of these undercover agents for Jesus who could no longer speak out.

But I would still like to complete my case for this writer. I would still like to have an airtight case against the greatest infiltrator of all time and a religious scam that all the other religious scams in history combined can't begin to match in scope or damage or loss of life.

Daniel's book tells much of what this *"arrogant"* and *"contemptible"* man did, but the rest of the clues, at least most of them, are found in the Acts of the Apostles. Paul's letters are the final pieces of evidence needed to solve the mystery, but like any good detective we have to continue to consider one piece of evidence and one eyewitness account at a time.

Perhaps a quick review Daniel's description of the "*arrogant, contemptible man,*" will help to solidify the case. Compare it with Acts stories about Paul and note the people who are present in the important scenes: King Agrippa, Queen Bernice, military tribunes, and prominent men of the city. Look at Paul and how he was treated while he was at Herod's headquarters. Listen to the story he told about his vision and the power he claimed was bestowed on him by Jesus. Daniel's visions and prophesies to which Luke's gospel directed us describes this very scene and the people in it:

"**In his place shall arise** *a contemptible person* **on whom royal majesty had not been conferred;** *he shall come in without warning and obtain the kingdom through intrigue.*

"Armies shall be utterly swept away and broken before him, and the prince of the covenant as well. And after an alliance is made with him, he shall act deceitfully and become strong with a small party.

"He shall come among the richest men of the province and do what none of his predecessors had ever done, lavishing plunder, spoil, and wealth on them. He shall devise plans against strongholds, but only for a time.

"The two kings, their minds bent on evil, shall sit at one table and exchange lies.

"He shall grow strong in power, shall cause fearful destruction, and shall succeed in what he does.

"He shall destroy the powerful and the people of the holy ones. By his cunning he shall make deceit prosper under his hand, and in his own mind he shall be great.

"He shall destroy many and shall even rise up against the Prince of princes.

"He shall be enraged and take action against the holy covenant.

"He shall turn back and pay heed to those who forsake the

holy covenant. Forces sent by him shall occupy and profane the temple and fortress.

"They shall abolish the regular burnt offering and set up the abomination that makes desolate.

"He shall seduce with intrigue those who violate the covenant; but the people who are loyal to their God shall stand firm and take action.

"The wise among the people shall give understanding to many; for some days, however they shall fall by sword and flame, and suffer captivity and plunder. When they fall victim, they shall receive a little help, and many shall join them insincerely.

"Some of the wise shall fall, so that they may be refined, purified, and cleansed, until the time of the end, for there is still an interval until the time appointed.

"The king shall act as he pleases. He shall exalt himself and consider himself greater than any god, and shall speak horrendous things against the God of gods.

"He shall prosper until the period of wrath is completed, for what is determined shall be done.

"He shall pay no respect to the gods of his ancestors, or to the one beloved by women; he shall consider himself greater than all.

"He shall honor the god of fortresses instead of these; a god whom his ancestors did not know he shall honor with gold and silver, with precious stones and costly gifts.

"He shall deal with the strongest fortresses by the help of a foreign god."

What could be more contemptible than to turn the Messiah into an idol of a bloodthirsty death cult? That may seem rather shocking on the surface but bear with me.

What was Jesus' background, his lifestyle, and his message? Even the most conservative biblical scholars now agree that in virtually all cases, Jesus is described as *"The Nazarene,"* not a man from the town of Nazareth. More can be learned about *The Nazarene Way of Life* from historians and the Pythagoreans than from biblical accounts. Acts did reveal that the Nazarene's governmental structure was one of common ownership. The appropriate word is "*communism*," but that word carries such an emotional charge because it's so closely associated with Marxism that I've avoided using it.

As strange as it might seem the most revealing information in the Bible about *The Nazarene Way of Life* is found in Paul's letters.

But to discover what Paul said about *The Nazarene Way*, we need to start with what the historians wrote about Jesus' brother James, the Nazarene/Essenes, and the Pythagoreans.

Most historians agree the following were key components of the lifestyle and doctrine. Some of this information also comes from various publications available for purchase from the Essene Church of Christ, Box 561, Elmira OR 97437, or, esseneinfo@aol.com:

They were strict vegetarians, and it was a requirement for membership. They had apparently adopted some Eastern philosophy and doctrine and killed no living thing for any selfish purpose. There seems to be one exception. If an animal was suffering severe pain and going to die painfully, they were obligated to kill it quickly.

They were excellent gardeners and able to produce large harvests with small amounts of land and minimal physical effort. They used the herbs and plants they produced for healing illnesses and injuries. In Egypt the Nazarene/Essenes were called Theraputae.

They did not cut their hair. Some modern scholars argue that the pictorial representations of Jesus with long hair are incorrect because the Jews cut their hair. Jesus was a Nazarene, and they did not cut their hair. Pythagoras was called "*the long hair*," and to this day a slang term for those with excessive knowledge, if there is such a thing, is "*a long hair*." Classical music is called "*long hair*" music.

They wore one-piece, white linen robes woven from the flax they harvested.

They held no slaves and were the first to openly oppose the practice of slavery.

They provided women with totally equal treatment and opportunities including the opportunity to serve as priestesses and teachers.

Their deity was One but consisted of aspects that were both male and female: YHVH; Jehovah (Jeh=male energy/ Ova=female energy); God/Goddess. They recognized that all of physical creation came from the balanced interaction of two complimentary forces, male/female, positive/negative, etc.

They believed in The One Law: Cause and Effect. Do good, good returns; do evil, evil returns.

They were baptized to signify their "*rebirth*" into the spirit of God/Goddess/Creator.

They did not circumcise; they trusted and honored the Creator's wisdom in all things. (The "*circmcision party*" were Pharisee and Sadducee Jews who had converted, not the Nazarene/Essene brother and sisterhood.)

Ancient historians agree that James the Just, Jesus' brother and a Nazarene, assumed a leadership role among the Nazarenes in Jerusalem after Jesus was crucified. Fourth century Church Father Eusebius, quoting the Palestinian historian, Hegesippus (90-180CE), described James the Just, Jesus' brother:

"*...he drank no wine or strong drink, nor did he eat meat...*"

"*...no razor touched his head, nor did he anoint himself with oil...*"

"*...he did not wear wool, but linen...*"

Hegesippus in describing Jesus' brother was describing portions of the doctrine called *The Way*. And the description also coincides quite nicely with the description of *Nazarites* in Numbers Chapter 6, previously quoted, as well as the doctrines reported by the modern Essene Church of Christ.

Historians have discovered that indeed women were among the principle teachers of *The Way* during the first century, conducting secret classes in their homes for all the Jews and Gentiles who had come to believe that Jesus was the long-anticipated Messiah.

Paul's letters contain vast amounts of information about

The Nazarene Way. It just has to be uncovered by some basic, beginning investigative work.

Since Paul's letters are not presented in the Bible in chronological order as they were written, my assumption is that they are presented in order of importance. I'm satisfied taking them in this order. I'm interested primarily in what can be learned about *The Nazarene Way of Life*. Did Paul support the doctrines of Jesus, or did he create his own doctrine that supported the Pharisees and the ruling King, Herod Agrippa II?

By starting with what is known about *The Nazarene Way*, we can see if Paul was aware of the doctrine and practices, and whether he supported them.

VEGETARIANISM/NO WINE OR STRONG DRINK

The Way, practiced and taught by Jesus the Nazarene: "*Eat no meat and drink no wine or strong drink.*" (Accounts of Jesus drinking wine and serving fish are probably interpolations inserted to support Paul and distance Jesus from the Nazarene Way.)

Paul's answers to those who sent word that there was disagreement about vegetarianism and/or drinking wine tell us two things: First, there was a question. Some of the teachers were saying no meat or wine or strong drink, and others said meat and wine were fine. Second, Paul's answers tell us whether he agreed with the Jesus' disciples who learned from Jesus and James, the Nazarenes. First, Paul's letter to the Roman church:

Romans 14:1: "*Welcome those who are weak in faith, but not for the purpose of quarreling over opinions. Some believe in eating anything, while **the weak eat only vegetables**. Those who eat must not despise those who abstain, and those who abstain must not pass judgment on those who eat; for God has welcomed them. Who are you to pass judgment on servants of another? It is before their own lord that they stand or fall. And they will be upheld, for the Lord is able to make them stand.*"

Romans 14: 20: "***Do not, for the sake of food, destroy the work of God**. Everything is indeed clean, but it is wrong for you to* *make others fall by what you eat; it is good not to eat meat or drink wine or do anything that makes your brother or sister stumble."*

Next to the church at Corinth:

I Corinthians 10:24-29: *"Do not seek your own advantage, but that of the other.* **Eat whatever is sold in the meat market without raising any question on the ground of conscience,** *for 'the earth and its fullness are the Lord's. If an unbeliever invites you to a meal and you are disposed to go,* **eat whatever is set before you without raising any question on the ground of conscience.** *But if someone says to you, 'This has been offered in sacrifice,' then do not eat it, out of consideration for the one who informed you, and for the sake of conscience--I mean the other's conscience, not your own."*

To the Colossians 2:16: *"Therefore,* **do not let anyone condemn you in matters of food and drink** *or of observing festivals, new moons, or Sabbaths."*

Colossians 2:20: *"If with Christ you died to the elemental spirits of the universe, why do you live as if you still belonged to the world? Why do you submit to regulations, 'Do not handle, Do not taste, Do not touch'? All these regulations refer to things that perish with use; they are simply human commands and teachings. These have indeed an appearance of wisdom in promoting self-imposed piety, humility, and severe treatment of the body, but they are of no value in checking self-indulgence."*

To Timothy, 5:23: *"No longer drink only water, but* **use a little wine** *for the sake of your stomach and your frequent ailments."*

It's clear from these letters to the new and potential converts that Paul was not a vegetarian and he did not object to the *"Christians"* eating meat. And most Christians today eat meat--lots of it. So on the first issue, vegetarianism and no wine or strong drink, yes or no:

Jesus/Nazarenes: *"Yes. Eat only from plants, drink no wine or strong drink."*

Paul: *"No. Eat meat and drink whatever you want."*

Pharisees: *"No. Eat and drink whatever is permitted under Judaic law."*

The winner on issue number one is Paul, not Jesus, with the Pharisees agreeing very closely with Paul.

LONG HAIR

Paul's response to the inquiry from Corinth as to whether men should let their hair grow long as the Nazarenes did:

I Corinthians 11:14: *"Does not nature itself teach you that for a man to wear long hair is degrading to him…"*

I don't know exactly to what he was referring, but *"nature"* appears to prefer long hair on humans because it grows long *"naturally."*

The vote on issue number two:

Jesus/Nazarenes: *"Men do not cut hair."*

Paul: *"To NOT cut hair is degrading to men."*

Pharisees: Wore short hair.

On this issue the winner again is Paul, and the Pharisees agree.

FREEDOM OF SLAVES, EQUALITY FOR WOMEN,

FREEDOM FROM OPPRESSION BY POWERFUL MEN

One of the first things Jesus did was address the church and read from Isaiah:

Luke 4:18-21: *"The Spirit of the Lord is upon me, because **he has anointed me to bring good news to the poor**. He has sent me to proclaim **release to the <u>captives</u>** and recovery of **sight to the <u>blind</u>**, to let **the <u>oppressed</u> go free**, to proclaim the year of the Lord's favor.' And he rolled up the scroll, gave it back to the attendant, and sat down. The eyes of all in the synagogue were fixed on him. Then he began to say to them, 'Today this scripture has been fulfilled in your hearing.'"*

Perhaps I'm taking too much liberty in my interpretation of this scene, but it sounds to me as if he was anointed to free the slaves, to educate the ignorant, and to free women and all other oppressed groups from the domination of those more powerful.

Paul wrote several letters about these very important issues. It seems as if virtually all the churches were questioning these two divergent teachings. Some of the disciples who walked with Jesus were teaching that slaves were to be freed and women were equal with men and free to teach the doctrine. And some were apparently teaching *"civil disobedience,"* possibly regarding the payment of excessive taxes:

Romans 13:1-7: *"Let every person be subject to the governing authorities; for there is no authority except from God, and those authorities that exist have been instituted by God. Therefore whoever resists authority resists what God has appointed, and those who resist will incur judgment. For rulers are not a terror to good conduct, but to bad. Do you wish to have no fear of the authority? Then do what is good, and you will receive its approval; for it is God's servant for your good. But if you do what is wrong, you should be afraid, for the authority does not bear the sword in vain! It is the servant of God to execute wrath on the wrongdoer. Therefore one must be subject, not only because of wrath but also because of conscience. For the same reason you also pay taxes, for the authorities are God's servants, busy with this very thing. Pay to all what is due them--taxes to whom taxes are due, revenue to whom revenue is due, respect to whom respect is due, honor to whom honor is due."*

Do you think Herod Agrippa liked hearing this? I doubt that Agrippa, himself, would have worded it any differently. This was written between 54 and 58 CE, during the reign of Herod Agrippa II. One must remember Paul's close to this letter:

*"Greet my **kinsman** Herodian..."* He also referred to Andronicus and Junias as *"kinsmen and fellow prisoners."*

Josephus mentioned Andronicus and reported that he was *"a royal governor who persuaded the king to determine that the temple at Jerusalem was built according to the law of Moses and **to put Sabbeus and Theodosious to death**."* Paul referred to others as *"my beloved in the Lord,"* and *"...our fellow worker in Christ,"* and *"...who is approved in Christ,"* and *"...those workers in the Lord,"* and *"...who has worked hard in the Lord."*

Interesting that the only references to *"kinsmen"* were Andronicus, Junias, and Herodian. One must not forget while reading this what Herod the First had done to Jesus or what Herod Agrippa II , at the time this was written, was doing to the remaining disciples.

Acts 11:29-30; 12:1-2: *"The disciples determined that according to their ability, each would send relief to the believers living in Judea; this they did, sending it to the elders by Barnabas and Saul."*

"About that time King Herod laid violent hands upon some who belonged to the church. He had James, the brother of John, killed with the sword." I doubt that Jesus' disciples would have agreed that the *"authorities had been instituted by God."*

I Corinthians 11:3-10: *"But I want you to understand that Christ is the head of every man, and the husband is the head of the woman, and God is the head of Christ. Any man who prays or prophesies with something on his head disgraces his head, but any woman who prays or prophesies with her head unveiled disgraces her head--it is one and the same thing as having her head shaved. For if a woman will not veil herself, then she should cut off her hair; but if it is disgraceful for a woman to have her hair cut off or to be shaved, she should wear a veil. For a man ought not to have his head veiled, since he is the image and reflection of God; but woman is the reflection of man. Indeed, man was not made from woman, but woman from man.* **Neither was man created for the sake of woman, but woman for the sake of man.** *For this reason a woman ought to have a symbol of authority on her head because of the angels."*

I Corinthians 14:33-36: *"As in all the churches of the saints,* **women should be silent in the churches.** *For they are not permitted to speak, but should be subordinate, as the law also says. If there is anything they desire to know, let them ask their husbands at home.* **For it is shameful for a woman to speak in church.** *Or did the word of God originate with you? Or are you the only ones it has reached?"*

Colossians 3:18-19: *"Wives, be subject to your husbands, as is fitting in the Lord. Husbands, love your wives and never treat them harshly."*

Colossians 3:22-25: **"Slaves, obey your earthly masters in everything,** *not only while being watched and in order to please them, but wholeheartedly, fearing the Lord. Whatever your task, put yourselves into it, as done for the Lord and not for your masters, since you know that from the Lord you will receive the inheritance as your reward; you serve the Lord Christ. For the wrongdoer will be paid back for whatever wrong has been done, and there is no partiality."*

I Timothy 2:11-15: *"Let a woman learn in silence with full submission. **I permit no woman to teach or to have authority over a man; she is to keep silent.** For Adam was formed first, then Eve; and Adam was not deceived, but the woman was deceived and became a transgressor. Yet she will be saved through childbearing, provided they continue in faith and love and holiness, with modesty."*

It is interesting that Paul says, *"**I permit no woman to teach**."* Jesus did permit women to teach, and those faithful to him continued to do the same.

I Timothy 6:1-5: *"**Let all who are under the yoke of slavery regard their masters as worthy of all honor**, so that the name of God and the teaching may not be blasphemed. Those who have believing masters must not be disrespectful to them on the ground that they are members of the church; rather they must serve them all the more, since those who benefit by their service are believers and beloved.*

"Teach and urge these duties. Whoever teaches otherwise and does not agree with the sound words of our Lord Jesus Christ and the teaching that is in accordance with godliness, is conceited, understanding nothing, and has a morbid craving for controversy and for disputes about words. From these come envy, dissension, slander, base suspicions, depraved in mind and bereft of the truth, imagining that godliness is a means of gain."

Of course, the *"sound words"* of Jesus said no to slavery!

Titus 2:3-5: *"Likewise tell the older women to be reverent in behavior, not to be slanderers or slaves to drink; they are to teach what is good, so that they may encourage the young women to love their husbands, to love their children, to be self-controlled, chaste, good manager of the household, kind, **being submissive to their husbands**, so that the word of God may not be discredited."*

Titus 2:9-10: *"**Tell slaves to be submissive to their masters and to give satisfaction in every respect**; they are not to talk back, not to pilfer, but to show complete and perfect fidelity, so that in everything they may be an ornament to the doctrine of God our Savior."*

If Jesus and the Nazarenes had said women were **not** allowed to speak in the churches, why was there a need for this instruction? We know the Judaism practiced by the

Pharisees and Sadducees didn't allow women to speak in the synagogues, so if Jesus the Nazarene, teaching from *The Way*, hadn't encouraged women to teach his message, why did Paul find it necessary to instruct the churches that women should **not** be allowed to speak in church? These edicts from Paul form the basis of the "*Christianity*" of the first century which was promoted by the Church of Rome, the Roman government, and later, with modifications of course, by Protestant churches.

Summarizing and comparing the doctrines:

Jesus/Nazarenes: "*All humankind is created equal: men and women, of all races, religions, and countries. No one may be forced to serve another.*"

Paul: "*Slavery is acceptable; women are to be submissive to men.*"

Pharisees: "*Slavery is encouraged; women are to be submissive to men.*"

The winners, again, are Paul and the Pharisees.

SHARING ASSETS

The Nazarene community government was communal. There was no individual ownership of property. Each family was provided with their own small home in which to sleep, but meals were usually communal. All people worked at all tasks, none valued above another. Remember from Acts 4:32, 34:

"*Now the whole group of those who believed were of one heart and soul, and no one claimed private ownership of any possessions, but everything they owned was held in common...*"

"*There was not a needy person among them, for as many as owned lands or houses sold them and brought the proceeds of what was sold. They laid it at the apostles' feet and it was distributed to each as any had need.*"

They did not "*give it to the apostles to use to build churches,*" or "*to give to God,*" or even "*to give to the saints.*" They gave it to the apostles "*and it was distributed to each as any had need.*" This was the benefit of living in a Nazarene community. There was a large room where all people met and shared in meals, giving thanks to the God/Goddess Creators that made possible the blessings they enjoyed. But there was no temple or synagogue apart from the Nazarene community. What served as a temple or synagogue was available for all to use all the time. In comparison, in Jerusalem at this time the temple priests were living in magnificent mansions adjacent to the magnificent temple. The money collected, whether contributions or from the sale of sacrificial lambs, goats, pigeons, and doves, went to support the lavish lifestyle of the temple priests. This was one of the major reasons Jesus took the Nazarene message to the people of Galilee and Judea. The people were often hungry while the temple priests and government authorities were living as kings, (as some of them were.)

In the Nazarene community there was no ownership of any property and no monetary exchange. They were totally self-sufficient, producing everything they needed, including flax for weaving linen and for making sandals and all other personal items. They shared the produce and products from their plants, first with the members of the Nazarene community, then with the poor beggars who were outside their community. This meant there was no *"monetary commodity"* that could be taxed by the government. This is the real reason they were persecuted by the government authorities and hated by those who lived under the government oppression felt most in the form of excessive taxes.

Paul made no effort to form cooperative communities. In fact he was strictly opposed to them.

Paul was apparently asked to comment on *"common ownership"* of property. He wrote about sharing but did not specifically address common ownership. However, from portions of several of his letters it's clear that Paul did not accept the practice of *"common ownership"* that Lux emphasized by describing it two times. And contrary to the annotation that *"it was only in Jerusalem that this type of communal living (similar to that of the Essenes) was practiced for a time,"* this communal living was a hallmark of the Nazarene/Essene communities. It was found at Mount Carmel in Galilee and at Qumran in Judea. In fact it was found wherever Nazarene/Essene communities flourished prior to the persecution and killing of its members and the destruction of its documents. Gone as well is virtually all biblical references to it ever having existed.

Romans 12:4-8: *"For as in one body we have many members, and all the members do not have the same function, so we, though many, are one body in Christ, and individually members one of another. Having gifts that differ according to the grace given to us, let us use them; if prophecy, in proportion to our faith; if service, in our serving; he who teaches, in his teaching; he who exhorts, in his exhortations;* **he who contributes, in liberality***; he who gives aid, with zeal; he who does acts of mercy, with cheerfulness."*

I Corinthians 13: *"If I give away all I have, and if I deliver my body to be burned, but have not love, I gain nothing."*

Paul's opinion about common ownership isn't stated overtly, but *"contribute liberally"* and *"share what you have"* certainly point to individual ownership rather than common ownership.

Paul's letter to the Romans supporting the *"authorities"* in all ways, including taxation, demonstrate his opposition to the Nazarene community way of life.

And what about *"money for the churches?"*

Romans 15:25-29: *"At present, however, I am going to Jerusalem with aid for the saints. For Macedonia and Achaia have been pleased to make some contribution* **for the poor among the saints at Jerusalem***; they were pleased to do it, and indeed they are in debt to them, for if the Gentiles have come to share in their spiritual blessings, they ought also to be of service to them in material blessings. When therefore, I have completed this, and have delivered to them what has been raised, I shall go on by way of you to Spain; and I know that when I come to you I shall come in the fulness of the blessing of Christ."*

I Corinthians 16:1-4: *"Now concerning the contribution for the saints: you should follow the directions I gave to the churches of Galatia. On the first day of every week, each of you is to put aside and save whatever extra you earn, so that collections need not be taken when I come. And when I arrive, I will send any whom you approve with letters to take your gift to Jerusalem. If it seems advisable that I should go also, they will accompany me."*

2 Corinthians 9:1-15: *"Now it is not necessary for me to write you about the ministry to the saints, for I know your eagerness, which is the subject of my boasting about you to the people of Macedonia, saying that Achaia has been ready since last year; and your zeal has stirred up most of them. But I am sending the brothers in order that our boasting about you may not prove to have been empty in this case, so that you may be ready, as I said you would be; otherwise, if some Macedonians come with me and find that you are not ready, we would be humiliated--to say nothing of you--in this undertaking. So I thought it necessary to urge the brothers to go on ahead to you, and arrange in advance for this bountiful gift that you have promised, so that it may be ready as a voluntary gift and not as an extortion.*

"The point is this: the one who sows sparingly will also reap sparingly, and the one who sows bountifully will also reap bountifully. Each of you must give as you have made up your mind, not reluctantly or under compulsion, for God loves a cheerful giver. And God is able to provide you with every blessing in abundance, so that by always having enough of everything, you may share abundantly in every good work. As it is written, 'He scatters abroad, he gives to the poor; his righteousness endures forever.'

"He who supplies seed to the sower and bread for food will supply and multiply your seed for sowing and increase the harvest of your righteousness. You will be enriched in every way for your great generosity, which will produce thanksgiving to God through us; for the rendering of this ministry not only supplies the needs of the saints but also overflows with many thanksgivings to God. Through the testing of this ministry you glorify God by your obedience to the confession of the gospel of Christ and by the generosity of your sharing with them and with all others, while they long for you and pray for you because of the surpassing grace of God that he has given you. Thanks be to God for his indescribable gift!"

Recall what was written in Acts 3:44-45 and 4:32-33: *"There are no needy among them"* (all who believed and were of one heart and soul). But also recall the scene in Acts 24:26: *"At the same time he (Felix) hoped that money would be given him by Paul, and for that reason he used to send for him very often and converse with him."* Quite frankly, I'm amazed that that little tidbit of information got past the eyes of the church fathers in charge of choosing, and fixing, the canonized books of the Bible.

And the final tally is:

Jesus and the Essenes held nothing individually but shared all things equally.

Paul did not support this type of governance nor did the Pharisees and Sadducees.

Chalk up another point for Paul and the Pharisees and Sadducees.

BAPTISM

Baptism was an important part of becoming a Nazarene. It was a ritual that signified birth or rebirth into *The Nazarene Way of Life* for babies or new converts.

Paul agreed that baptism was part of the entry into his religion. But for Paul baptism was into Jesus' death, not into *The Nazarene Way of Life*.

Romans 6:3-11: *"Do you not know that all of us who have been baptized into Christ Jesus were baptized into his death? Therefore we have been buried with him by baptism into death, so that, just as Christ was raised from the dead by the glory of the Father, so we too might walk in newness of life.*

"For if we have been united with him in a death like his, we will certainly be united with him in a resurrection like his. We know that our old self was crucified with him so that the body of sin might be destroyed, and we might no longer be enslaved to sin. For whoever has died is freed from sin. But if we have died with Christ, we believe that we will also live with him. We know that Christ, being raised from the dead, will never die again; death no longer has dominion over him. The death he died, he died to sin, once for all; but the life he lives, he lives to God. So you also must consider yourselves dead to sin and alive to God in Christ Jesus."

The Pharisees did not baptize.

Although Jesus, the Nazarenes, and Paul agree on the ritual of baptism, they do not come close to agreeing on the meaning of the ritual.

If I understand baptism as explained to me by my fundamental friends, Paul wins again.

CIRCUMCISION

Jesus and the Nazarenes did not circumcise. The Creations of the Creator were honored as being perfect as they were.

Paul claimed to argue for uncircumcision, but at Acts 16: 8 is the strange tidbit that *"Paul circumcised Timothy."* It was certainly a huge issue with Paul. In his letters to the various churches he used the words *circumcised* or *circumcision* fifty-seven times. He used the word *forgiveness* only four times. He claimed to be the apostle to the uncircumcised, with Peter being the apostle to the circumcised. Peter was not born a Nazarene. He was probably a Pharisee and had, therefore, been circumcised. He must have known that the Nazarenes did not consider circumcision to be a *"covenant with God,"* but Peter may very well have continued in the tradition of circumcision. Jesus did after all admonish Peter, saying, *"Get behind me, Satan! For you are not on the side of God, but of men"* (Mark 8:33). Perhaps the issue of circumcision was one that Peter continued to *"side with men"* on.

To the Pharisees, of course, circumcision was the covenant Moses made with God and it was a requirement under any and all circumstances.

So on the question of circumcision Paul appears to agree with Jesus and the Nazarenes, but in practice, according to Luke's gospel, he continued to circumcise his disciples who had Jewish blood.

GOD/GODDESS AS CREATOR

The Nazarenes' knowledge about Creation's dual nature led them to honor the duality of Creation. Their ceremonies of thanksgiving were to recognize and honor the action of male energies (Father), female energies (Mother), and the unseen, unknowable action of Law (Holy Spirit) in the process of Creation. They recognized the earth and waters as the symbols of the female energy; the sun (fire) and air were the symbols of the male energy. The invisible, dimensionless consciousness, or

Law, directed the male and female energies to create all physical matter.

Their deity was both male and female: God/Goddess. They recognized that all of physical creation came from the balanced interaction (or sexual union) of two balancing and complimentary forces: male/female, positive/negative, etc.

Most people have forgotten, if they ever knew, that *God* was originally *YHVH*. Someone decided to place vowels between these letters, making it *Yahveh*, and changed the "*V*" to "*W*" to symbolize the correct pronunciation. Later transliterations changed it to Jehovah. But look at these letters carefully: Y represents male; V represents female. Ancient written words were visual; they created picture images. Notice how the Y and V can be visualized to "*mate*."

Y

V

Think about the shape of the womb. It forms a V. The Y is the shape of two legs and a penis. The H which follows both the Y and V could be a visual representation of intersecting vortexes. Envision two tornadoes, one upside down, merging at their points. Or picture two triangles, one upside down above the other with their points overlapping. This is a pretty good visual image of how light and energy spin to form matter. The two H's that follow the Y and V actually form a shape that could symbolize the two energies spinning in "*marital*" union.

The word, *Jehovah*, contains two parts: *Jeh* is male, *ovah* is female (ovaries, ova, etc.). The word *God* came from a word which means *good*. Later, some man or group of men decided to make God into their male image. After all "goodness" can't be personified. There is great irony that this man, or men, used a word for *good* and created a vengeful, terrifying deity that would strike fear into the hearts of the superstitious people they wanted to control. So *YHVH* (Father/Mother), became *Jehovah* (Father/Mother), became *God* (good), which became *God*, male deity and not so good.

(The original, of course, was probably in Hebrew letters

shaped differently than the Y and V, but this visual image was just too good to keep to myself.)

Jesus the Nazarene was the promised Messiah, or Christos. Jesus was the all good, all loving expression of the Jeh portion of Jehovah. But Jesus was male, and what is missing from the traditional Christian doctrine is the feminine balance to Jesus' perfection. Lux gave us that balanced mate when the seven evil spirits were driven from Mary Magdalene, making her the "*Missiah*," or "*Christas*." Jesus and Mary Magdalene represent the ultimate goal of Nazarene/Essenes: the perfecting of the human body, mind, and soul, both male and female.

Jesus/Nazarenes' *God*: One but consisting of both male and female energies mated to become One.

Paul's "*God*": One, male, with human emotions. He demanded the shedding of blood. Jesus was the blood sacrifice that would replace the scapegoat to assuage God's thirst for blood. As before, all who acknowledged that Jesus' blood was shed so that God would forgive them for their shortcomings. The goats could now be killed strictly for food, rather than for their sins.

Pharisees' "*God*": One, male, with human emotions. He demanded the shedding of blood. Jesus was not the long anticipated Messiah. The prophesies of ancient men, according to their Torah, did not describe Jesus. Until the real messiah arrived, men and women were required to purchase lambs, goats, pigeons, and doves from them, fatten them, pay the priests to "*sanctify*" the offering, then purchase for food the edible remains, not burned to pacify "*God*" who loved the smell of burning flesh. This was the primary source of income for the temple priests. (From materials published by The Essene Church of Christ.) The goats still had to die.

Paul wins with the Christians, the Pharisees win with most Jews (modified somewhat to fit modern mores.)

Only scientists and philosophers accept the concept of the Nazarene/Jesus message. They typically have no ceremonies to acknowledge these Laws, although they may find themselves feeling some sense of awe at how it all works.

Paul claimed to be a Nazarene who accepted the doctrine of the Nazarenes, called *The Way*. However, that seems incredulous since what he taught directly contradicts in every case the teachings of the Nazarenes, Jesus, and the loyal disciples who tried to keep the doctrines alive.

Paul's ideas are not from *The Way*. These doctrines were not from the Nazarenes. These "*laws*" are not from Jesus! These ideas came from Paul, who never met Jesus and who did not teach what Jesus taught. Paul's doctrine is not the doctrine of the Nazarenes. Paul's instructions in his letters were necessary because Jesus did not cut his hair and the Nazarenes permitted women to teach the doctrine! But Paul did not accept these two Nazarene traditions, among others, including vegetarianism, abolishing slavery, and communal sharing of assets. Or maybe he knew the religion he was determined to spread could not possibly succeed if women were given equal rights and equal importance in the teachings. And the early Church certainly agreed! Giving women power in the churches must have horrified the patriarchal leaders of the time.

Although most biblical scholars agree that Paul did not write all the letters attributed to him, I've presented the comparisons from all the letters as if he had. The introduction to Colossians includes "*Scholars are divided about how to interpret these differences*" (language differences between letters known to be Paul's and this letter). "*Some hold that they are strong enough to conclude that Colossians was not written by Paul, as it claims, but by a disciple of Paul shortly after his time, to give Paul's authority to the continuing tradition of his teaching. Others think that the letter was written by Paul, while in prison (4.4,18), presumably at Rome; the particular situation and, perhaps, changes in Paul's thinking, account for the contrasts.*"

The same problems exist with Thessalonians, I and II. Few dispute that the letters to Timothy and Titus were not written by Paul but by a disciple at least a generation after Paul. Who actually wrote the letters is irrelevant to the comparisons between Paul's doctrine and Jesus and the Nazarene's.

THE ONE LAW: CAUSE AND EFFECT

Jesus' primary message has been condensed to what is known as *"The Golden Rule."* But he taught this message as something far more important than simply a *"good way to live."* He taught that it was unfailing and that it mattered not whether you did something good or something evil. The first half of the cycle was the *cause*, the second half the *effect*.

Luke 6:38: *"...give, and it will be given to you. A good measure, pressed down, shaken together, running over, will be put into your lap; for the measure you give will be the measure you get back."*

Jesus spoke and acted against the *"laws of men,"* but the Universal Law of Cause and Effect was certain:

Luke 16:16: Jesus said: *"'The law and the prophets were in effect until John came; since then the good news of the kingdom of God is proclaimed, and everyone tries to enter it by force. But it is easier for heaven and earth to pass away, than for one stroke of a letter in the law to be dropped.'"*

Paul knew nothing of this *"Universal Law"* of cause and effect. He knew only of the *"laws of men"* established for those who had no knowledge or understanding of the *Universal Law* about which Jesus taught.

I Timothy 8: *"Now we know that the law is good, if one uses it legitimately. This means understanding that the law is laid down not for the innocent but for the lawless and disobedient, for the godless and sinful, for the unholy and profane, for those who kill their father or mother, for murderers, fornicators, sodomites, slave traders, liars, perjurers, and whatever else is contrary to the sound teaching that conforms to the glorious gospel of the blessed God, which he entrusted to me."*

Romans 3:27: *"Then what becomes of boasting? It is excluded. By what law? By that of works? No, but by the law of faith. For we hold that a person is justified by faith apart from works prescribed by the law."*

The Pharisees and Sadducees were slaves to the laws of men.

On this point there is no agreement. One thing is certain, Jesus' words were neither understood by Paul nor were they present in his doctrine.

CHAPTER SIX

"By rejecting conscience, certain persons have suffered shipwreck in the faith;
among them are Hymenaeus and Alexander,
whom I have turned over to Satan,
so that they may learn not to blaspheme."
I Timothy 1:19-20

WOODEN HORSES
AND
SHEEP'S CLOTHING

Accoding to Acts Paul was a brutal force opposed to Jesus the Nazarene's message. That is until his conversion. The original remaining disciples weren't convinced.

Acts 9:26-32:

"When he had come to Jerusalem, he attempted to join the disciples; and they were all afraid of him, for they did not believe that he was a disciple. But Barnabas took him, brought him to the apostles, and described for them how on the road he had seen the Lord, who had spoken to him, and how in Damascus he had spoken boldly in the name of Jesus.

"So he went in and out among them in Jerusalem, speaking boldly in the name of the Lord. He spoke and argued with the Hellenists; but they were attempting to kill him. When the believers learned of it, they brought him down to Caesarea and sent him off to Tarsus.

"Meanwhile the church throughout Judea, Galilee, and Samaria

had peace and was built up. Living in the fear of the Lord and in the comfort of the Holy Spirit, it increased in numbers."

First the apostles doubted Paul's sincerity, then they sent him home to Tarsus. And then the church began to grow and there was peace within the church. That's what it says!

Later Barnabas went to find Saul in Tarsus, and he took him to Antioch where they stayed for a year. And then according to Acts 11:29-30:

"The disciples determined that according to their ability, each would send relief to the believers living in Judea; this they did, sending it to the elders by Barnabas and Saul." Coincidentally, Saul's name is *immediately* followed by Herod's.

Acts 12:1-3: *"About that time King Herod laid violent hands upon some who belonged to the church. He had James, the brother of John, killed with the sword. After he saw that it pleased the Jews, he proceeded to arrest Peter also."*

An important annotation accompanies this text:

"Herod Agrippa's persecution: James the son of Zebedee is martyred; Peter is arrested but escapes. Herod Agrippa I, grandson of Herod the Great and the Maccabean Mariamne, was made king by Claudius, ACE 41. **He was popular because he favored Pharisaism."**

Lots of info here from our friend Lux. After Saul was sent to Tarsus the church was growing peacefully. Then Saul comes back from Tarsus, and at the very same time Herod, who was popular because he favored Pharisaism, began to persecute the church in Jerusalem where the old apostles were now headquartered. It's the location of the original apostles, John, son of Zebedee, and Peter.

Acts 12:25: *"Then after completing their mission Barnabas and Saul returned to (footnote: or from) Jerusalem and brought with them John, whose other name was Mark."*

Apparently the footnote indicating "other ancient authorities read 'from'" is correct, for in the next verse Barnabas and Saul reappear in Antioch. And six short verses later they run into *"the false prophet magician named "Bar-Jesus,"* or *Elymas,* and **Sergius Paulus.**

Paul's letter to the Galatians describes his split from Peter:

Galatians 2:7-21: *"On the contrary, when they saw that I had been entrusted with the gospel for the uncircumcised, just as Peter had been entrusted with the gospel for the circumcised (for he who worked through Peter making him an apostle to the circumcised also worked through me in sending me to the Gentiles), and when James and Cephas and John, who were acknowledged pillars, recognized the grace that had been given to me,* **they gave to Barnabas and me the right hand of fellowship, agreeing that we should go to the Gentiles and they to the circumcised.** *They asked only one thing, that we remember the poor, which was actually what I was eager to do.*

"But when Cephas came to Antioch, I opposed him to his face, because he stood self-condemned; for until certain people came from James, he used to eat with the Gentiles. But after they came, he drew back and kept himself separate for fear of the circumcision faction. And the other Jews joined him in this hypocrisy, so that **even Barnabas was led astray by their hypocrisy.** *But when I saw that they were not acting consistently with the truth of the gospel, I said to Cephas before them all, 'If you, though a Jew, live like a Gentile and not like a Jew, how can you compel the Gentiles to live like Jews?'*

"We ourselves are Jews by birth and not Gentile sinners; yet we know that a person is justified not by the works of the law but through faith in Jesus Christ. And we have come to believe in Christ Jesus, so that we might be justified by faith in Christ, and not by doing the works of the law, because no one will be justified by the works of the law. But if, in our efforts to be justified in Christ, we ourselves have been found to be sinners, is Christ then a servant of sin? Certainly not! But if I build up again the very things that I once tore down, then I demonstrate that I am a transgressor. For through the law I died to the law, so that I might live to God. I have been crucified with Christ; and it is no longer I who live, but it is Christ who lives in me. And the life I now live in the flesh I live by faith in the Son of God, who loved me and gave himself for me. I do not nullify the grace of God; for if justification comes through the law, then Christ died for nothing."

Notice here that Paul did not cease his railing with the issue of circumcision. He rolled into, without stopping, a dissertation on *"living by the law"* versus *"living in the faith of the blood sacrifice of Jesus."* Maybe it's just me, but it sounds as if this were the real reason for the face-off with Peter. Peter and John and the other apostles were teaching the *"One Law"* which Paul always interprets as being *"man's laws,"* whereas Paul was teaching the blood sacrifice of Jesus.

Galatians 3:1-5: *"You foolish Galatians! Who has bewitched you? It was before your eyes that Jesus Christ was publicly exhibited as crucified! The only thing I want to learn from you is this: Did you receive the Spirit by doing the works of the law or by believing what you heard? Are you so foolish? Having started with the Spirit, are you now ending with the flesh? Did you experience so much for nothing?--if it really was for nothing. Well then, does God supply you with the Spirit and work miracles among you by your doing the works of the law, or by your believing what you heard?"*

Galatians 3:10-14: *"For all who rely on the works of the law are under a curse; for it is written, 'Cursed is everyone who does not observe and obey all the things written in the book of the law.' Now it is evident that no one is justified before God by the law; for 'The one who is righteous will live by faith.' But the law does not rest on faith; on the contrary, 'Whoever does the works of the law will live by them.' Christ redeemed us from the curse of the law by becoming a curse for us--for it is written, 'Cursed is everyone who hangs on a tree'--in order that in Christ Jesus the blessing of Abraham might come to the Gentiles, so that we might receive the promise of the Spirit through faith."*

Galatians 3:19-29: *"Why then the law? It was added because of transgressions, until the seed would come to whom the promise had been made; and it was ordained through angels by a mediator. Now a mediator involves more than one party; but God is one.*

"Is the law then opposed to the promises of God? Certainly not! For if a law had been given that could make alive, then righteousness would indeed come through the law. But the scripture has imprisoned all things under the power of sin, so that what was promised through faith in Jesus Christ might be given to those who believe.

"Now before faith came, we were imprisoned and guarded under the law until faith would be revealed. Therefore the law was our disciplinarian until Christ came, so that we might be justified

by faith. But now that faith has come, we are no longer subject to a disciplinarian, for in Christ Jesus you are all children of God through faith. As many of you as were baptized into Christ have clothed yourselves with Christ. There is no longer Jew or Greek, there is no longer slave or free, there is no longer male and female; for all of you are one in Christ Jesus. And if you belong to Christ, then you are Abraham's offspring, heirs according to the promise."

Galatians 5:7-12: *"You were running well; who prevented you from obeying the truth? Such persuasion does not come from the one who calls you. A little yeast leavens the whole batch of dough. I am confident about you in the Lord that you will not think otherwise. But whoever it is that is confusing you will pay the penalty. But my friends, why am I still being persecuted if I am still preaching circumcision? In that case the offense of the cross has been removed. I wish those who unsettle you would castrate themselves!"*

Paul wrote to Timothy that he was being deserted by some:

I Timothy 1:19-20: *"By rejecting conscience, certain persons have suffered shipwreck in the faith; among them are Hymenaeus and Alexander,* **whom I have turned over to Satan,** *so that they may learn not to blaspheme."*

I assume Paul had them killed, or killed them himself?

I Timothy 5:15: *"For some have already turned away to follow Satan."*

I Timothy 6:1-5: *"Let all who are under the yoke of slavery regard their masters as worthy of all honor, so that the name of God and the teaching may not be blasphemed. Those who have believing masters must not be disrespectful to them on the ground that they are members of the church; rather they must serve them all the more, since those who benefit by their service are believers and beloved.*

"Teach and urge these duties. Whoever teaches otherwise and does not agree with the sound words of our Lord Jesus Christ and the teaching that is in accordance with godliness, is conceited, understanding nothing, and had a morbid craving for controversy and for disputes about words. From these come envy, dissension, slander, base suspicions, and wrangling among those who are depraved in mind and bereft of the truth, imagining that godliness is a means of gain."

2 Timothy 1:15-18: *"You are aware that **all who are in Asia have turned away from me**, including Phygelus and Hermogenes. May the Lord grant mercy to the household of Onesiphorus, because he often refreshed me and was not ashamed of my chain; when he arrived in Rome, he eagerly searched for me and found me--may the Lord grant that he will find mercy from the Lord on that day!"*

2 Timothy 4:9-15: *"Do your best to come to me soon, for **Demas, in love with this present world, has deserted me and gone to Thessalonica; Crescens has gone to Galatia, Titus to Dalmatia.** Only Luke is with me. Get Mark and bring him with you, for he is useful in my ministry. I have sent Tychicus to Ephesus. When you come, bring the cloak that I left with Carpus at Troas, also the books, and above all the parchments. Alexander the coppersmith did me great harm; the Lord will pay him back for his deeds. You also must beware of him, for he strongly opposed our message."*

Paul may have been the first to label all who disagreed with him as *"Satan."* Certainly the later church took his lead when they *"sent to Satan all who blasphemed,"* which meant they rejecting the church's teachings. How many millions of people have died, and are still dying, because the church beginning with Paul taught that disagreement with the official doctrine, *"God's word,"* was punishable by death?

Paul proclaimed himself to be converted. He proclaimed his relationship with Jesus was through visions. He convinced the old apostles that he was *"just one of them."* And he probably was initially working *"for Jesus"* with the blessings of Peter and John. But it didn't take long for them to learn that his doctrine did not come from Jesus but from the Pharisee environment in which he was raised. And they surely learned of his close ties to the Herodians. If ever there was a *"wolf in sheep's clothing"* or *"a soldier in a wooden horse,"* the apostles must have known that Paul was it. But it was too late.

CHAPTER SEVEN

"When they had gone through the whole island...
they met a certain magician, a Jewish false prophet, named Bar-Jesus."
Acts 13:6

BAR-JESUS
BAR-MARY

The big question, perhaps the question of all time, is this: Why did Luke/Acts place such emphasis on "*The Holy Seed?*" Was it simply to portray Jesus as "*Holy?*" And was Jesus the "*Holy Seed*" of Isaiah 6:13? That might be the conclusion but for one thing: Acts provides other references that tell more of the story, and the additional story is the most important message Luke/Acts left to Theophilus.

Acts Chapter 8 immediately follows the vividly portrayed stoning death of Stephen. And it opens with an important message about Saul:

Acts 8:1: *"And Saul was consenting to his death. And on that day a great persecution arose against the church in Jerusalem; and they were all scattered throughout the region of Judea and Samaria, except the apostles."*

Acts 8:3: *"But Saul was ravaging the church, and entering house after house, he dragged off men and women and committed them to prison."*

Acts 8:5-6: *"Philip went down to a city of Samaria, and proclaimed to them the Christ. And the multitudes with one accord heed to what was said by Philip, when they heard him and saw the signs which he did."*

Acts 8:26: *"But **an angel of the Lord** said to Philip, 'Rise and go at noon to the road that goes down from Jerusalem to Gaza.' This is a desert road. And he rose and went. And behold, an **Ethiopian, a eunuch**, a minister of the Candace, queen of the Ethiopians, in charge of all her treasure, had come to Jerusalem to worship and was returning; seated in his chariot, he was reading the prophet Isaiah."*

Notice how this story suddenly grabs your attention? For one thing, *"the angel"* shows up, and that's always important. This time the angel sends Philip off by himself, into the desert, at high noon. What's amazing is that Philip finds a black eunuch (*Ethiopian* means *black skin*) sitting in a chariot reading Isaiah. Come on, now! Isn't it blatantly clear that Lux is really, really trying to get our attention? A black eunuch in a chariot reading Isaiah out loud so that Philip and Theophilus can know what portion of Isaiah the black eunuch is reading!

Acts 8:29: *"Then the Spirit said to Philip, 'Go over to this chariot and join it.' So Philip ran up to it and heard him reading the prophet Isaiah. He asked, 'Do you understand what you are reading?' He replied, 'How can I, unless someone guides me?' And he invited Philip to get in and sit beside him. Now the passage of the scripture that he was reading was this: 'Like a sheep he was led to the slaughter, and like a lamb silent before its shearer, so he does not open his mouth. In his humiliation justice was denied him. Who can describe his generation? For his life is taken away from the earth.'"*

Lux had the black eunuch reading Isaiah 53:8-9. I wondered why? I found a little help answering this question from an expert--a biblical scholar. Warren Gage, assistant professor of Old Testament, Knox Theological Seminary, wrote an essay, *"The Ethiopian Eunuch Finds Joy,"* which I found at: www.knoxseminary.org/Prospective/Faculty/KnoxPulpit/wgage_eunuch.html.

Gage asks a pertinent question:

"Isn't it ironic that the verse this eunuch is reading as Philip comes alongside his chariot describes a man who dies childless? The eunuch is intrigued that part of the pain and suffering of this man is that

*he would die childless. He knew the same pain because that was his
destiny as well."*

Ironic, indeed! Gage continues:

*"Verse 35 reports: 'Then Philip opened his mouth, and beginning
at this Scripture, preached Jesus to him.'* **He unfolds the NT
understanding that Isaiah's Suffering Servant is Jesus of
Nazareth.** *The prophecy of Isaiah 53 may be the clearest description
of the events surrounding Jesus' death of any passage in all the Bible!
Certainly by the number of quotations and allusions to Isaiah 53 in the
NT (which is somewhere around 40 references),* **we know Isaiah 53
was the central passage of the OT for interpreting the passion/
death of Jesus.** *Isaiah was a primary instructor of the apostolic
community of the first century, and in particular Isaiah 53 was central
to the development of the gospel. So Philip could begin right there, he
could pick right at that point and unfold the gospel to the eunuch with
great ease."*

Well! Go figure!!! Lux just happens to have the black
eunuch reading the very passage that all early Christians knew
referred to Jesus the Nazarene! Gage's observations are about
to get very, very important, so please pay attention to what
follows:

*"So what would the eunuch think as they read down to vs. 10?
In verse 8,* **he read that Jesus died without descendants,** *so how
could He see* **His seed** *and prolong His days? This is where Philip
would teach him about the resurrection, that this Jesus was not just
crucified and buried, but that* **He rose from the grave!** *His life was
cut short without descendants in vs. 8,* **but He was awakened from
death in the resurrection to behold His offspring in vs. 10! Jesus
prolonged his days when He rose from the dead!** (Emphasis
added.)*

*Isaiah 53:10: "Yet it was the will of the Lord to crush him with
pain. When you make his life an offering..., He shall see* **His seed**
*(offspring), and shall prolong His days; through Him the will of the
Lord shall prosper."*

There's that seed again! And although the King James
Version used the word *seed,* the newer translations now use
offspring. Isaiah clearly said that *"he shall see His seed"* and Lux has

the black eunuch reading this very verse! Is it just me, or does it sound as if Lux used Isaiah to report that Jesus *"saw his seed"* and fathered children after the resurrection? Why couldn't he? He appeared to Mary Magdalene and the apostles alive.

Without the knowledge of the information Lux has already made available to Theophilus, the *"Paulian Indoctrinated Christian"* would not be able to find the message hidden within the words. However, Theophilus is looking for *"The Truth"* that Paul's doctrine tried to destroy. At the very least they would be asking if it were possible that this allusion to Isaiah's barren man who *"...shall see his seed, and shall prolong his days,"* was a message that Jesus actually had children after the resurrection. That isn't what the Paulian Christians want to believe, but we're looking for the truth here!

Of course this isn't enough to draw the conclusion that Jesus had children. But we aren't through, either. Lux has more to say to Theophilus:

You will recall that Luke Chapter 9 opened with descriptions of Saul's violence against the disciples, just as Chapter 8 did:

"Meanwhile Saul, still breathing threats and murder against the disciples of the Lord, went to the high priest and asked him for letters to the synagogues at Damascus, so that if he found any who belonged to the Way, men or women, he might bring them bound to Jerusalem."

As previously shown, Lux describes Paul's *"conversion"* and reports that *"he attempted to join the disciples; and they were all afraid of him, for they did not believe that he was a disciple."*

Throughout Chapters 10 and 11, Peter travels about the countryside healing people (Aeneas) and raising people from the dead (Tabitha, in Greek, Dorcas). He then stays in Joppa for *"some time with a certain Simon, a tanner."*

Peter has a vision, leaves Joppa, and travels to Caesarea then back to Jerusalem.

Acts Chapter 11 ends with these words: *"...this they did, sending it to the elders by Barnabas and Saul."*

Acts 12:1: *"About that time King Herod laid violent hands upon some who belonged to the church. He had **James**, the brother of*

John, killed with the sword. After he saw that it pleased the Jews, he proceeded to arrest Peter also."

(It has already been pointed out that Lux frequently places Saul's name next to Herod's while Herod is persecuting the apostles; this time it's James who is killed and Peter who is thrown into prison.)

Acts 12:11: *"Then Peter came to himself and said, 'Now I am sure that **the Lord has sent his angel** and rescued me from the hands of Herod and from all that the Jewish people were expecting."*

Peter is rescued from prison by *"an angel of the Lord."* If Lux continues with the same pattern, we're about to be given very important information. Where there's an angel, there's hidden meaning, and it's important.

Acts 12:12: *"As soon as he realized this, he went to the house of **Mary, the mother of John whose other name was Mark**, where many had gathered and were praying."*

Mary who? Which Mary? Keep in mind, the angel has just appeared in the previous verses, and now *"Mary, the mother of John whose other name was Mark"* enters the scene, and there are many people in her house praying. This is the first description of a *John* with another name, *Mark*. This seems to be a new person on the scene. And it sounds as if his mother *"Mary"* might be a teacher, or perhaps a disciple, of Jesus. Hold that thought.

The maid Rhoda heard Peter knocking on the door and recognized his voice, but she was *"so overjoyed that, instead of opening the gate, she ran in and announced that Peter was standing at the gate."*

The people in the house didn't believe her at first:

Acts 12:16: *"Meanwhile Peter continued knocking; and when they opened the gate, they saw him and were amazed."*

Then Peter enters the house, and it appears Lux wants to convey Peter's concern that they not be heard:

Acts 12:17: *"He motioned to them with his hand **to be silent**, and described for them how the Lord had brought him out of the prison. And he added: 'Tell this to **James** and to **the brothers**.' Then he left and went to another place."*

I quoted, using the word *brothers* because according to a

footnote that is the word used in the Greek text. The word used in *The New Oxford* is *believers*. But based on what we've learned in Isaiah and what is about to occur, *brothers* is probably the correct word, and it could have a more specific meaning than the Christian term *brethren*.

Time to stop and examine the clues just presented:

First Acts 12:1 reported that "*Herod had **James the brother of John** killed with a sword.*" Now Peter shows up at "*Mary's*" house, and "*Mary*" is described as "*the mother of John Mark.*" How can they "*tell James*" when James was killed in verse 1? Apparently this is another James. But who? Mary's son, John Mark's brother. Don't we know Lux well enough by now to know there was careful planning in how these stories are told and how the names are used as well as their placement relative to other names? And there is always a hidden meaning.

Could this "*Mary*" be *Mary Magdalene*? Keep in mind the action in this mystery movie is taking place during Paul's early exploits. According to Lux Paul just finished overseeing the stoning of Stephen and the killing and imprisoning of other Christians. He has just converted, and is now preaching his doctrine. That places this scene between 50 and 60 CE, plus or minus a couple of years.

Jesus was crucified between 28 and 34 ACE if the biblical timeline is correct. If this is Mary Magdalene, and if she and Jesus were about the same age, she would now be somewhere between fifty and sixty. And if she had children they would be between twenty and thirty.

What happens after "*Mary*" shows up with her son, "*John Mark*" who has a brother, "*James*" (apparently not the James killed by Herod's men), who has other "*brothers*"?

Acts 12:23: "*And immediately, because he (Herod) had not given the glory to God, an **angel of the Lord** struck him down, and he was eaten by worms and died.*"

Did that get your attention? And did you notice that the angel just showed up again? The following verses might be really important:

Acts 12:24-25: "*But the word of God continued to advance and* *gain adherents. Then after completing their mission Barnabas and Saul returned from Jerusalem and **brought with them John, whose other name was Mark.***"

Acts 13:1: "*Now in the church at Antioch there were prophets and teachers: Barnabas, **Simeon who was called Niger,** Lucius of Cyrene, Manaen a member of the court of **Herod the ruler, and Saul.***"

There's "*Herod the ruler, and Saul*" again. *Niger* means *black*, so we have another man of color! What in the world does this mean? There weren't a lot of black people traveling around Judea and Galilee, were there? Isn't it kind of strange that so many would show up in Acts at almost the same time? Lux must be trying to send a message, but what might it be? Is one of the main characters a person of color?

Acts 13:2-4: "*While they were worshiping the Lord and fasting, the **Holy Spirit** said, 'Set apart for me Barnabas and Saul for the work to which I have called them.' Then after fasting and praying they laid their hands on them and sent them off. So, being sent out by the **Holy Spirit**, they went down to Seleucia; and from there they sailed to Cyprus.*

An "*angel of the Lord*" and two "*Holy Spirits*" just made an appearance. What follows should be of extreme importance:

Acts 13:5: "*When they arrived at Salamis, they proclaimed the word of God in the synagogues of the Jews.*"...

Not much there, but suddenly, lumped within the same verse, Lux give us additional information. It is set apart in a separate, single sentence--almost as if it were an afterthought:

Acts 13:5: "*...And they had **John also to assist them.***"

This time he's referred to only as "*John,*" not "*John Mark.*" But we know it is John Mark because 12:25 told us John Mark accompanied them from Jerusalem. I'll remind you, because it's easy to forget and I sometimes do myself, that what Lux writes isn't necessarily historical. Luke's purpose was to convey "*The Truth*" about the things that were being written and taught. These hidden messages were mixed in with stories from the texts and letters that had already been written. The purpose was to plant clues (angels, Holy Spirit) just before the hidden information appears. We are to watch for the juxtaposition of names and events; we are to look for messages within the quotes from Old Testament texts or familiar Greek books and plays. With this reminder, look at what comes next:

Acts 13:6: *"When they had gone through the whole island as far as Paphos, they met a certain **magician, a Jewish false prophet, named Bar-Jesus.**"*

Bar means *son of*, so *Bar-Jesus* means *son of Jesus*. In verse 5 Paul is traveling with a young man named *John Mark*, and in verse 6 Paul meets Bar-Jesus.

Time for another review: First we met Mary, her sons, James and John Mark, and their *"brothers."* Now in the next chapter, we encounter Jesus, Jr.

Another unique feature of this section is that John Mark and James are said to be brothers, and their mother is said to be Mary, but their father's name is noticeably absent. It is highly unusual for a biblical text to give the mother's name and not the father's. Why here? Why did Lux leave out this information? Do you think it's something Theophilus is supposed to consider, considering this is a mystery and we're trying to solve it? Is this another clue? Is this a clue to some very important knowledge about this *"Mary"* and this *"Bar-Jesus"*?

Lux has Bar-Jesus meet Saul, Barnabas and John Mark and tells us that Bar-Jesus is a magician, and that:

Acts 13:7-8: *"He was with the proconsul, **Sergius Paulus**, an intelligent man, who summoned Barnabas and Saul and wanted to hear the word of God. But the magician Elymas (for that is the translation of his name) opposed them and tried to turn the proconsul away from **the faith.**"*

Knowing what we now know about Paul's total disregard and disagreement with Jesus' teachings and *The Nazarene Way*, it's no wonder Lux has Paul say:

Acts 13:9-10: *"But Saul, also known as Paul, filled with the Holy Spirit, looked intently at him and said, 'You son of the devil, you enemy of all righteousness, full of all deceit and villainy, will you not stop making crooked the **straight paths** of the Lord? And now listen--the* *hand of the Lord is against you, and you will be blind for a while, unable to see the sun.'"*

These are the words Saul would have used if he had come face-to-face with Jesus prior to his *"conversion"* on the road to Damascus. As one of Herod Agrippa's henchmen, a Pharisee, Saul stood against everything that Jesus stood for. If Saul's conversion had been a sham, which Lux tells us it was, then these words are what Saul would have uttered against Jesus' son, Jesus, Jr. And it's noteworthy that Lux had previously referred to the Nazarenes' doctrine as *The Way*, but in this verse Bar-Jesus tries to turn the proconsul away from *"the faith."* There's a difference, and Lux knew Theophilus would know that.

Once I began connecting Plutarch's works with Lux and Acts and realized that virtually all of the characters who appeared with Saul/Paul in Lux and Acts were people about whom Plutarch had written biographies, it became almost a habit for me to search those names. The name *Sergius Paulus* was especially curious since Paul's name was attached to *Sergius*.

Plutarch wrote of a *Lucius **Sergius** Catilina* in 75 ACE, in the life of *Cicero*. Another historian, Sallust, who lived between 86 and 34 BCE, wrote a more detailed essay of Lucius Sergius Catilina in *The Cataline Conspiracy*. The information quoted here comes from a web site that can be accessed at: www.hoocher.com/catilina.

Some of the highlights contained in Sallust's biography of Lucius Sergius Catilina that might be *"hidden information"* about Saul/Paul:

"He was a patrician member of a noble family and propraetorian governor of Africa (66-67 BCE.)"

"He was accused of several murders, including the beheading of Marcus Marius Gratidianus."

"Cicero accused him of: planning to murder him in 64 BCE; planning to murder Cicero as well as his rival consular candidates in the election of 63 BCE; planning to massacre the consuls and other leading men, as well as the entire Senate, on the 29th of December 66 BCE in order that he might take the place of one of the consulares for 65 BCE who were also to be murdered.

"*These statements about Catiline's plans for violence at the end of 66 BCE merit further study. In the speech 'In Toga Candida' Cicero says that he will pass over the plot to massacre the Optimates, but the speech 'Pro Sulla' can shed light on the origin of the myth. Cicero is engaged in the defence of Publius Cornelius Sulla and the prosecution has pointed out that in his letter to Pompey Cicero had linked the earlier affair with the conspiracy of 63 BCE. Cicero therefore has to extricate Sulla from the complicity in 66 BCE, and one of the devices he employs is the substitution of Catiline for Sulla as a principal in the affair and the implication that Catiline was to have taken the place of one of the murdered consuls.*"

"*Sallust accepts Cicero's story and gives Catiline the leading role. The story is highly appropriate for a man ever driven to violence and crime by the corruption of the times and by his bad conscience.*"

"*In his 'Second Speech Against Catiline' Cicero identifies six groups among Catiline's supporters:*

1. Wealthy men who are heavily in debt and who could repay their debt by selling land but are unwilling to do so.

2. Men who are in debt and see revolution as their road to power.

3. Veterans of Sulla's army who had been settled in colonies, but have lived beyond their means and now want new proscriptions from which to recover their fortunes.

4. Men deep in financial difficulties who seek to evade their problems by joining Catiline.

5. The criminal element in society.

6. The dissolute youth of the capital.

"*Catiline's support was thus not confined to the lower classes, but there is a significant omission from this list--the urban plebs. There is no doubt that the Roman masses did at first support the conspiracy and their omission is capable of explanation. The 'Second Speech Against Catiline' was delivered to a meeting open to the whole populace in which Cicero seeks to present Catiline's supporters in the worst possible light and to urge the lower classes not to join a conspiracy under the leadership of depraved aristocrats whose interest have nothing in common with theirs. He must therefore avoid identifying his audience with those whom he is attacking.*"

"*Those efforts to split the urban plebs from the other conspirators were successful. Cicero was able to convince his listeners that Catiline's aim was anarchy, but anarchy or the liberation of the slaves was not what they sought. No more was it the temporary alleviation of an economic crisis which would leave its root causes untouched. The prospect of radical social reform offering them a permanent improvement of their position in society might have led them to join Catiline, but this was not--according to Cicero--what they were being promised."*

Jesus declared that he had come to free the slaves and the oppressed and to help the poor.

Luke 4:18: *"The Spirit of the Lord is upon me, because he has anointed me to preach good news to the poor. He has sent me to proclaim release to the captives and recovering of sight to the blind, to set at liberty those who are oppressed..."*

Paul's advice to the slaves and the oppressed was to serve their masters willingly and obediently, and the poor were to continue to pay taxes to the authorities without complaint.

Colossians 3:22-25: ***"Slaves, obey your earthly masters in everything**, not only while being watched and in order to please them, but wholeheartedly, fearing the Lord. Whatever your task, put yourselves into it, as done for the Lord and not for your masters, since you know that from the Lord you will receive the inheritance as your reward; you serve the Lord Christ. For the wrongdoer will be paid back for whatever wrong has been done, and there is no partiality."*

Romans 13:1-2: *"Let every person be subject to the governing authorities; for there is no authority except from God, and those authorities that exist have been instituted by God. Whoever resists authority resists what God has appointed, and those who resist will incur judgment."*

Romans 13:5-7: *"...one must be subject, not only because of wrath but also because of conscience. For the same reason you also pay taxes, for the authorities are God's servants, busy with this very thing. Pay to all what is due them--taxes to whom taxes are due, revenue to whom revenue is due, respect to whom respect is due, honor to whom honor is due."*

This link to Lucius **Sergius** Catilina, especially incorporating Paul's name with *Sergius* serves as yet another clue that Paul had close ties to the wealthy leaders and was not truly interested in freeing the slaves and the oppressed or helping the poor who were burdened by excessive taxation.

After Saul's tirade against Bar-Jesus, Lux writes:

Acts 13:11: "*...Immediately mist and darkness came over **him**, and **he** went about groping for someone to **lead him by the hand**.*"

Lux leaves the identity of "*him*" and "*he*" unclear. I think it was intentional. It has always been assumed that "*he*" and "*him*" in this sentence was Bar-Jesus, but it's just as likely that both pronouns referred to Saul. And in fact, it's more likely it was Saul who was struck blind, not Bar-Jesus. Saul proclaimed that Bar-Jesus would be blind and unable to see, but the "*angels*" and/or the "*Holy Spirit*" would have blinded one who would try to attack Jesus or one of his disciples--or his son.

The words highlighted in this story are virtually the same as those found in Acts 9 which describes Paul's "*conversion*" and what occurred at that time:

Acts 9:8: "***Saul** arose from the ground; and when his eyes were opened, **he could see nothing**; so they **led him by the hand**...*"

Acts 9:11: "*And the Lord said to him, 'Rise and go to the **street called Straight**, and inquire in the house of Judas...*"

Acts 9:12: "*...And he has seen a man named Ananias come in an **lay his hands on him...***"

Acts 9:8, 11, and 12 openly describe Saul as being blind. To use so many of the same words just four chapters later, Lux seems to want Theophilus to know that Saul is the "*blind guy*" and Bar-Jesus is the "*good guy*."

Lux knew of Paul's letters and knew Paul's doctrine was being promoted by Herod Agrippa and the temple priests. He knew Jesus' message was being abandoned and Paul's doctrine adopted. Lux was trying to get the truth out! He knew Paul had written to the church at Galatia:

Galations 4:13-17: "*You know that it was because of a physical infirmity that I first announced the gospel to you; though my condition put you to the test, you did not scorn or despise me, but welcomed me as an angel of God, as Christ Jesus. What has become of the goodwill you felt? For I testify that, had it been possible, **you would have torn out** *your eyes and given them to me. Have I now become your enemy by telling you the truth? They make much of you, but for no good purpose; they want to exclude you, so that you may make much of them."*

The annotation for these verses is:

"On his first visit through the region of Galatia (Acts 16:6) an illness (was it eye trouble? See v. 15) detained Paul; though he was a care to the Galatians, they treated him with special consideration."

The suggestion here is that the *"physical infirmity"* and *"you would have torn out your eyes and given them to me"* indicate the illness was eye trouble of some sort. I agree, and I believe Acts 13:1-12 used the knowledge of the content of Paul's letter to the Galatians to send more information to the Theophilosophers about Paul.

Lux created the story of Bar-Jesus and the proconsul because one of the narratives being circulated, about which he wanted to get out *"the truth,"* was Paul's letter to the Galations.

Lux used the name *Bar-Jesus* and described him as a *"Jewish false prophet"* who was with *Sergius Paulus* (note this *Paulus* is another government official; the writer consistently puts Paul with government officials). This *"son of Jesus"* *"opposed them and tried to turn the proconsul away from "the faith."* The *faith* this *"son of Jesus"* tried to turn him away from is Paul's *faith not works* doctrine.

And what about Luke's insertion of this phrase: *"But the magician Elymas (for that is the translation of his name)..."*? I looked up the meaning of *Elymas*. It's Arabic and it means *a wise man*. *Magi* also means *a wise man*. And *Nazar* means *wise man*. So in this story, this *Bar-Jesus*, or *son of Jesus*, is called *"a wise man"* two times. Remember this gospel had to pass the scrutiny of the church leaders. If there was any appearance that it contained a message contrary to the official doctrine people would be killed. On the surface it had to appear to be in favor of Paul's doctrine because that was the official doctrine that was being spread.

And what exactly is meant by *"a Jewish false prophet"*? Paul called anyone who disagreed with his doctrine a *"false prophet."* The Nazarenes, although considered a branch of Judaism, were considered *"false prophets"* by the Pharisees and Sadducees. Herod and Pontius Pilate considered Jesus to be just another in a long line of false prophets. Jesus--our Jesus--was considered a false prophet by the government and temple rulers! And if this *"Bar-Jesus"* was preaching the doctrine of The Nazarene Way, Paul would have called him a false prophet, too!

Saul travels with his companions, minus *"John who returned to Jerusalem"* (13:13), to Paphos, Perga in Pamphylia, to Antioch in Pisidia. There they went into the synagogue and sat down.

Acts 13:15: *"After the reading of the law and the prophets, the officials of the synagogue sent them a message, saying, 'Brothers, if you have any word of exhortation for the people, give it.' So Paul stood up and with a gesture began to speak."*

Lux begins to put words into Paul's mouth that lead to the Old Testament:

Acts 13:19: *"After he had destroyed seven nations in the land of Canaan..."* This links to:

Deuteronomy 7:1-4: *"When the Lord . . brings you into the land that you are about to...occupy, and he clears away many nations before you...Canaanites,...seven nations mightier and more numerous than you--and when the Lord...gives them over to you and you defeat them, then you must utterly destroy them. Make no covenant with them and show them no mercy. Do not intermarry with them, giving your daughters to their sons or taking their daughters for your sons, for that would turn away your children from following me, to serve other gods."*

Deuertonomy 7:14: *"You shall be the most blessed of peoples, with neither sterility nor barrenness among you or your livestock."*

Acts 13:21: *"Then they asked for a king; and God gave them Saul son of Kish, as man of the tribe of Benjamin..."*

This links to I Samuel 9:1, but it must be placed in context if the message Lux wants to send is to be fully understood. It's a story similar to Daniel's Nebuchadnezzar; the people continue to turn away from the Lord and worship other gods and false idols:

I Samuel 8:6-9: *"But the thing displeased Samuel when they said, 'Give us a king to govern us.' Samuel prayed to the Lord, and the*

Lord said...'Listen to the voice of the people...for they have...rejected me from being king over them. **Just as they have done to me, from the day I brought them up out of Egypt to this day, forsaking me and serving other gods....** *Now then, listen to their voice; only--you shall...warn them and show them the ways of the king who shall reign over them.'*

I Samuel 8:10-18: "*So Samuel reported all the words of the Lord to the people who were asking him for a king. He said, 'These will be the ways of the king who will reign over you; he will take your sons and appoint them to his chariots and to be his horsemen, and to run before his chariots; and he will appoint for himself commanders of thousands and commanders of fifties, and some to plow his ground and to reap his harvest, and to make his implements of war and the equipment of his chariots. He will take your daughters to be perfumers and cooks and bakers. He will take the best of your fields and vineyards and olive orchards and give them to his courtiers. He will take one-tenth of your grain and of your vineyards and give it to his officers and his courtiers. He will take your male and female slaves, and the best of your cattle and donkeys, and put them to his work. He will take one-tenth of your flocks, and you shall be his slaves. And in that day you will cry out because of your king, whom you have chosen for yourselves; but the Lord will not answer you in that day.'*"

I Samuel 8:19-22: "**But the people refused to listen** *to the voice of Samuel; they said, 'No! but we are determined to have a king over us, so that we also may be like other nations, and that our king may govern us and go out before us and fight our battles.' When Samuel had heard all the words of the people, he repeated them in the ears of the Lord. The Lord said to Samuel, 'Listen to their voice and set a king over them.' Samuel then said to the people of Israel, 'Each of you return home.'*"

I Samuel 9:1: "*There was a man of Benjamin whose name was Kish son of Abiel...a man of wealth.* **He had a son whose name was Saul...**"

Acts 13:22: "*When he had removed him, he made David their king. In his testimony about him he said, 'I have found David, son of Jesse, to be a man after my heart, who will carry out all my wishes.'*"

This links to:

I Samuel 13:14: *"Samuel said to Saul, 'You have done foolishly; you have not kept the commandment of the Lord your God, which he commanded you. The Lord would have established your kingdom over Israel forever, but now your kingdom will not continue; the Lord has sought out a man after his own heart; and the Lord has appointed him to be ruler over his people, because you have not kept what the Lord commanded of you.'"*

This needs no comment from me; it's clear what the message is. And this one even calls Saul by name!

Acts 13:32-41: *"And we bring you the good news that what God promised to our ancestors he has fulfilled for us, their children, by raising Jesus; as also it is written in the second psalm, 'You are my Son; today I have begotten you,' As to his raising him from the dead, no more to return to corruption, he has spoken in this way, 'I will give you the holy promises made to David.' Therefore he has also said in another psalm, 'You will not let your Holy One experience corruption.' For David, after he had served the purpose of God in his own generation died, was laid beside his ancestors, and experienced corruption; but he whom God raised up experienced no corruption. Let it be known to you therefore, my brothers, that through this man forgiveness of sins is proclaimed to you; by this Jesus everyone who believes is set free from all from which you could not be freed by the law of Moses. Beware, therefore, that what the prophets said does not happen to you: 'Look, you scoffers! Be amazed and perish, for in your days I am doing a work, a work that you will never believe, even if someone tells you.'"*

That last quote comes from Habakkuk 1:5: *"Be astonished! Be astounded! For a work is being done in your days that you would not believe if you were told."*

How true are those words sent to us by Lux?! The Christians will not believe it!

⟋⟍

There are many people who are convinced that Jesus and Mary Magdalene married and had children. The *"wise man,"* Bar-Jesus, who spoke against Paul's faith, could be just another of Luke's devices to impart Paul's opposition to Jesus' teachings.

But couldn't it also be possible that they wanted to leave a message about something almost as important? Could it be they wanted the world to know that Jesus did father children?

Some writers who have proposed that Jesus and Mary Magdalene married and had children claim ancient texts exist that document this is exactly what happened. Sir Laurence Gardner's, *Bloodline of the Holy Grail*, is one that I'm familiar with. It is quite interesting and thought-provoking, and I can highly recommend it. And there are others.

I have to say, when I found the numbers of Light in Luke's first chapter, I never dreamed that it would lead to this discovery in Acts. I just saw a mystery unfolding and thought it might be in need of solving, and I love solving mysteries. I'm not complaining.

CHAPTER EIGHT

"When Paul noticed that some were Sadducees and others were Pharisees,
he called out...'Brothers, I am a Pharisee, a son of Pharisees...'"
Luke 23:6

DISDAINFUL DECEIVER

W as Paul a deceiver? I have no desire to work through all the scriptures Paul quotes out of context and with questionable transitional phrases clearly designed to mislead. I will urge you to get a Bible with annotations and read the Old Testament scriptures from beginning to end whenever Paul quotes them. It will be clear he omits phrases that contradict the point he is trying to make.

Acts, combined with historical documents by Josephus and others, point to a close relationship between Paul and the Roman government and between Paul and the Pharisee high priests. He boasted that his teacher was Gamalial, a noted Pharisee of high rank.

Was Paul arrogant?

Paul heard of Jesus, his lifestyle, his doctrine, his philosophy, and his knowledge. He rejected all of that and replaced it almost totally with the Pharisee doctrine. In my opinion that's arrogant.

The only two issues which Paul didn't completely reject were non-circumcision and baptism. Yet, Acts reports that he circumcised Timothy because he wanted Timothy to accompany him; coded message for "*Paul said one thing but did another*"? Or perhaps, "***Paul lies!***"

Acts 16:1-3: "*Paul went on also to Derbe and to Lystra, where there was a disciple named Timothy, the son of a Jewish woman who was a believer, but his father was a Greek. He was well spoken of by the believers in Lystra and Iconium. Paul wanted Timothy to accompany him; and he took him and circumcised him because of the Jews who were in those places, for they all knew that his father was a Greek.*"

Two points have to be made here. First, Titus was Greek and uncircumcised, and Paul, according to the introduction to "*The Letter of Paul to Titus*," (New Oxford Annotated Bible, 1994, p 311 NT), "*resisted all efforts made in demanding that he (Titus) be circumcised.*"

Second, with a Jewish mother, had she been Pharisee or Sadducee, Timothy would have been circumcised on the eighth day following his birth. Reading between the lines it seems clear that Timothy's mother (and his grandmother, as well) were Nazarenes who did not circumcise their boys.

Paul was a Pharisee. His tutor was the most famous Pharisee priest of the time, Gamaliel. He was circumcised and had been taught the absolute necessity of circumcision from the time he was born. Why would he "*resist all efforts*" to circumcise Titus, but circumcise Timothy? His second letter hints at a relationship with Timothy that was, for lack of a more eloquent word, "*special.*"

2 Timothy 1:3-5 (From the 1973 edition of *The New Oxford Annotated Bible*):

"*I thank God whom I serve with a clear conscience, as did my fathers, when I remember you constantly in my prayers. As I remember your tears, I long night and day to see you, that I may be filled with joy. I am reminded of your sincere faith, a faith that dwelt first in your grandmother Lois and your mother Eunice and now, I am sure, dwells in you.*"

It certainly sounds as if Timothy was third generation Nazarene, and his grandmother would have been a contemporary of Jesus and his original disciples including Mary Magdalene.

I don't want to try to read anything into the *"tears"* or *"longing night and day"* or *"that I may be filled with joy."* But it did bring to my mind Paul's letter to the Romans. In one section he seems to bear his soul:

Romans 7:15-20: *"I do not understand my own actions. For I do not do what I want, but I do the very thing I hate. Now if I do what I do not want, I agree that the law is good. But in fact it is no longer I that do it, but sin that dwells within me. For I know that nothing good dwells within me, that is, in my flesh. I can will what is right, but I cannot do it. For I do not do the good I want, but the evil I do not want is what I do. Now if I do what I do not want, it is no longer I that do it, but sin that dwells within me."* (Sort of like, "The Devil made me do it!")

Romans 7:21-7: *"So I find it to be a law that when I want to do what is good, evil lies close at hand. For I delight in the law of God in my inmost self, but I see in my members another law at war with the law of my mind, making me captive to the law of sin that dwells in my members. Wretched man that I am! Who will rescue me from this body of death? Thanks be to God through Jesus Christ our Lord! So then, with my mind I am a slave to the law of God, but with my flesh I am a slave to the law of sin."*

Paul's definition of sin was his own. I don't know with total confidence what *"evil"* he is referring to, but it may not be evil in my eyes or yours.

A reminder: The Nazarenes, and Jesus, taught that *The Law* was unfailing. Any sinful act under the *Law of Cause and Effect* would bring punishment and pain to the person acting against the law. The Nazarenes and Jesus taught that the Law could not be broken. They taught that the law could not be avoided. It worked for both good and evil. Jesus taught that people should think and act with loving kindness and immediate forgiveness so that the action of the law would bring desired reward.

Luke 6:35-38: Jesus said, *"But love your enemies, and do good, and lend, expecting nothing in return; and your reward will be great, and you will be sons of the Most High; for he is kind to the ungrateful and the selfish. Be merciful, even as your Father is merciful. Judge not, and you will not be judged; condemn not, and you will not be*

*condemned; forgive, and you will be forgiven; give, and it will be given
to you; good measure, pressed down, shaken together, running over, will
be put into your lap.* **For the measure you give will be the measure
you get back."**

The Pharisees believed that man's *"sins of the flesh"* could
be transferred to a goat (hence the term *scapegoat*), the goat
consecrated and sacrificed to *God*, and the *"sins of the flesh"*
would be forgiven. Even some of the pagan doctrines provided
for this *"transference"* of sins to something or someone else.

Modern *"Christians"* believe that a man's *"sins of the flesh"*
can be transferred to Jesus, Jesus volunteered to be sacrificed to
God, and the *"sins of the flesh"* are thereby forgiven.

In principle, where payment of sin is concerned, Pharisee,
Pagan, and Christian doctrine is the same. The only difference
is to what or to whom is the sin transferred: a goat or some
other animal or to Jesus.

But the Nazarene doctrine is rather harsh to the sinner
because the sinner must bear the cost and pay the price of the
sin. *"The measure you give is the measure you get back." The Law* is
the same whether the act is good or bad.

For centuries the Pharisee and Sadducee Jews, and some
Pagans, had their scapegoats. The Nazarene/Essenes never
did. The Nazirites had taken a vow to God to live according to
certain guidelines not imposed on the Sadducees or Pharisees:
no meat, no wine or strong drink, no cutting of hair. As time
passed certain modifications were made. The Nazarene/Essenes
vowed to care for the sick (including lepers) and other outcasts,
to share with each other equally, to care for the poor, and to
treat all life with honor and respect with daily thanksgiving
for the gifts received from their Father/Mother source of all
things.

For countless generations Pharisees, Sadducees, and
Pagans had been able to pass off to something else the penalty
for their sins. No wonder they were bloody, brutal, and cruel to
each other. Why in God's name would they want to reject that
benefit and assume the responsibility of their sins themselves
if they had a choice? Herod was no fool. He had to have had a

pretty good idea which doctrine would be the easier to sell. If he could get someone inside the movement, a trusted relative or a relative of one of his trusted advisors, the average man, Jew, Gentile, or Pagan, could be easily directed away from the difficult and harsh lifestyle of the Nazarenes and back to the *"pass the sin"* religions of the Jews and Pagans. All Herod needed was a large wooden horse and some soldiers to hide inside it. Actually all he needed in this case was some sheep's clothing for the soldiers. The *"flock"* was looking for an easier way than *The Way* anyway.

CHAPTER NINE

"Many of them therefore believed, with not a few Greek women of
high standing."
Acts 17:12

CRACKING THE CASE

The final question to be answered in this mystery is who specifically wrote Luke's gospel and the Ax of the Apostle. The answer can be found by asking a couple more questions:

Who benefited most from Jesus' the Nazarene's true doctrine *The Nazarene Way of Life?* And who had the most to lose when Paul took over the new movement, rejected Jesus' doctrine and *The Way of the Nazarenes,* and replaced it with the traditions of the Pharisee Jews?

Three groups primarily: the poor, the slaves, and the women.

Who had the most to gain by acknowledging the arrival of a *"true messiah"* who taught a doctrine that agreed on virtually every point with the Pharisees and Sadducees' doctrines?

The powerful (the king, governors, proconsuls, temple priests), etc., the wealthy property and slave owners, and free men.

Both before and after Jesus the Nazarene arrived in Galilee, Judea, Syria, Sumaria, and the rest of the region, there were others claiming to be the long awaited messiah that had been prophesied. Many managed to gather support, some more than others. It had been an irritation to both the temple priests and the Roman government. Virtually all except Jesus stirred up anger and violence by trying to get the oppressed to wage battle against the oppressors.

But Jesus' message was one of passive resistance. He simply suggested that *The Nazarene Way of Life* provided the best means of escape from the tyranny of the church and the state. To the poor, the women, and the freed slaves, he said: *"Forget owning property. The taxes will eat you alive anyway. Sell what little you might have and come with us to the Nazarene communities where everyone shares equally in all things. Come to a community where the value of any one person does not exceed the value of any other. Come live with us where the preparation of food, the weaving of cloth, tending gardens, treating the sick, and nurturing the children is as valuable as work that requires physical strength or holding a position of authority or preaching in the temple. Waging war is not necessary. Simply refuse to play their game and come live The Nazarene Way of Life."*

This message was a real threat. The Roman armies would always be more powerful than some grassroots movement by a rebel claiming to be the messiah. Those skirmishes did nothing more than keep the armies in shape. But this threat was quite different, and it had to be dealt with differently. This threat had to be infiltrated and dismantled from within by discrediting the real doctrine and replacing it with a false doctrine that supported the government and church leaders.

Paul's doctrine did that. The disciples and teachers of the true doctrine had to be demonized and persecuted. *The Nazarene Way* had to become something feared and hated by the new converts to Paul's religious movement. The knowledge of the use of herbs and plants for healing illness had to be turned into the practice of witchcraft. The knowledge of the Creation of the heavens and earth, of mass and matter, and the sizes and distances and interrelationship of the heavenly bodies had to be turned into *gnosticism*, or as Paul called it, *"false knowledge."* Once the ball got rolling the church and government joined forces to kill those who tried to teach the secret knowledge, and they burned all the documents that contained it. This information is history, folks. Know your history and you'll know this is what happened to Jesus' message.

When the writer/writers of Luke and Acts inserted a story or a phrase that seems out of place, it is quite likely it contains a message. Why else would it be there, sticking out like a sore thumb?

Some additional examples:

Acts 13:50: *"But the Jews incited the **devout women of high standing** and the leading men of the city, and stirred up persecution against Paul and Barnabas, and drove them out of their region."*

Acts 16:13-14: *"On the Sabbath day we went outside the gate to the riverside, where we supposed there was a place of prayer; and we sat down and spoke to **the women** who had gathered there. A certain woman named Lydia, a worshiper of God, was listening to us; she was from the city of Thyatira and a dealer in purple cloth."*

Acts 17:4: *"Some of them were persuaded and joined Paul and Silas, as did a great many of the devout Greeks and not a few of **the leading women**."*

Acts 17:12: *"Many of them therefore believed, with not a few **Greek women of high standing."***

Acts 17:34: *"But some of them joined him and became believers, including Dionysius the Areopagite **and a woman** named Damaris, and others with them."*

Acts 18:2: *"There he found a Jew named Aquila, a native of Pontus, who had recently come from Italy with **his wife Priscilla**, because Claudius had ordered all Jews to Leave Rome."*

Who is most likely to have believed it important to insert these superfluous tidbits of information in Lux and Acts?

Luke 24:10: *"Now it was Mary Magdalene, **Joanna**, Mary the mother of James, and the other women with them who told this to the apostles."*

Joanna is mentioned only two times in the scriptures, both times by Luke. And both times she is with Jesus and Mary Magdalene. Lux clearly wants to demonstrate her importance or she would not be named in these two important scenes.

The virgin Mary's parents, according to ancient texts, were

named Joachim and Anna. Traditionally children were named after parents, aunts, uncles, or grandparents. What a perfect name for a grand daughter of Joachim and Anna! Or what a perfect clue to suggest that Jesus had a daughter.

Are there any other clues that might support this outrageous proposal? There is an unusual section of Luke's gospel that might:

Luke 8:41-42: *"And there came a man named Jairus, who was a ruler of the synagogue; and falling at Jesus' feet he besought him to come to his house, for he had an only daughter, about twelve years of age, and she was dying."*

What causes these verses to stand out is that the scene suddenly shifts to a woman, and *"coincidentally,"* she has had a flow of blood twelve years, the age of Jarius' daughter just mentioned. Perhaps we're to connect the two stories. If so, the pertinent verse might be Luke 8:48, for Jesus addresses the woman as *"Daughter."* This is the only recorded scene in any of the gospels in which Jesus calls someone *"Daughter."* With that, Lux immediately returns to Jarius' daughter:

Luke 8:54-56: *"But he took her by the hand and called out, 'Child, get up!'...Then he directed them to give her something to eat. Her parents were astounded; but he ordered them to tell no one what had happened."*

There are some who claim that to the Nazarene/Essenes/Pythagoreans, *death* meant *"birth into the physical world"* (the spirit *"died"* to the spiritual realm as it was born into the earthly realm). In that case, those of *The Way* would know from this story that a daughter was born, and Jesus addressed the woman whose story interrupted the death and rebirth of Jarius' daughter as *"Daughter."*

Granted this may not be a lot in the way of proof, but Lux was sending coded messages, and this is certainly a rational solution to these unusual scenes that are juxtaposed in such as way as to draw attention.

༄

Who originally wrote the story that eventually reached

the Bible under the names, Luke's Gospel and the Acts of the Apostles?

I'll venture a guess at some possible names: Elizabeth, Anna, Susanna, Joanna, Salome, Martha, Sarah, Mary, Druscilla, Bernice, Lois, Eunice, Rhoda, Damaris, Lydia, and, of course, *"the other women,"* and *"Greek women of high standing."*

Was there a specific woman who was in charge of the project? Probably. I'm going to guess Joanna led the group. I base this guess on her prominence at the crucifixion and because she was named with Mary Magdalene as they traveled around with Jesus and the other disciples. And if the name *Joseph* is a designation that refers to the eldest son, wouldn't *Joanna* be the equivalent, or the eldest daughter, making Joanna a High Priestess in the Nazarene/Essene community?

There were no doubt others not named, and their names may never be known. I would love to be able to list all of them and be able to honor each and every one of them. But all I can do is present this case for their actions and honor them as we do the unnamed men and women who fought for American independence--in a general way. Just knowing how they managed to get the message written and included in the Church canon may be enough. I do believe they should be recognized and praised each Sunday as their knowledge of the Universe and their doctrine of love and forgiveness is preached from the pulpits of the Reorganized and Renewed Church of the Nazarenes and Essenes.

To our Father/Mother Creator of all life, thanks be to the brave women who took refuge in *Lux* the goddess of Light. Their contribution to the reawakening of Jesus and the Nazarene Way and the *Tree of Life* cannot be overstated. At this particular time in our evolution, with complete annihilation of every form of life on the planet just a button-push away, never before has humankind been more in need of his message.

The scientist and film maker David Suzuki explains it this way: *"The canaries are already dead. Now it's our children, our sisters, our mothers who are dying from the poison in the air we breathe, the food we eat and the water we drink."*

If we don't take a step back and look at what we've done to the earth, the air, the water, and each other, it won't take the bombs to kill us all. If it hasn't already been passed, there is a point of no return. If Jesus were here in physical form, and he may be for all I know, he would do what he did then. He would say *"Love and respect all life, all things, all of Creation. Think first of others, then of yourself. In this is the key to living life abundantly."*

It's obvious the women had to have help to get their story published and accepted as *"gospel."* It had to be a man, because no woman would have been given any voice in the matter at the time the gospels were being collected and judged. I figured since all the other information was tucked neatly in Lux and Ax, surely the identity of the man responsible for bringing the message to the public was tucked in there someplace, too. Since Luke opened with the information about who the story was really about, the Nazarenes, I suspected the man's name would be at the end of Acts. I started with chapters 27 and 28, and I really didn't have to go any further.

I noticed that one first century character's name kept showing up: Plutarch. Now I began a process which led me over and over to him. I noted the names of characters and locations in Acts 27 and 28. Here's what happens when Internet searches of some of those characters and locales are combined with *Plutarch*:

Acts Chapter 27:

Plutarch Augustan Cohort Julius led to web sites for Plutarch's *Life of Mark Anthony, written in 75 ACE;*

Plutarch Adramyttium led to www.bartleby.com: *Cicero* by Plutarch, written in 75 ACE; *"He (Cicero) sailed from Athens for Asia and Rhodes. Amongst the Asia masters he studied with Xenocles of* **Adramyttium, Dionysius** *of Magnesia, Menippus of Caria; at Rhodes he studied oratory with* **Apollonius,** *the son of Molon...";*

Plutarch Aristarchus led to www.hao.ucar.edu: *"Aristarchus' only surviving text is his Treatise on the Sizes and Distances of the Sun and Moon. However, largely through the writings of Archimedes*

(287-212 BC) and **Plutarch, Aristarchus** *is known to have been the first proponent of the heliocentric hypothesis, with the Earth ascribed a movement of orbital rotation about the Sun, as well as a daily axial rotation. Aristarchus argued that the lack of observed annual parallax in the fixed stars could be explained, within his heliocentric model, by assuming that the distance to the fixed stars is very much larger than the size of the Earth's orbit. The very same argument was to be made by Nicholas Copernicus, seventeen centuries later."*

Plutarch Fair Havens led to *Timoleon,* written by Plutarch in 75 ACE. Timoleon is a legendary character who died in 337 BCE. According to Plutarch, Timoleon is a Corinthian; his friend is Paulus Aemilius, and one of the other characters in the story is Dionysius;

Plutarch Cnidus led to www.livius.org: Ctesias of Cnidus; *"This part of Ctesias' work is relatively well known because it is quoted at great length by the Greek author* **Plutarch of Chaeronea,** *who wrote a biography of Artaxerxes."*

Plutarch Lycia led to www.allaboutturkey.com: *"Plutarch recorded Brutus's feelings on this second mass suicide."* Plutarch wrote *Marcus Brutus* in 75 ACE.

Remember, those are just the names and places recorded in Chapter 27! The same results occur when the names and places in Luke's gospel are linked with Plutarch, as well as the names and places in earlier chapters of Acts.

Acts 28:11-15: *"Three months later we set sail on a ship that had wintered at the island, an Alexandrian ship with the* **Twin Brothers** *as its figurehead. We put in at Syracuse and stayed there for three days; then we weighed anchor and came to* **Rhegium.** *After one day there a south wind sprang up and on the second day we came to* **Puteoli.** *There we found believers and were invited to stay with them for seven days. And so we came to Rome. The believers from there, when they heard of us, came as far as the* **Forum of Appius** *and* **Three Taverns** *to meet us. On seeing them, Paul thanked God and took courage."*

Plutarch Pollux Castor led to www.geocities.com: *Theseus* by Plutarch, 75 ACE.

Plutarch Rhegium led to *"Pythagoras of Rhegium"*; Plutarch wrote about *"Pythagoras of Rhegium."*

Plutarch Puteoli led to *Apollonius of Tyana* and the resurrection story about him (he appeared to Damis at Puteoli);

Plutarch Appius led to *Appius Claudius Caecus* who constructed both the Via Appia, or Appian Way, and the Aqua Appia during Plutarch's lifetime. *Caecus* means *blind*, which reminds one of Paul's mysterious affliction, assumed to be blindness, and the blindness that struck him during his Damascus trip according to Lux.

Virtually all of Paul's companions and travel destinations were named in Plutarch's *Lives* and/or *Moralia*. And there are quotations attributed to characters about whom Plutarch wrote. For example, Lux has Paul quote Epimenides:

Acts 17:28: "...'*In him we live and move and have our being.*'" Epimenides is named in Plutarch's *Solon* written in 75 ACE.

In the same verse Lux has Paul quote Aratus:

Acts 17:28: "...'*For we too are his offspring.*'" Plutarch wrote *Aratus* in 75 ACE, as well.

The links between Plutarch and *Acts* are incredibly strong. In fact, they add up to quite a long chain of evidence that Plutarch's works were used extensively in the writing of both Lux and Ax. It appears that Plutarch wrote virtually all of the essays and books, from which the characters and locations in Luke and Acts were taken, in 75 ACE. This is very close to the estimated time frame during which Luke and Acts were also written. Another clue?

Perhaps there's another loose string to tie up, and it relates to the stoning of Stephen/Jacob, and his insistence that his family had fled to Alexandria, Egypt, and this "*Alexandrian ship with the Twin Brothers as its figurehead.*" If Jesus and Judas the twin (a.k.a. *Apollonius*) had fled to Alexandria, as Luke's gospel seems to report through Stephen's speech, this last chapter of Acts would apparently report that they, or their descendants, left Alexandria and headed across the Mediterranean Sea. There are legends that Mary Magdalene and the Holy Grail arrived at Gaul, and from there spread Christianity to the British Isles and elsewhere across Europe. This information from between the lines of Acts would suggest that the legend may be based in fact.

The documents found at Qumran, occupied by Essenes in the first century and earlier, have begun to provide some interesting footnotes to the religion that became "*Christianity.*" Surely this will be the very last web site referenced: www.livius.org/men-mh/messiah/messiah_14.html:

"*Several texts are considered to be written by members of the sect: the Damascus document for example, and the Messianic rule. In these texts, we may expect to find the sect's own messianology. The distinguishing characteristic is that the Qumranites expected the coming of not one, but two Messiahs. This must have been an attempt to make sense of such contradictory messianic images as we have encountered up till now.*

"*The root of this idea may be the lines of Zechariah...:*

"*Here is the man whose name is the Branch, and he will branch out from his place and build the temple of the Lord. It is he who will build the temple of the Lord, and he will be clothed with majesty and will sit and rule on his throne. And he will be a priest on his throne. And there will be harmony between the two.' (Zechariah 6.12-13).*"

"*This refers to prince Zerubbabel and the high-priest Joshua, but it is certain that it was understood in a messianic sense in the early Hasmonaean period. For example, the author of the Testaments of the twelve patriarchs expected a priestly and a kingly ruler:*

"*My children, be obedient to Levi and to Judah. Do not exalt yourselves about these two tribes because from them will arise the Savior from God. For the Lord will raise up from Levi someone as a high-priest and from Judah someone as king. He will save all the gentiles and the tribe of Israel.' (Testament of Simeon 7.1-2)*"

"*...The word 'Messiah' is not used, however. This step was taken by the sect at Qumran. Its members were looking forward to a 'Messiah of Israel' and a 'Messiah of David', who resemble the kingly and priestly descendants of Judah and Levi in the Testaments of the twelve patriarchs.*"

"*The first text we must study is the Damascus document, which is, as so often at Qumran, a combination of texts. Its first part is a kind of theological history which proves that the sect is the true Israel and that*

God will reward the faithful; then follows a kind of law; and a brief penal code is added as an appendix. Our first quote does not mention the Messiah, but must without any doubt be interpreted in a messianic fashion, because it alludes to Bileam's prophecy.

"And the star is the seeker of the law, who came to Damascus; as it is written A star has journeyed out of Jacob and a scepter is risen out of Israel. The scepter is the Prince of the whole congregation, and at his coming he will break down all the sons of Seth.' (Damascus document 7.18-21)"

"This is a very interesting text, because it not only mentions two Messiahs, but also shows that one of them is a military leader and the other a sage. Moreover, the expression 'seeker of the law' usually signifies the Teacher of Rightousness (the founder of the sect); the fact that this title is now used to describe one of the Messiahs suggests that the members of the Qumran sect believed that he would one day return. We will discuss this idea below.

"In this first quote, the word 'Messiah' is not used. But the Damascus document is sometimes more explicit.

"(...) during the time of ungodliness until the appearance of the Messiahs of Aaron and Israel (...)' (Damascus document 12.23-13.1)"

"This is the exact statement of the ordinances in which they walk until the Messiah of Aaron and Israel appears and expiates their iniquity.' (Damascus document 14.18-19.)"

"Those who heed Him are the poor of the flock; they will be saved at the time of visitation. But others will be delivered up to the sword at the coming of the Messiah of Aaron and Israel.' (Damascus document 19.9-11)"

"...The most interesting text, however, can be found in the Messianic rule (also called the Rule of the congregation). It describes the table arrangement during a sacred, messianic meal. The interesting point is the hierarchy between the two Messiahs.

"This is the sitting of the men of renown called to the assembly for the council of the community when God will have begotten the Messiah among them. The Priest shall enter at the head of all the congregation of Israel, then are all the chiefs of the sons of Aaron, the priests, called to the assembly, men of renown. And they shall sit before him, each according to his rank.

'Afterwards, the Messiah of Israel shall enter. The chiefs of the tribes of Israel shall sit before him, each according to his rank, according to their position in the camps and during their marches; then all the heads of family of the congregation, together with the wise men of the congregation, shall sit before them, each according to their rank.

'And when they gather for the community table, or to drink wine, and arrange the community table and mix the wine to drink, let no man stretch out his hand over the first-fruits of bread and wine before the Priest. For it is he who shall bless the first-fruits of bread and wine, and shall first stretch out his hand over the bread. And afterwards, the Messiah of Israel shall stretch out his hands over the bread. And afterwards, all the congregation of the community shall bless, each according to his rank.' (1Q28a 2.11-21)"

Certainly it must have been seen as a message from God when the High Priestess, Miriam, gave birth to identical twin boys. They must have known that the two Messiahs of prophecy had been born into their Nazarene/Essene community.

There can be little doubt who wrote the gospel of Luke and the Acts of the Apostles, or Luke's gospel and the Ax of the Apostle. He left his name throughout Ax, and especially in Chapters 27 and 28. Virtually every proper noun in these two chapters links to one of Plutarch's books, and most of those to which they link were written in 75 ACE. According to most biblical scholars, Luke and Acts were written between 80 and 120 ACE, exactly the time Plutarch was writing between 200 and 300 books, and shortly after his prolific year, 75 ACE. The proper nouns Pyrrhus, Sopater, Secundus, Adramyttium, Cnidus, Appius, Twin Brothers, Puteoli, Rhegium, and Lycia appear only in Acts. And just as the subtle change from *"Jesus the Nazarene"* to *"Jesus of Nazareth"* points to an intentional deception, the removal of *"Pyrrhus"* from the King James version adds more evidence of deception on the part of the church leaders.

It may be that Paul's letters had reached Plutarch through the Nazarene/Essene women named throughout Acts. The question is, did the fourth century church leaders, especially Jerome, *"touch up"* Paul's letters to include all of the characters Plutarch placed with him, or did Plutarch write stories about Paul's companions named in the epistles?

Because so many of the names link to legends that predate Paul and Plutarch, it seems reasonable to conclude that the sequence of events was as follows:

Paul wrote some letters: to the Thessalonians in the early 50's, to the Corinthians between 51 and 56, to the Galatians around 55, to the Romans between 54 and 58, to the Colossians and the Epehsians in the early 60's, and to the Philippians between 61 and 63. Most biblical scholars agree that Paul did not write the letter to the Hebrews , although it was probably written before 70 ACE. The letters to Timothy and Titus were probably written at least a generation after Paul's death by one or more of his disciples who became the early church leaders.

Plutarch wrote Lux and Ax, using the names that link to Greek legends, history, and to his own books, between 80 and 120 ACE. In the fourth century some of the Church fathers caught onto the links and were forced to attempt to cover it. They inserted Plutarch's names used in Acts, into the salutations and/or to the closing verses of Paul's epistles, making it appear that all the characters in Acts were actually traveling around with Paul and that Paul had written letters about them. And it worked until now, thanks to the Internet and the ease of finding the connections. The early church leaders may have written Timothy and Titus at that time. Or Timothy and Titus might have been added earlier in order to solidify Paul's new doctrines. Since all the original letters and gospels were destroyed, one can only make educated guesses about some of the issues.

What I think cannot be disputed is that Luke's gospel and the Acts of the Apostles were written by Plutarch, a student of Plato and Pythagoras. He wrote them in order to preserve the knowledge of what Paul did to Jesus the Nazarene's message of Truth.

I pondered the irony of the False Apostle Paul infiltrating the Nazarene/Essene movement, Plutarch's use of the Trojan

Horse as a way of revealing it, and the greater irony that Plutarch then "hid" the truth inside the Bible, making it a *"Trojan Horse"* of sorts. I went back to the Internet; I entered *Plutarch* and *Irony*, since *Irony* is one of the genre of Ancient writing, along with *tragedy* and others that I can't recall. I got a hit: *"On Progress and Irony: with particular reference to the abandonment of human sacrifice,"* by Carl Pfluger (www.azothgallery.com).

The essay begins:

"Plutarch, in his Life of Themistocles, tells us that just as the battle of Salamis was about to begin, '...Themistocles was offering sacrifice alongside the admiral's trireme. Here three remarkably handsome prisoners were brought before him...At the very moment that Euphrantides the prophet saw them, a great bright flame shot up from the victims awaiting sacrifice at the altar and a sneeze was heard on the right, which is a good omen. At this, Euphrantides clasped Themistocles by the right hand and commanded him to dedicate the young men by cutting off their forelocks and then to offer up a prayer and sacrifice them all to Dionysus, the Eater of Flesh, for if this were done, it would bring deliverance and victory to the Greeks. Themistocles was appalled at this terrible and monstrous command from the prophet, as it seemed to him. But the people, as so often happens at moments of crisis, were ready to find salvation in the miraculous rather than in a rational course of action. And so they called upon the name of the god with one voice, dragged the prisoners to the altar, and compelled the sacrifice to be carried out as the prophet had demanded.' (c.13; tr., Ian Scott-Kilvert, Penguin Classics)"

Pfluger continues the essay with another example of Plutarch's treatment of blood sacrifices:

"...Plutarch again tells the tale in his Life of Pelopidas, a Theban general who, on the eve of the battle of Leuctra (371 B.C.) had a dream in which he was commanded to sacrifice 'a red-haired virgin' in order to ensure victory. When Pelopidas reported the dream to his colleagues, a typically Greek debate ensued, with generals sounding incongruously like sophists, philosophers, and antiquarians, as they argued the pros and cons of carrying out the bloody command to the letter. (Precedent was generally in favor of it, philosophy against.) At last the prophet Theocritus threw his weight on the side of humanitarian opinion by

declaring that a red-maned filly (which had opportunely intruded herself into the proceedings) would be an acceptable offering.

"Plutarch's relief at this equus ex machina outcome is palpable; and in his summary of the arguments brought against human sacrifice he clearly presents his own view:

"'...that such a barbarous and impious sacrifice could not be pleasing to the powers above, because it is not the Typhons of Giants or other monsters who rule in heaven, but the father of gods and men. They argued that it is probably foolish in any case to believe that there are deities who delight in bloodshed and in the slaughter of men, but that if they exist, we should disregard them and treat them as powerless, since it is only weak and depraved minds that could harbour such cruel and unnatural desires.' (c.21; tr., Ian Scott-Kilvert, Penguin Classics)"

But by far the most important clues to the character and philosophy of Plutarch are found later in the essay:

"One of Plutarch's most characteristic works is his essay 'On Superstition,' which begins with these words:

"'The flood of ignorance and misunderstanding of the gods has divided from the very beginning into two separate streams. One, flowing as it were over stony ground, has in hard dispositions produced atheism; the other, as if over moist soil, has in tender minds produced superstition.'" (tr., L.R. Loomis, Classics Club Editions)"

"And then, although he himself was in so many ways the most 'tender-minded' of writers, and one of the most sincerely religious people who have ever lived, Plutarch, in confronting this antithetical pair of spiritual vices, says that we must come down unequivocally harder against superstition than against atheism. Throughout this essay he reiterates that it is better to believe nothing about the gods than to hold superstitious beliefs about them--among which, of course, he counted the belief that they could ever be pleased by human sacrifice, or by bloodshed of any sort. If he could observe us today, I suspect that Plutarch would say that virtually all modern people are hopelessly enmeshed in one of these twin snares, atheism or superstition. Either we ignore the gods, for all practical purposes, or we adhere mindlessly and slavishly to some arbitrary cultus, and thereby mutilate our own essence, our humanity, with a shameful lack of regard for our own dignity."

I can add nothing to that observation.

CHAPTER TEN

"...I am coming soon; my reward is with me, to repay according to everyone's work.
I am the Alpha and the Omega, the first and the last, the beginning and the end.
Blessed are those who do his commandments...they will have the right to
the Tree of Life and may enter the city by the gates."
Revelation 22:12-14

SECRET CODE
HOLY SEED

Has the case been made beyond a reasonable doubt that Lux gospel and the Ax of the Apostle were written as mysteries and filled with clues? Will the jury agree that the cleverly disguised clues revealed the truth about Jesus, his message, and what really happened to his loyal disciples? Can the Theo-detectives wrap up the case and move on to the next? Does the prosecutor have enough to work with?

Lux opened with the appearance of the angel Gabriel. Gabriel links only to the book of Daniel. There we found the missing books of *Susanna*, a name recorded in Luke's Chapter 8, and *Bel and he Dragon*. Both are *"examples of ancient mystery novels,"* and both depict corruption among the leaders of their communities. *Susanna* demonstrates the corruption of government leaders and their abuse of women; *Bel* depicts corruption and abuse of powers by religious leaders.

Susanna contained puns and wordplay that provided clues that I originally missed. I found *Susanna* before I realized the importance of the Tree. Of course that was the purpose of using her story as an early clue. The words are memorable if one knows the Greek language. "'*Under a clove tree...the angel will cleave you'; 'under a yew tree...the angel will hew you asunder.*" Had the story not been retained in the apocrypha, I wouldn't have known of its existence when Lux was writing. Had it not been for the annotations and footnotes, I couldn't have known of the art and skill of its author, nor could I have been aware that Lux used the same device.

The Tree is so very important to the biblical writers. Imagine their horror when they realized it was Paul's ax that felled the *Tree of Life*!

One of the most compelling visions from the book of Daniel is his vision of what happened to "*The King.*"

Daniel 4:23-27: "*And...the holy watcher came down from heaven...saying, 'Cut down the tree and destroy it, but leave its stump and roots in the ground...As it was commanded to leave the stump and roots of the tree, your kingdom shall be reestablished... when you learn that The Most High is Supreme*" (or, *The Law is unfailing*). "*Therefore...break off your sins with righteousness, and your iniquities with mercy to the oppressed, so that your prosperity may be prolonged.*'"

(The above quotation is somewhat paraphrased for clarity.)

The Ax of the Apostles ended with a quote from the book of Isaiah 6:9-10:

"*And he said, 'Go and say to this people: 'Keep listening, but do not comprehend; keep looking, but do not understand. Make the mind of this people dull, and stop their ears, and shut their eyes, so that they may not look with their eyes, and listen with their ears, and comprehend with their minds, and turn and be healed.'*'"

The quotation ends there, but the most important message immediately follows, and any theological philosopher would have known what it was.

Isaiah 6:13: "*Then I said, 'How long, O Lord?' And he said:*

'Until cities lie waste without inhabitant, and houses without people, and the land is utterly desolate; until the Lord sends everyone far away, and vast is the emptiness in the midst of the land. Even if a tenth part remain in it, it will be burned again, like a terebinth (tree) **or an oak whose stump remains standing when it is felled.' The holy seed is its stump."**

Jesus taught exactly the same thing Daniel was told in his vision: The One Law is unfailing in its operation. Our actions create our experiences, and those experiences will be painful until we learn this One Truth: Jehovah is All; Jehovah is Everything; Jehovah is One and Oneness. We are the *"molecules"* that make up the Oneness which is Jehovah; we are like a single water molecule in the clouds or the ocean. Therefore, it is for our own well-being that each individual must care for the whole.

I used the word *Jehovah* rather than *God* for a reason. *God* is masculine no matter how hard one tries to Spiritualize the word. For the Nazarene/Essenes the duality of the Creator was the basis for their religion and for their philosophy of living. They recognized and practiced equality of male and female and maximized the strengths and purposes of each. Their understanding of the Oneness of the Creator and the Duality of the physical Creation is the basis for their *Tree of Life*.

If I should be asked to make a guess as to which of the Nazarene doctrines Lux most wanted to convey to Theophilus, I would answer immediately: The absolute importance of the male/female balance in all things and that the Nazarenes not only taught it but produced two perfected examples: Jesus the Nazarene and Mary the Magdalene/Nazarene; God and Goddess manifest on earth; the foundation of the *"Christian/ Christina"* movement.

The understanding of the importance of the *Tree of Life*

has waned over two thousand years. The Bible first introduces it in Genesis and ends Revelation describing it again. But modern Christianity's focus on the blood sacrifice has all but destroyed the *Tree of Life*. Most Christians have no idea what it represented to the Nazarene/Essenes and others two thousand years ago. Since Lux and Ax placed such emphasis on it, it might be important to know just what it meant to them. One of the best explanations is at www.thenazareneway.com:

"The Essene Tree of Life represented fourteen positive forces, seven of them heavenly or cosmic forces and seven earthly or terrestrial forces. The Tree was pictured as having seven roots reaching down into the earth and seven branches extending up toward the heavens, thus symbolizing man's relationship to both earth and heaven.

"Man was pictured in the center of the tree halfway between heaven and earth.

"The use of the number seven is an integral part of the Essene tradition which has been transmitted to Western cultures in various outer ways, such as the seven days of the week.

"Each root and branch of the tree represented a different force or power. The roots represented earthly forces and powers, the Earthly Mother, the Angel of Earth, the Angel of Life, the Angel of Joy, the Angel of the Sun, the Angel of Water and the Angel of Air. The seven branches represented cosmic powers, The Heavenly Father, and his Angels of Eternal Life, Creative Work, Peace, Power, Love and Wisdom. These were the Essene angels of the visible and invisible worlds.

*"In ancient Hebrew and Medieval literature these heavenly and earthly forces or angels were given names: Michael, **Gabriel**, and so on; and they were pictured in religious art as human figures with wings and clad in flowing robes, such as in the frescoes of Michael Angelo (sic).*

"Man, in the center of the Tree, was seen to be surrounded as in a magnetic field, by all the forces, or angels, of heaven and earth. He was pictured as in the meditation posture, the upper half of his body above the ground and the lower half in the earth. This indicated that part of man is allied to the forces of heaven and part to the forces of earth. This concept closely parallels that of Zoroaster who represented the universe as a framework of realms with man in its center and the various forces

above and below him. It also corresponds to the Toltec ritual performed on the steps of their pyramids with man in the midst of all the forces.

"*This position of man in the center of the Tree, with the earthly forces below him and the heavenly forces above, also corresponds to the position of the organs in the physical body. The gastric and generative tracts in the lower half of the body, being instruments of self-preservation and self-perpetuation, belong to the earthly forces. Whereas the lungs and brain, in the upper half of the body, are the instruments of breathing and thinking and thus connect man with the finer forces of the universe.*

"*Contact with the angelic forces represented by the Tree of Life was the very essence of the daily life of the Essenes. They knew that to be in harmony with these forces they must make conscious effort to contact them. The Essenes were spoken of by the ancient writers as an extremely practical people. Their concepts were not just theories; they knew exactly how to be continually aware of the forces about them and how to absorb their power and put them into action in their daily lives.*

"*They had the deep wisdom to understand that these forces were sources of energy, knowledge and harmony by which man can transform his organism into a more and more sensitive instrument to receive and consciously utilize the forces. Furthermore, they considered that to put himself into harmony with the forces of the Heavenly Father and the Earthly Mother was man's most important activity in life.*

"*The characteristics of each one of the different forces was very clear to them and they knew what the force meant in each individual's life and how it should be utilized.*

"*They also understood the relationship between the forces. They considered that each heavenly force has an earthly force corresponding to it and each earthly force a corresponding heavenly power. These corresponding heavenly and earthly forces were placed on the Essene Tree of Life diagonally across from each other, one above and one below man. A line drawn between any two corresponding forces consequently passed directly through man in the center of the Tree.*

"*The forces which correspond with each other, above and below, are as follows:*

"*The Heavenly Father and the Earthly Mother;*

"The Angel of Eternal Life and the Angel of Earth;

"The Angel of Creative Work and the Angel of Life;

"The Angel of Peace and the Angel of Joy;

"The Angel of Power and the Angel of the Sun;

"The Angel of Love and the Angel of Water;

"The Angel of Wisdom and the Angel of Air.

"These correlations showed the Essenes that when an individual contacts any earthly force he is also in touch with a certain heavenly power. This enabled them to understand how necessary it is to be in perfect harmony with each and every one of the forces and angels, both in the visible and invisible worlds.

"The symbolical Tree of Life made it clear to the people how inseparably they are linked to all the forces, cosmic and terrestrial, and it showed them what their relationship is to each."

Gabriel showed me the *Tree of Life* in a slightly different way. The Trunk represents the Earthly Mother and Heavenly Father Energies. Together they nourish the twelve extensions that spring from this foundation Trunk. The trunk reaches into the Earth with six angelic forces in its roots and into the Heavens with six angelic powers in its branches.

The entire Holy Bible is really about the *Tree of Life*. All the rules and rituals, the *"shalts"* and *"shalt nots,"* were man's attempts to control others. Anyone dedicated to living according to the doctrine of Jesus the Nazarene didn't need rules. Love of the Creator and Creation and respect for all living things superseded the laws of men and made them meaningless.

The *"Inspired"* writers kept the Tree in the foreground when they could, underground when it was being threatened with destruction. But the Tree is always the central figure in the lives and stories of the Spiritual Teachers.

ᔕᕈ

I'll ask the question one last time: If the church had approved of and accepted the scientific knowledge that Luke's gospel transmitted, why were the numbers hidden within the stories?

If Lux was in agreement with the narratives being circulated at the time (and at the time the narratives being circulated were Paul's letters to the various churches), why did they feel the need to set the record straight?

The government (Herod, supported by his governors, proconsuls, magistrates, praetors, and other subordinates) had an agenda. That agenda was to quell the expanding peaceful protest of the people, instigated by Jesus and the Nazarenes against the government tyranny. Imprisoning and killing the converts was not working. Subverting the doctrine would.

There is a pattern in Acts that becomes apparent to a detective looking for clues: Herod seems to always show up when Paul's around. At Acts 11:30-12:1 Paul returns from Tarsus immediately preceding Herod's reign of terror, the death of James, and the beginning of the persecution of Jesus' disciples. At Acts 13:1 a member of Herod's court is traveling with Saul. Herod's *"doctrine"* can be found throughout Paul's letters to the churches:

"Whoever resists authority resists what God has appointed, and those who resist will incur judgment." (Romans 13:2)

"...one must be subject, not only because of wrath but also because of conscience. For the same reason you also pay taxes, for the authorities are God's servants, busy with this very thing." (Romans 13:5-6)

In order to pass under the radar of the early church leaders and Jerome's editing a couple of centuries later Luke's gospel had to sound as if it supported Paul and Paul's doctrine. On the surface it does. Paul is honored with words even while he is being described as the most dishonorable and contemptible of characters. It's easy at times to *"hear"* only the praises for Paul.

But the true message is just below the surface. It's in the myths and ancient biblical stories. It's in the names and the numbers. It's in the knowledge of historical accounts combined with the proximity of names with one another. It is there for those with ears to hear and hearts that want to know The Truth.

Lux/Ax tells us that the Nazarenes' *Tree of Life* was felled by the Ax of the Apostle Paul; it became the cross of Calvary. The blood sacrifice cult hung the corpse of Jesus on it and created rituals to praise his death, ignoring the lessons of his Life and resurrection and what it means for us. His dead body has hung on that dead tree for nearly two thousand years. It is a symbol of death, darkness, and fear. The seed is in the stump, waiting for attention and rebirth. It is our responsibility to give it the nourishment it needs to spring back to life.

The *Tree of Life* is more than just a symbol. Studied and understood it contains the knowledge of the forces and powers of Creation. Through it comes the true knowledge of The Nazarene Way of Life, The Truth of their message, and The Life eternal.

The cleverness with which Lux and Ax were composed is truly amazing. *Luke's Gospel*, once the code is broken, is clearly *Lux Gospel*. Bringing the stump of the tree in *Daniel* into the first chapter of *Lux*, and closing the last chapter of *Acts* with a speech from Isaiah that brings back that stump, creates the amusing play on one of the words in the title of the second book to Theophilus, making it *The Ax of the Apostle*.

The device used in Susanna (clove/cleave; yew/hew) and adopted by *Luke/Lux* is used again in this title of *Acts*. The Greek word for *acts* is *agein*; *ax* is *axien*. And isn't it just incredible how those two words translated into English are *Acts/Ax*? Go figure! This demonstrates a wonderful sense of humor, as well as a great love of the mystery novel.

But as I wrap up this project, which has been a source of immense joy for me, I have to wonder. When I started I had no idea where it would lead. I had discovered the numbers of Light in Luke Chapter 1, and I only suspected there might be more than just the numbers. I was gently led to everything revealed in this work by Gabriel, who knows where the answers lie. I have finally for the most part submitted to "*It.*" I'm quite certain the *Energetic Impulses* are there for anyone who can put aside their own thoughts and prejudices, even if only temporarily. That may be the most important thing I can tell you: "*It*" is there for you when you submit to it with all love and trust and desire for Truth. And once experienced life can never be the same.

I know the proof I wanted to find was revealed. Jesus

delivered The Truth to resurrecting the promised *Tree of Life*, and *The Nazarene Way of Life* is it. Paul appeared to be a disciple, and the Apostles believed him and welcomed him into their sacred movement. But Paul's purpose was to destroy the movement from within, and he succeeded. His Ax left just the stump of *The Tree*. But the seed of Truth remained in that stump. It's up to us to shine the Light on it so that it can again spread its branches to the Sky and its roots into the Earth.

I wonder: What will be the reaction of those faithful Christians who have been deceived by Paul and believed the lies? Will they be so protective of their religions that they'll reject Jesus again? And will they reject the importance of Mary Magdalene to the movement? When they cannot deny that *Lux Gospel* and *The Ax of the Apostle* were written so that the words could travel through time and deliver The Truth at this moment in the history of the world, will they then reject this faithful servant of their Lord Jesus Christos and Lady Mary Christas, known for over two thousand years as *Luke*? Will Paul and the cult of the blood sacrifice continue to hold them in servitude to the useless rituals and evil actions of the Angels of Darkness?

The Light has always been there for those who were looking for Truth. Will it be Jesus and the Light of his everlasting Love which nourishes the *Tree of Life*? Or will it be Paul's cross of death and more generations and lifetimes of darkness lived in its shadow?

EXCERPTS FROM GOTT'S NEXT BOOK, A NOVEL

FROM
HOLY SEED
TO
SACRED LOVE

As they walked along the path on the banks of the gently flowing river, Jeshua took Miriam's hand. They walked in silence; a soft breeze tossed strands Miriam's dark hair about her face. Her heart pounded with excitement from the warmth of the touch of the Teacher's strong hand.

When they reached a grove of trees about a quarter mile from the Nazarene camp, Jeshua stopped and faced her. "How do you feel about what we're trying to do?"

Miriam thought for a moment before answering. "I know how important this is and how blessed we are to have been chosen. Sometimes I worry that I'm not truly worthy of such an important task."

His head tilted as he posed the question. "Why do you say that?" He took her other hand and looked into her soulful eyes.

She hesitated again as she tried to gather the appropriate words. "I still feel many human emotions. Sometimes... sometimes I feel jealous of the time you spend with the men. I see the love in your eyes when you look at the women, and some of them are so beautiful. I feel jealousy enter my heart that you feel deep love for them. I know these feelings are weaknesses of human ego, and I know you don't have such emotions. I am just not where you are in being able to love everyone and all they do with the same unconditional acceptance."

"You do know how very much I love you," he said softly, "and how differently I love you."

"I do," she replied, dropping her head. After a brief pause and a deep sigh she looked back into his eyes. "I am able to stop and observe my emotions and discuss this with myself. I am able to see that your love for your disciples is deep and true and that your love for me is also...and is more, as well. But I want to be rid of the need to stop and think. I want to be as you are. I want to be so infused with the knowing of my Godliness that every act of love comes without thought. I want it to be because Love is what I am, not what I know."

Jeshua smiled at the wisdom of her words and the honesty of her heart. "You know I have access to the power to heal the sick of disease and the power to drive demons out of their bodies."

"I have seen you do all these things," she replied.

"These ego frailties you describe are nothing more than small areas of darkness within your body. You can be healed of these dark areas, just as you have seen others healed of disease and evil spirits."

"Are you saying I am possessed of demons?"

"The angels of darkness fight very hard to hide the Light of wisdom from people. You have demonstrated your understanding of the importance of Love to overcome the attempts made by the angels of darkness to work in and through you. But these dark areas still give them a place to rest from time to time."

"But you can heal me?"

"You can heal yourself. It is your desire and your faith that provides the opening for the power of Love to fill you completely and to clear your body of all areas of darkness and fear."

"I do very much want to be purified."

Jeshua brought her hands to his lips and kissed them lightly, first the left, and then the right. As he did so he continued to look deeply into her eyes.

Miriam felt a jolt of electricity when his lips touched her hands. She saw the Light of Love in his eyes, and she relinquished herself to his power. As he began to speak, she took a deep breath and closed her eyes.

His voice was soft and low; he said, "Attachment to matter is the first darkness that possesses people, and it is the easiest to heal. Your Love has recognized the reality of Spirit and the illusion of the material world. Now remember your Spiritual Nature and release the human nature that would keep you bound to earthly matter."

He paused and watched her steady, deep breathing.

"The second darkness is the desire to possess, and it works hand-in-hand with the first. This is what creates jealousy. Your Love has already recognized the pain this darkness can cause. Now remember your Spiritual Nature and release the human nature that would keep you bound to earthly matter." He paused again to allow his words to wash over her.

"The third darkness is laziness and contentment with things of the earth. Your Love has already recognized the value of Knowledge of Truth, and you are now willing to exert the effort to acquire the Knowledge I bring. Now remember your Spiritual Nature and release the human nature that would keep you bound in ignorance."

"The fourth darkness is anger, and it is sevenfold, for it is the desire to retain the darknesses that have inhabited the body: attachment to matter, the desire to possess, ignorance, deadly jealousy, pride, inflated earthly wisdom, and false worldly wisdom which justifies horrendous acts of evil. Your Love has opened your eyes to all the darkness, and your Wisdom has opened your heart to healing. Now remember your Spiritual Nature and release the human nature that would keep you bound in darkness."

As he spoke Miriam began to hear a soft whirring sound--like the wings of a flock of birds taking flight. Then she felt a warm whirlwind enter the bottom of her feet; it began to work its way upward through her body, spinning, spinning, spinning. The whirlwind moved slowly upward, delivering warmth through her legs, slowly upward through her hips, her abdomen, around her heart, her chest, her neck, and finally upward and out from the top of her head. She suddenly felt as if a light had been placed at her heart; the warmth spread outward from the center of her being. She opened her eyes and looked into his.

"It is done," Jeshua said softly. "You are purified and freed of the limitations of darkness." He smiled as he enjoyed the warmth of her hands and the beauty of the light streaming from her body.

As tears of joy welled up in Miriam's eyes, Jeshua put his arms around her and pulled her to his chest. "I love you so very much, Miriam," he said into her hair. "You make me complete by providing the feminine energy that enables us, both of us, to spread this message of Love and Light. Without you I cannot touch all the people because I am not complete. Your energies combined with mine give us the balance we must have to touch the feminine and the masculine in all the people. You embody the Spirit of Mother Earth, which is Life and emotion, and I embody the Spirit of the Sun, which is Light and knowledge. Together we represent the wholeness of Creation. And we can demonstrate the relationship of unconditional Love that all should aspire to achieve."

"I feel the Light of your Love throughout my entire body and soul. You have healed me of the sevenfold curses of darkness."

"Your Love has made you whole, Miriam. I only guided you through the process of recognizing your True Nature, which is Spirit and Love and Light. Now our work can begin. Now we can deliver The Truth to all the people. My need for you is equal to your need for me. Now, Miriam, we are both complete and we can, together, teach the perfected Love of the Creator to all men and women who truly desire to know." He kissed her gently on her lips. "And you now have the power to heal, just as I have. We are equal in all ways."

"You brought me here to do this for me, didn't you?"

"It is for both of us and all of them, Miriam, and for all of those throughout this age. And until the end of time."

BIBLIOGRAPHY

BOOKS AND PUBLICATIONS

The Scripture quotations, contained herein, unless otherwise noted, are from the New Revised Standard Version Bible, copyright 1989 by the division of Christian Education of the National Council of the Churches of Christ in the U.S.A., and are used by permission. All rights reserved.

The New Oxford Annotated Bible copyright circa 1973, 1977, by Oxford University Press, Inc.

The New Oxford Annotated Bible copyright circa 1994, by Oxford University Press, Inc.

The Dimensions of Paradise, by John Michell, Adventures Unlimited Press, 2001.

The Energy Grid, by Bruce Cathie, Adventures Unlimited Press, 1990, 1997.

Bloodline of the Holy Grail, by Laurence Gardner, Fair Winds Press, 2002.

The Book of Doctrines of Essene Church of Christ, by Brother Nazariah.

The Case for Christ, by Lee Strobel, Zondervan Publishing House, 1998

BIBLIOGRAPHY: WEB SITES

www.touregypt.net/godsofeygyp/maat.htm

www.touregypt.net/godsofegypt/maat2.htm

www.crosswalk.com/Dictionaries/Eastons

www.crosswalk.com/Dictionaries/Smiths

www.crosswalk.com/Dictionaries/BakersEvangelicalDictionary

www.wikipedia.org/wiki/Pliny_the_Elder

www.e-classics.com/pyrrhus.htm

www.depts.drew.edu/jhc/mcdonald.html: "Luke's Eutychus and Homer's Elpenor: Acts 20:1-12 and Odyssey 10-12," Dennis R. MacDonald, Iliff School of Theology; excerpted from: Journal of Critical Studies (Fall 1994), 4-24; copyright Institute for Higher Critical Studies, 1996. Quoted with permission.

www.4literature.net/Euripides/Bacchae

www.theatrehistory.com/ancient/erripides009.html

www.depts.drew.edu/jhc/eisenman.html: "Paul as Herodian," Robert Eisenman, Institute for Jewish-Christian Origins, California State University at Long Beach; excerpted from Journal of Critical Studies (Spring 1996), 110-122; copyright Institute for Higher Critical Studies, 1996.

www.thenazareneway.com

www.space.com/scienceastronomy/astronomy/dobson_
astronomer_000507.html

www.azothgallery.com/progress_irony.html

www.livius.org/men-mh/mssiah/messiah_14.html

www.knoxseminary.org/Prospective/Faculty/KnoxPulpit/
wgage_eunuch.html. Gage

www.probertencyclopaedia.com

www.apollonius.net/bernard 1 e.html

www.winshop.com

www.livius.org/pi-pm/plutarch/plutarch

www.abacon.com/-jkrause/jesus.html

www.apollonius.net/golgotha.html

www.hoocher.com/catilina

OTHER BOOKS BY GOTT

Fiction-Women's Mystery

ENCHANTED CIRCLE (By Paula Gott), www.globalbookpu
blisher.com
IBSN: 1-59457-185-6

Non Fiction-Spiritual

JESUS: MASTER OF SCIENCE, LESSONS OF LIGHT,
www.globalbookpublisher.com
IBSN: 1-59109-284-1

Non Fiction-Children's Science Series #1

THE LIFE AND ADVENTURES
OF LITTLE WATER MOLLY CULE, www.globalbookpubli
sher.com
IBSN: 1-59457-186-4

Comments and questions are encouraged.
Books may be ordered from the publisher,
Globalbookpublisher.com;
Amazon.com; Renaissance Books & Gifts, Springfield,
Missouri;
and most other bookstores (provide the IBSN).
One complimentary copy may be ordered for Churches
and other not-for-profit groups: (417) 443-3152

PaxAmoLux/Gott
PO Box 21
Highlandville MO 65669